THE FINANCIAL
GUIDE TO
BUSINESS
FINANCE

THE FINANCIAL TIMES GUIDE TO

BUSINESS FINANCE

ERNEST JONES

Managing Director, Mobile Training Ltd

PITMAN PUBLISHING
128 Long Acre, London WC2E 9AN

A Division of Pearson Professional Limited

First published in 1994

British Library Cataloguing in Publication Data
A CIP catalogue record for this book can be obtained from the British Library.

ISBN 0 273 60905 X

5 7 9 10 8 6 4

Typeset by Northern Phototypesetting Co. Ltd, Bolton
Printed and bound by Bell and Bain Ltd., Glasgow

*The Publishers' policy is to use paper manufactured
from sustainable forests*

CONTENTS

1

AN INTRODUCTION TO BUSINESS FINANCE

Business management attracts words and never more so than in the field of money. The simplest financial transaction is couched in phrases that both defy understanding and humiliate the curious. However, the fact remains that business – its progress and success – has existed far before such terms and jargon were invented. So let us begin this study of business finance by returning to its roots. Roots that reveal the fact that business is a partnership in which the skills, energy and enterprise of people are linked with money – its sources and investment – so as to create success: success that is measured by the wealth – termed profit – the business creates.

THE BUSINESS GAME

In fact the ingredients of business success are not dissimilar from the attributes that might be ascribed to a successful football team.

- First, it must be match-fit – obtain its money from the right sources and invest it in the right places.
- Second, it must continue to do so as the business continues to operate.
- Third, it must score – which is the whole purpose of becoming and remaining match-fit in the first place and which is measured in terms of profit.
- Fourth, the ball – cash itself – must be there as and when it is needed. After all, a star striker can be right in front of the empty goalmouth but if the ball is off the field he won't score. And so it is in business. The availability of cash can be crucial in so many decision-making situations.

These then are the fundamental 'understanding' points that must be achieved if we are to understand business finance. Of course we shall introduce the terms, phrases and jargon as appropriate but never before we understand their meaning and significance within the practical business environment. After all, we are not discussing the lilies in the fields as they grow that toil not neither do they spin. We are addressing a very real commodity: money, which both *toils* and *spins*!

OUR BASIC APPROACH

So we shall approach our understanding of business finance with our feet firmly on the ground. We begin with a fundamental appreciation of the sources and uses of money in a business so as to recognise its fitness to create profit in the first place; following this with an examination of the measurement of profit and its sinister alternative, loss – whilst not forgetting that the need for fitness to make profit does not end at the birth of a business. It is a continuing concern. And for this reason a business must be regularly re-examined. This it does, in a listing of where its money is invested and where it came from, in the balance sheet.

Finally, we must recognise that beyond and within the man-made measurements of fitness and profit, there is the reality of cash itself: how much is available – you can jingle in your pocket – at any particular point in time; revealing – if the amount is inadequate – what is euphemistically called the cash-flow problem which, in the language we shall prefer, is called being skint!

The fitness of a business to make profit depends, from a money point of view, upon its sources and uses: from where it obtains its money and upon what this is spent – or, if you prefer the word, invested. Mind you, what must never be forgotten is its partnership with people – their skills, energy and enterprise are the vital complement to money in any profit achievement. And the role of management is that of the *inquisitor* : questioning whether or not the business has obtained its money – its funds – from the right sources and, second, whether such funds have been invested in the right places. This study of business finance indeed has only one overall objective: to improve such questions – recognising that everything we learn will seldom create answers, simply better questions.

THE BUSINESS MODEL

To start our understanding we shall return to the question of match-fitness through a money model. We shall begin by looking at the 'money position' – its sources and uses – when a business starts. Follow this with the questions management must pose if profits are to be maximised and losses minimised.

To help us to do this, look at Illustration 1.1. This sets out a model of business investment. What we will do is put a name into each numbered circle – and to discover these names I shall pose the questions you would need to ask yourself if it were your own business you were starting. If you prefer not to mark the illustration, why not take a copy?

THE SOURCES OF MONEY

First, in the case of circle 1, what must we have financially if we start a business? Oh yes. I know we must have policies, plans, ideas and so on, but what else? Yes, we certainly need money. We have a very special word for the area from which we get money. We call it capital. So we can put the word 'capital' into circle 1.

When anyone starts a business capital is obtained from two sources: their own resources – savings, for example – and borrowings from people or businesses such as banks who do not want their money back immediately. In limited companies these two sources of capital are termed the share capital (provided by the shareholders, the owners of the business), and loan capital (provided by lenders).

Illustration 1.1 The business model

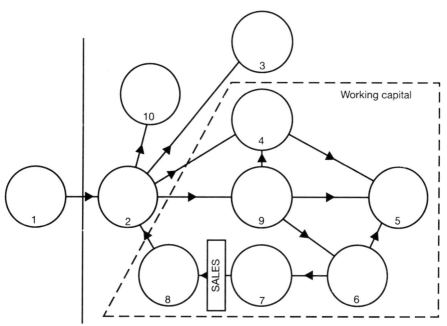

From where capital   In what areas capital has been invested
has been obtained

Gearing

It is the division of capital between these two sources which is called the gearing of a business. High gearing is when the majority (more than 50 per cent) of the capital has been obtained by means of borrowing, while the reverse situation is known as low gearing. The significance of gearing lies in the relationship between the providers of the capital and its recipient, the particular business. In the case of loan capital, for exampie, interest must be paid on the amount borrowed over the life of the loan and the amount itself must be repaid to the lender on the due date. This means that if a business borrowed, say, £100,000 repayable after six years at 10 per cent interest per annum, each year it would have to find £10,000 interest on the loan and at the end of the sixth year a further £100,000 to repay the amount borrowed.

However, a very different situation is created in the case of the owners' capital. We do not have to repay owners – the shareholders, as owners are called in the case of limited companies – the money they have invested as capital: it is, as we say, permanent. And their rewards – dividends in the case of limited companies – do not have to be paid to them. Owners' capital is, as we say, 'at risk'. It may do well or badly but this will depend upon how the business does.

It therefore follows that a high-geared business may well find the need to pay interest on – and finally to repay – its borrowed capital financially embarrassing and even disastrous during difficult times. It might be said that the need to pay interest and to repay loans creates pressure on a business.

The question of pressure

Gearing is therefore concerned with pressure. High gearing means more and low gearing less pressure, which brings us to the first principle of understanding business finance: that is, understanding rarely supplies answers, just better questions.

For instance, in the case of a high-geared business, the question is: can the business take the pressure? There is nothing pejorative about the question; after all, there is nothing wrong with pressure – in fact many businesses, like people, work better under pressure – but you must always question their ability to work in this way.

It is the same with low gearing – there is nothing right or wrong about such a situation, just questions which need to be raised. For instance, is the business living under too little pressure and, if so, does this mean that it is not working as hard as it could?

Under-gearing

Finally there can be the situation of 'under-gearing'. This is when a business has good things on which it could borrow, i.e. use as security or collateral, such as land or buildings and it has not done so. And again we are left with further questions. For instance, 'under-gearing' may be a sign that the business is not using its resources as well as it could, or there could be other reasons. It could be that the business is waiting for some future event for which funds will need to be raised by means of borrowing and it wishes to preserve its ability to do so.

THE USE OF MONEY

We have now considered the sources of finance and so can turn to circle 2. This relates to the way money comes into the business. In other words, what are we looking for financially to start a business? The answer is of course cash, so we can put the word 'cash' in circle 2.

Of course, it is possible that owners might bring into the business, as their capital, things that they own like office equipment, machinery and motor vehicles. Loans may also be made specifically to purchase such items. However, this presupposes the conversion of cash into such things which are then used in the business. So we shall assume that capital introduced into a business always starts as cash and is then converted into the things the business uses. Now we come to the next question: what do we do with the cash we put into a business? Yes, we buy things – but what things? If we sat down and listed the things which we would have to buy in any business we might produce a selection – a 'shopping list' – such as this: land and buildings, people things (like wages and salaries), plant and machinery, materials, merchandise, office equipment, shop fittings, motor vehicles … And then there are those things like rent and advertising, insurance, and heat and light, things which are often called collectively (in the case of light rather appropriately) the overheads!

In fact we could go on and on with this list. However, at this point let us pause and think about the items just mentioned from a cash spending point of view, because if we do we shall find that they fall quite naturally into two main divisions. To understand this I want you to think about the items we have mentioned and ask yourself: if it was your money and your business, would you consider these all in the same way?

I believe that if you thought of them in this way you would find that from a money point of view the items mentioned very broadly divide themselves into two. Some are things we buy with no intention of selling, for example the land and buildings, plant and machinery, office equipment and the motor vehicles – what in business we call the 'fixed assets'. On the other hand, items such as wages and salaries, materials, advertising, rent, insurance, and so on are going into what we do sell.

Fixed assets

We can now fill in some more circles. Circle 3 relates to those items which we have no intention of selling, and we can therefore place in it the words 'fixed assets'. (And just to confuse matters the money spent on fixed assets is often referred to as capital expenditure. Do I hear an example of duplicate jargon?)

Working capital

Next we come to circles marked 4, 5, 6, 7 and 8, flowing out of and back into cash, and circle 9 in the middle.

There is a broken line around these circles in Illustration 1.1 as they are referred to collectively as 'the working capital'. They show, as circles 4, 5 and 6 respectively, materials, labour and all those other items named overheads, and these can now be filled in. These in turn are converted into finished goods, services or saleable merchandise which are shown as circle 7. Such goods, services or merchandise may then be sold for cash, which is shown by the line leading from circle 7 eventually back to the cash circle 2.

It may also be of interest to mention that just as fixed assets are referred to by a duplicate term (capital expenditure), expenses which form the working capital are not deprived of the same treatment. They are collectively referred to as 'revenue expenditure'.

Credit taken

Both goods and services are often sold to customers – people and businesses – who do not pay immediately. They hesitate before they pay. In England such customers are collectively called the 'debtors' whilst Americans, who shorten everything, refer to them as 'accounts receivable'! In Illustration 1.1. these are shown as circle 8, which interrupts the line between circles 7 and 2.

Credit received

Finally, circle 9 (in the middle), which connects to circles 4, 5, 6 and 2, represents the fact that, just as a business's customers do not pay immediately for the goods and services sold to them, neither does a business pay immediately for all it owes.

For example, it receives materials and merchandise from its suppliers before it pays for them. It also incurs overheads in the form of electricity, advertising and other expenses before having to pay for them, and in most cases it does not pay for its labour before the end of each month. In all these cases the businesses and people supplying such goods and services are waiting for their money, and we refer to them collectively as the 'creditors' of the business, or as the Americans would say 'accounts payable'. Circle 9 therefore stands for these creditors or accounts payable and indicates the delay between the receipt of materials, merchandise, labour and other services and the subsequent payment for them.

Working capital investment

The investment in working capital is therefore a net amount. It is the sum of circles 4, 5, 6, 7 and 8 minus circle 9. However, we have been considering this area in terms of money spent, while if it were our own money we would see it more clearly as an investment. For instance, if we were considering a manufacturing business, working capital would be calculated in the following terms. First, there would be the stocks of raw materials we would have to carry at any particular time. Second, there would be stocks of work in progress – the goods in part production – made up of the cost of the materials, labour and overheads which have gone into them up to their stage of production. Third, there would be the stocks of finished goods – again containing the materials, labour and overheads in the completed items. And finally there would be the debtors, or accounts receivable made up also of the materials, labour and overheads and, in this case we hope, the profit making up the prices of the goods sold but unpaid for.

It is from the total of these items that there must be deducted the credit the business has taken before paying for its materials, labour and overhead costs which have gone into its stocks of raw materials, work in progress, finished goods and debtors or accounts receivable. This way of looking at working capital is set out in Illustration 1.2.

The financial luggage

The working capital of a business can be likened to the financial 'luggage' that it carries on its journey to a sale. For a manufacturing business there are four pieces of financial luggage, namely the raw material, work in progress, finished goods stocks and the debtors or accounts receivable. It is from the total of these that we deduct what it owes to the people or businesses who help it carry its luggage – the financial 'sherpas' as they might be called – known as the creditors or accounts payable.

Illustration 1.2 Alternative business model for a manufacturing business

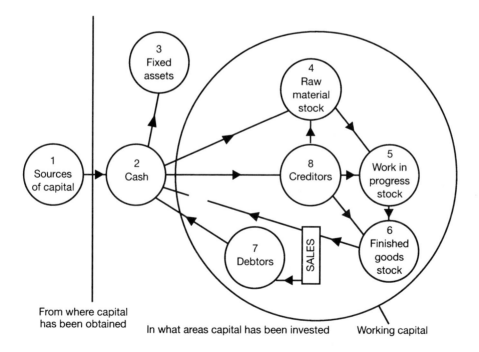

Recapitulation

So we have now discovered that when we invest money in a business we have two investment areas: first, in the things we are not intending to sell – the fixed assets sometimes referred to as capital expenditure – and, second, in things specifically intended to go into what is sold: revenue expenditure, which as an investment area is termed working capital.

FIXED ASSET QUESTIONS

The right assets?

Now to return to the questions. When viewing the fixed assets of a business, two very specific questions need to be posed. First, because fixed assets are purchased with no intention of their resale, there is a prime requirement that the assets – things of value – a business owns in this area are the 'right ones'. After all, once fixed assets are purchased the business is stuck with them! For this reason it is important that people looking at fixed assets have the necessary technical knowledge to decide whether they are the right ones. So, for example, the knowledge of an engineer is vital when looking at the plant and machinery of an engineering enterprise, as is the knowledge of a property person when looking at land and buildings owned by a hotel group.

Their replacement

At the same time as posing this first question, the second needs to be asked when looking at some of the fixed assets of a business: those which over their lives wear out and/or become obsolete. In such cases the question is whether or not the business is preparing for their replacement. In other words, has it set aside sufficient money for this purpose, either in cash or investments which can easily be converted back into cash? Or is the business building itself in such a way that it will at the appropriate time be able to obtain the necessary funds from outside sources – for example by borrowing on the security of the land and buildings it owns?

These then are the two questions that must be asked when we look at the fixed assets of a business. First, are they the right ones and, second, when it becomes necessary, will the business be able to replace those which wear out and become obsolete?

WORKING CAPITAL QUESTIONS

The cash flow

But what about the working capital? Which questions need to be raised here? Once again, two questions need to be asked, the first relating to a very important commodity indeed – cash itself.

If you look at Illustration 1.1 you will see just how central cash is to working capital. The line joining each of the circles in working capital is continuously moving out of and back into cash. It is for this reason that when managers or investors consider this area they need to pose the classic cash question which haunts everyone, in both their business and personal lives: 'Will I have the money available to pay the bills (in business, the creditors or accounts payables) as and when they become due?' If you examine the business model you will see that this is very much a timing problem, ensuring that money is available as cash as and when it is needed. If this is not done and creditors demand their money immediately, the business will either have to sell its fixed assets in a hurry – not the best or easiest thing to do in most cases – or obtain a loan in a hurry, again not the best way to borrow money!

A business that finds itself in such a situation is said to have a liquidity or cash-flow problem: precisely the same problem that, when faced by individuals, is described as 'being skint'!

Cash might be said to provide the lubrication for every meaningful business decision. If cash is not available managers do not make decisions – decisions are forced upon them. It is for this reason that the question of liquidity is so important for a business. After all, if you do not have the money you may be unable to buy the best materials from the best suppliers but be forced to deal with those who give the longest credit, however poor the quality of their goods. Or again, you may be forced to sell goods to people who pay the quickest, even though the price you charge them to attract prompt payment is much less than to people who take longer.

As well as the question of liquidity, however there is the second working capital question: the amount of the investment itself.

The amount?

To understand this second question let us pretend that we are the manager or investor in a business and ask ourselves how much of our capital would we wish to invest in the working capital area? This is not a trick question – the answer does not differ between large or small businesses or between different types of trade. Every manager and every investor has an identical wish so far as the amount of the investment in working capital is concerned. It is to minimise it as far as possible – to reduce it to nil, or even in some cases to a minus amount.

The ambition of every manager or investor is to sell their goods or services as soon as possible and to convert the sale back into cash; at the same time maximising the time taken before paying for the materials, labour and other expenses which go into such sales. It is indeed by doing this that a business minimises its working capital investment. And why should this be the ambition of managers and investors alike? Simply ask yourself what is everyone's ambition regarding investment anywhere, whatever the proposition, whether on a horse or in a business. The answer, quite clearly, is to maximise the odds, the return or the profit made, on the capital invested or employed.

Odds, return, profit

The words 'odds', 'return' or 'profit' refer to precisely the same thing: the growth the investment creates. If the odds are ten to one, it means that if we put £1 on the horse to win and it does, the £1 becomes £11. We still have the original £1 invested and it has grown by £10. So, in the case of a business, profit is the measurement of the growth created on the capital invested – or employed, as we say – over a given period of time.

If we invested £100,000 in a business on 1 January and on 31 December it was discovered that the business had made a profit for the year of £20,000, the amount invested would now equal £120,000 signifying that the investment had grown by £20,000 – the profit made for the year.

Minimising

The purpose of minimising the working capital investment is to maximise the return or profit in relation to the capital employed. It follows therefore that if a business can make the same profit with less capital invested, it must be right.

You can see an example of this in Illustration 1.3 where for A Ltd the profit of £60,000 represents a return of 10 per cent on the total capital employed – fixed assets of £400,000 and working capital £200,000, a total of £600,000. However, the same profit made by B Ltd on capital employed of £500,000 – fixed assets of £400,000 and working capital £100,000 – represents a return of 12 per cent on the total capital employed.

Illustration 1.3 Comparisons of return on capital employed

	A Ltd £	B Ltd £
Fixed assets	400,000	400,000
Working capital	200,000	100,000
Total capital employed	600,000	500,000
Profits	= 60,000	= 60,000
Return on capital employed	10%	12%

On the other hand, however strong the desire to minimise the working capital investment it must be reconciled with the need to meet the amounts owed to creditors, or accounts payable, as and when they become due. This is essential because if it cannot be achieved the business then has to raise cash speedily with things it has no intention of selling – its fixed assets. In working capital there is always a need to strike a balance between minimising the amount invested and avoiding the risk of being unable to meet bills as and when they become due.

Outside investment

Having understood the two major investment areas we still have one more to consider: the investment of cash not in fixed assets or in working capital but in outside investments in the form of shares in or loans to other businesses or individuals.

Mind you, we must be careful about definitions even at these initial stages of our understanding of business finance. Recently accountants have decided (foolishly I believe) to class outside investments held with no intention of resale as fixed assets. Formerly they have (rightly) placed them in a separate category so that they could be reviewed quite independently from the fixed assets used within the business. However, we will treat them at this stage for our purposes as a category on their own although we shall 'return to the fold' later in our studies.

Reasons

We can therefore fill in circle 10 in Illustration 1.1. as 'outside investments'. Such investments are not normally made when a business is first started, but when it has been in operation for some time situations may well arise where an outside investment might be felt desirable. One reason which might attract a business to invest outside itself is to spread its investment risk: that is, to divert some capital away from the main business into one that is totally dissimilar or to gain an interest in a business which is complementary to its own. An investment in the supplier of a key raw material is an example of this type of investment. In this way it may be possible to guarantee supplies if they become difficult to obtain as well as sharing in any prosperity demand for those supplies has created, which will include that of the investing company.

It might also be felt desirable to invest in another enterprise in order eventually to take over its control and thus obtain a second, ready-made business. In the case of limited companies control is normally obtained by purchasing more than 50 per cent of the voting shares of the company. As a share is normally an equal division of the total capital this will mean that the investing company will also own more than 50 per cent of the total capital of the business. In such a case the business in which the investment is made is referred to as a subsidiary company and the investing business as its parent company.

These then are examples of outside investments and the questions that need to be posed in respect of these are first 'Why the investment?' (does the reason seem logical?) and, second, as in the case of all business investment, 'Is the return gained commensurate with the value of the investment made?'

MODELS FOR A SERVICE INDUSTRY OR RETAIL BUSINESS

We have now examined business investment in terms of a manufacturing enterprise and a complete example is set out in Illustration 1.4. In the case of a service industry the finished goods circle 7 will be described by the term 'finished services'. In such cases it may also be found that materials are so small as not to warrant a separate circle. However, the model that we have been discussing will be found, with very few exceptions, to be adaptable to every conceivable type of business. Illustrations 1.4 and 1.5 should be examined together to see how the model for a manufacturing business (Illustration 1.4) compares with that for a service business (Illustration 1.5).

In a retail enterprise material is referred to as merchandise, and as there are no manufacturing processes there will be no finished goods, just saleable merchandise. It will also be found that, as most sales by retailers are for cash, the interruption caused by credit being taken by customers (circle 8, the debtors) will be the exception and not the rule as in the case of most manufacturing and many service industries. A business model for a retail enterprise is included as Illustration 1.6. Again, this should be compared with the business models for manufacturing and service enterprises.

SUMMARY OF THE BUSINESS MODEL

What must be stressed is that the pattern of investment described above has not been invented by experts but follows the natural investment of cash in any business. After all, even Adam and Eve had fixed assets – they called them trees; they also had working capital which they called apples!

Now to summarise – in any business money can be invested only in three areas, namely fixed assets (things we have no intention of selling), outside investments and working capital. It has always been, always will be, invested in these three areas. It must also be noted that there are no natural barriers between them. Amounts invested in one can be taken out of that area and transferred to another and vice versa. In other words, when we are looking at business investment we are looking at a very fluid situation. We are also looking at one in which those taking on the role of management have complete freedom in the movement of funds under their control. They have, however, complete responsibility!

Illustration 1.4   Business model: manufacturing industry

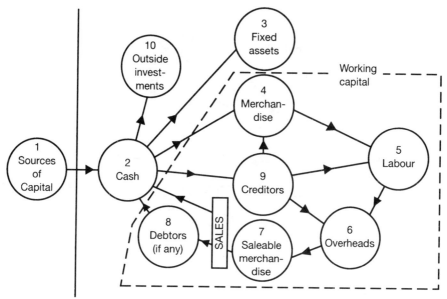

From where capital
has been obtained

In what areas capital has been invested

Illustration 1.5   Business model: service industry

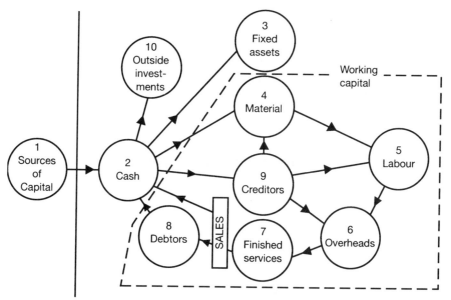

From where capital
has been obtained

In what areas capital has been invested

Illustration 1.6 Business model: retail industry

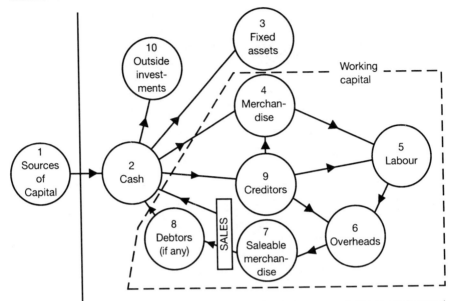

From where capital
has been obtained

In what areas capital has been invested

It must also be noted that all the rules regarding how much money we should invest in particular areas are always subject to alteration. Even the rule mentioned in this chapter about minimising the money in working capital can and may need to be broken. For instance, if someone running a business can see that material or merchandise costs are likely to rise over the year ahead he or she might well believe it right to buy more material or merchandise than is needed immediately. This will involve holding more stock than is required for immediate use. However, by taking such action, those running the business would be doing the right thing, although they would be breaking the rule of minimising the working capital investment.

The money questions

The movement of money is central to an understanding of business finance. It is this movement which calls for the need to control and examine money in business by the techniques which we introduce and examine in this and future chapters. It must always be remembered that financial information is produced to meet the natural desire to know what is happening to the business investment as it progresses. Thus so far we have directed our attention to the match-fitness of the business when it starts: whether it has obtained its money from the right places and spent – invested – it on the right things. But what next? – what else do we want to know? To answer this we will consider ourselves, once again, as though we are starting our own business, and seek to answer this primary question: 'What do we want to know about the financial progress of the business?' Or to put it into our sporting context – match-fit for what?

The return

To answer this question we need to consider what investment is all about. Why do we invest in the first place? Earlier in this chapter we saw that business investment has much in common with all other investments, whether backing a horse or buying jewellery or a car. In every case, whenever an investment proposal is raised investors and business managers need to ask two primary and obvious questions: first, what is the return? In other words, what will get in return for your investment, for example the odds on the horse.

It is to examine this question of return, the growth made by the investment, that in business a statement known as the profit and loss account is produced.

The risk

Whilst the first question is therefore to ascertain the return, the second – equally important and obvious to any investor – is: what is the risk of the investment giving you a return, i.e. the chances of the horse winning?

This is, however, a peculiar question because, although we raise it, we are not really seeking an answer. We want to work it out for ourselves. Consider for a moment a situation in which I recommend a horse and tell you it is bound to win a particular race. Would you take my word? I doubt it. I think you would suspect me. In fact, although you would clearly want to know the chances of the particular horse winning, you would want to do your own homework. And what you would really need would be a starting point based on fact not opinion. In the case of the horse the obvious choice would be its name. After all, that could hardly be invented and, once you know that, you could enquire into whether or not a horse with that name has ever won a race before? Who rode it? And which horses and jockeys was it riding against when it did?

It is just the same in the case of the chances or risk of a business making a profit. What is supplied is a starting point in the form of a statement from which to do one's own 'homework', called a balance sheet. In reality this is an agenda setting out the business model we have just been looking at, so we can see what the business owns as fixed assets, outside investments and working capital, and how such investments were financed from – in the case of limited companies, for example – the share capital and borrowed sources. It is from reading this agenda that the chances of a business making future profits can be considered, by asking such questions as:

- Has the business the right fixed assets to make future profits and are they being replaced as required?
- Are the investments appropriate for the particular business?

- Does the working capital investment reveal liquidity and does it seem to be minimised?
- Have all these investments been financed from the right sources – the question of pressure or gearing?

The two primary questions, then, for all investors, whether the investment is on a horse or in a business, are those concerned with the return and the risk. And it is in response to these two questions that in business we produce, in the case of the return, the profit and loss account and, in the case of the risk, the balance sheet.

The ready

At this stage, however, we meet a difference between business and other investment propositions. This is because when we put money into a business something happens to the money itself which does not happen in other investment situations – it moves. Business, as we have seen, is all about the movement of money and this is what makes it different from putting money into other investments. For instance, when you put money on a horse the one thing you do not want to move is the money – you want the horse to move and the money to stand absolutely still!

It is for this reason that we have a third information requirement regarding business: to know exactly how much money we will have as cash at any particular point in time. Because money is continually moving within a business we will find that the amount in the form of cash and bank balances (circle 2 in Illustrations 1.1, 1.2, 1.4, 1.5 and 1.6) will not necessarily stay the same. Sometimes the business will be spending money on fixed assets and material and so on, and sometimes money will be coming in from sales or dividends on its outside investments. We have also seen, when discussing the cash-flow situation within working capital, how important the question of cash availability can be.

Remember the 'lubrication to make a decision' we mentioned? It is this situation which makes it essential for those running a business to try to forecast its cash position over the period ahead so that they can be sure whether or not the business will have the money to pay its bills as and when they are due. We refer to the statement that sets out this prediction as the cash flow forecast, and it could be described as the forecast of the availability of cash within a business over the period ahead.

The profit and loss account, balance sheet and cash flow forecast

You can say therefore that a profit and loss account measures the *return* on and the balance sheet sets out the *risk* in the capital invested within the business, while the cash flow forecast lets us know if we will have the money when it is needed – the *ready*. These three statements form the basis of all financial information in business and might be termed the three Rs of financial literacy. Or if we prefer to remain in the sporting world, the profit and loss account is the score-line of business, the balance sheet is the position of the money-making players and cash is the ball. So remember the star striker and the empty goalmouth – which in business leads to the need for the cash flow forecast.

We must also emphasise that what the interested investor needs to know, the manager needs to know also. After all, the manager is simply acting on behalf of the investor and their needs as regards financial information are therefore iden-tical. In later chapters we examine each of these three financial statements indi-vidually, and create a real understanding of their content and use to those running a business. We will also see that effective managers are those who iden-tify themselves with investment.

Consolidation and conclusion

Before we look into these three financial statements, we must first consolidate our understanding of the way business money moves. We must recognise the two aspects of money in business which are set out in Illustrations 1.1, 1.2, 1.4, 1.5 and 1.6. These are the sources of money – where we get our capital from – and the application of such money: where it is invested; on what it is spent. We must also become familiar with each source – the owners' funds and money bor-rowed – and each area of application: fixed assets, outside investments and working capital.

In this understanding we must be aware that whether we are looking at a one-man business or a multi-million-pound enterprise our main sources and our main applications of money remain identical. To illustrate this point refer to Illustra-tion 1.7, in which you will find a management model together with a list of items on which money might be spent in a business and a model with empty circles. You should insert the appropriate number into the appropriate circle in the model. For instance, if you think raw materials are a fixed asset, item 2 should be placed in the fixed assets circle. (I may have made a mistake, so I will not help you any more!) Again, if you prefer not to mark the illustration, why not take a copy?

When you have completed this test turn to Illustration 1.8 and check your answers. When you have done this proceed to chapter 2, which deals with the first of the three primary financial statements: the profit and loss account.

Illustration 1.7 Financial transactions and unfinished business model

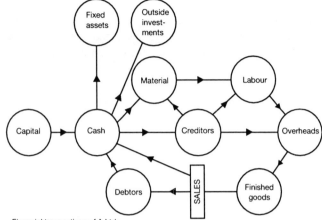

Financial transactions of A Ltd:
(to be placed in appropriate circles)

1	Plant and machinery	10	Buildings
2	Raw materials	11	Monthly salaries
3	Customers who have not paid	12	Advertising not paid for
4	Delivery vehicles	13	Rent
5	Components	14	Share capital
6	Cash in bank	15	Advertising
7	Freehold land	16	Loan capital
8	Wages for operatives	17	Shares purchased in S Ltd
9	Materials not paid for	19	Finished goods stock

Illustration 1.8 Financial transactions and finished business model

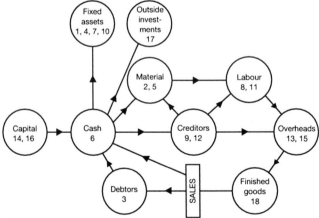

Financial transactions of A Ltd:
(to be placed in appropriate circles)

1	Plant and machinery	10	Buildings
2	Raw materials	11	Monthly salaries
3	Customers who have not paid	12	Advertising not paid for
4	Delivery vehicles	13	Rent
5	Components	14	Share capital
6	Cash in bank	15	Advertising
7	Freehold land	16	Loan capital
8	Wages for operatives	17	Shares purchased in S Ltd
9	Materials not paid for	19	Finished goods stock

2

THE PROFIT AND LOSS ACCOUNT

INTRODUCTION

The definition of profit or loss

This chapter is concerned with the score-line of business. The measurement of the return on the business investment which is set out in the profit and loss account. To begin with we must understand the meaning of return, and to do this let us go back to the simple situation of the return on a horse – the odds. What does it mean when we say the 'odds are quoted at ten to one'?

It means, of course, that if you put 1 on the horse to win and it does, the 1 will grow by 10, and if it loses the 1 will shrink. In fact it will disappear altogether. Return is therefore the measurement of the growth or shrinkage in the amount invested, and this is precisely what is being measured in the profit and loss account. The definition of profit and loss is the measurement of the growth or shrinkage that has taken place in the business investment, wherever it may be, over a period of time.

The bias of the profit and loss account

In practice, however, we seldom find a profit and loss account follows this definition in its entirety. It is biased. It concentrates on one area of growth or shrinkage more than others. This is because people who wish to examine the growth or shrinkage of the business investment are concerned mainly with how much of this is being created by its trading or operating activities.

It is because of this that the profit and loss account concentrates upon the items that reflect the working capital of the business. In other words, it spends most of its time recording whether the products, merchandise or services the business produces, presents or renders have been sold for more than they cost. Look back at the business models set out in Illustrations 1.4, 1.5 and 1.6 to see the areas we are talking about. It does not *ignore* the other areas – the fixed assets and outside investments – but it deals with them only if something obvious has happened: for instance, if dividends or interest have been received on the outside investments or losses or profits made on the sale of fixed assets or outside investments.

Capital and revenue expenditure

It is because of this bias that occasional difficulties of definition may arise. These occur when comparing trading or operating expenses with sales income because of what might be termed the 'mixed' nature of some expenditure. Expenses which might be going either into fixed assets, often termed capital expenditure, or into things which go into what is to be sold, often termed revenue expenditure.

The problem that arises is that at times expenditure may be partly capital and partly revenue. However, unless this is correctly defined the wrong costs will be set off against the sales for the particular period and so the wrong trading or operating profit or loss presented. An example of this is when repairs are made to buildings or machinery and during the process of the repair the particular item is improved. In such a case only the repair should be treated as a revenue expense and deducted from sales in the profit and loss account before striking the trading or operating profit or loss. The improvement part should be treated as capital expenditure and therefore included as a fixed asset.

The period of the profit and loss account

It is also necessary to recognise that because of the bias towards the trading area, the period covered by the profit and loss account is crucial if a true measurement of such profits is to be gauged. We normally associate the period of the profit and loss account with a year and this is not coincidental or because of a legal or even a taxation rule. Rather, if you are examining the growth of a business within the context of its trading or operating activities, the period measured must extend over its full trading cycle which will normally be a year. Businesses are in most cases seasonal and only by looking at the full year can a balanced view of the trading or operating profits or losses be provided.

It might be said that a month's profit and loss account is just a step along the way. For this reason any statement of profit or loss which does not embrace the full trading cycle – usually one year – must be treated with caution or wrong conclusions may be drawn from it.

The structure of the profit and loss account

Let us now examine Illustrations 2.1 and 2.2. They set out two simple profit and loss accounts, showing sales for the period, from which are subtracted the materials, labour and overhead costs pertaining to such sales. If sales exceed these costs we have a trading or operating profit as shown in Illustration 2.1; if not we have a trading or operating loss, as in Illustration 2.2.

Illustration 2.1 A Ltd: profit and loss account for the year ended 31 March

	£ 000	£ 000
Sales or turnover		10,000
Less:	£ 000	
Material costs	4,000	
Labour costs	2,000	
Overhead costs	3,000	9,000
Trading or operating profit		1,000

Illustration 2.2 B Ltd: profit and loss account for the year ended 31 March

	£ 000	£ 000
Sales or turnover		8,000
Less:	£ 000	
Material costs	3,000	
Labour costs	4,000	
Overhead costs	3,000	10,000
Trading or operating loss		2,000

In Illustration 2.1 we show sales of £10,000,000, material costs of £4,000,000, labour costs of £2,000,000 and overheads of £3,000,000, and we have a trading or operating profit of £1,000,000. In Illustration 2.2, on the other hand, we have sales of £8,000,000, material costs of £3,000,000, labour costs of £4,000,000 and overheads of £3,000,000, so in this case we have a trading or operating loss of £2,000,000.

At this stage we are not trying to examine details but principles. It is useful therefore to look back at the business model set out in Illustrations 1.4, 1.5 and 1.6 to see that a trading or operating profit means that more comes out of the working capital cycle than goes in, while a loss means the opposite. To illustrate this point in more detail, a profit will arise if the sum of circles 4, 5 and 6 is less than sales, and a loss if that sum is more than sales.

CASH AND PROFIT AND LOSS

It will be seen therefore that a profit means more and a loss means less cash generated within a business. Mind you, we have rather simplified this situation as cash and profit are not necessarily the same. The prime reason for this is the 'matching' context in which the profit and loss account is set. What is meant by this is that in order to calculate profit (growth) or loss (shrinkage) we must compare like income with like expenditure, and cash will not serve this purpose. After all, the cash received from sales will depend on which customers have paid at any point in time. And the amount may bear little relationship to the payments made over the same period – expenditure upon materials, labour and overheads which have gone into such sales.

Matching expenses with sales

It is in order to find a like for like comparison – to match sales income with sales expenditure – that the profit and loss account concerns itself with invoiced sales, regardless of whether the money has come in. In the same way the materials, labour and overhead costs in the profit and loss account are those which relate to – or as we say, 'match' – the sales invoiced for the period under review, again whether or not the money has been spent.

This means that you can in fact be making a profit but at the same time be short of money, i.e. be skint. On the other hand, you can be making a loss and at the same time have money, i.e. be flush! Profit or loss will eventually affect cash but there may well be a considerable time gap before this happens.

Accruals and prepayments

In order to match expenses with sales there is a need when assessing the profit or loss over a period of time to make sure we relate income and expense to that period. This will very often call for the adjustment of expenses and income to ensure that the full amount of each is set out under each head. To illustrate the adjustments necessary, let us consider electricity used but not yet billed. In this case it will be necessary to bring in the amount of this unbilled expense if the full charge for electricity is to be correctly set off against the sales for the period under review. This adjustment is referred to as an accrual.

Equally, in the case of rent paid in advance it will be necessary to restrict this expense to the rent for the period covered by the profit and loss account. This adjustment is referred to as a prepayment. If either of these adjustments is ignored the profit or loss of the business would be misstated.

Accrual adjustment

For instance, if in Illustration 2.3 materials received but not invoiced amounted to £20,000 the material figure of £450,000 would be understated by £20,000. It should therefore read £470,000, and if this item was not adjusted, the profits would be overstated by £20,000. In this case it would therefore be correct for the profit to read £80,000 and not £100,000 because an accrual adjustment of £20,000 would need to be made.

Illustration 2.3 A Ltd: profit and loss account for the year ended 31 March

		£
Sales		1,000,000
Less:	£	
Material	450,000	
Labour	200,000	
Overhead	250,000	900,000
Net profit		100,000

Prepayment adjustment

Again, if the overhead expenses of £250,000 included insurance of £3,000 relating to the period from 1 April to 30 June a further adjustment would be required. Overheads would have to be reduced by this £3,000, and if this were not done profits for the period ended 31 March would be incorrectly reduced by £3,000. To correct this a prepayment adjustment of £3,000 would be made to reduce overheads from £250,000 to £247,000.

Stock and matching

A profit and loss account is concerned fundamentally with the difference between sales made and the cost relating to such sales, and it is for this reason that all expenses deducted from the sales must match those sales. Due to this need to match expenses against sales a difficulty can arise after having arrived at the cost of each expense, i.e. material, labour and overheads, for the period under review – that is, after having made all the necessary accrual and prepayment adjustments. At the close of a period a business may have incurred material, labour or overhead costs for the period under review which have not yet gone into what has been sold. To adjust for such expenses it is necessary to take 'stock'. This is the term used to describe such material, labour and overhead costs.

Types of stock

In a manufacturing business there may well be three types of stock: raw material stock which is made up of the value of unsold raw material, work in progress stock and finished goods stock. Both of these latter stocks will include the value of the labour and overheads as well as the materials which have gone into the finished and partly completed items which have not yet been sold.

At this stage we must understand the logical need for these stock adjustments. Take raw materials: Illustration 2.3 shows a figure of £45,000 deducted from sales. In fact the materials expense in a profit and loss account is a calculated figure, and that in Illustration 2.3 would be made up as shown in Illustration 2.4. This assumes an opening stock figure of £30,000 (the stock figure at the close of the previous year) and current closing stock of £50,000 (also note the inclusion of the accruals figure of £20,000, already explained, to complete the calculated deduction).

Illustration 2.4 Calculation of materials figure in Illustration 2.3

Amount deducted from sales calculation:	£
Opening stock of materials	30,000
Add: Purchases for period (including £20,000 accruals)	470,000
	500,000
Less: Closing stock of materials	50,000
Deducted from sales	450,000

It will be seen from this that the closing stocks of one year become the opening stocks of the next and this applies not only to raw material but also work in progress and finished goods as stocks.

Work in progress and finished goods stock

The valuation of both work in progress and finished goods stock requires a calculation not only of the materials but also the labour and other expenses or overheads which have gone into such partly finished and finished goods. The adjustments required for these closing stocks will therefore reflect all these expense items. At this stage suffice it to say that we will examine these adjustments and the basis of their valuation in more detail later in our studies.

Cash and profit – the timing difference and the matching need

It can therefore be seen that because of the need to adjust for accruals and prepayments and to provide the matching adjustments known as stock, the profit or loss determined in the profit and loss account will not necessarily be identified with cash in the bank. There is a timing difference and a matching need. A business can be making a profit and at the same time be short of cash and vice versa.

To understand this point fully, refer back to Illustration 1.4, 1.5 or 1.6 and trace the making of profit or loss and the effect this has upon circle 2, cash. Remember debtors – a sale is a sale in the profit and loss account when a customer is invoiced, not when it is paid for. Remember also creditors: a cost is a cost against sales if it relates to the period of the profit and loss account and matches the sales made, whether or not the expense has been paid.

MANAGEMENT JUDGEMENTS

Finally, we come to the need to recognise that in determining profit or loss adjustments have to be made based on management judgements.

Stock

In fact we have just been considering an item – stock – whose value depends very much upon the judgement of management. After all, in assessing stock someone has to consider its quality and quantity before any valuation can take place, and both these considerations require judgement. Such judgements can never be claimed to be precisely accurate, and yet they have an immediate effect upon the profit or loss shown. Change the stock figure by one penny and you change the profit or loss figure by precisely the same amount. If you doubt this go back to the examples of the stock adjustment and its effect on profit and loss set out in Illustrations 2.3 and 2.4.

Depreciation

Again, consider the need to take account of the fact that many fixed assets lose value. To illustrate this point let us return to the model in Illustration 1.2, where we showed that money in a business is either invested in the things we have no intention of selling (fixed assets) or in working capital – the money-moving area as it might be called.

However, it must be appreciated that there are many fixed assets which over their lives, and although we may have no intention of selling them, lose their value due to wear and tear and obsolescence. They cease to work or grow out of date. Indeed, we might say that there is a 'secret shrinkage' which goes on in many fixed assets throughout their lives. To deal with this secret shrinkage – the erosion of value that goes on all the time – it is necessary to bring in another adjustment before arriving at the profit or loss of a business: the adjustment termed depreciation. To illustrate how this adjustment affects the profit or loss of a business imagine that we have bought a piece of plant and machinery for £40,000 and expect it to have a five-year life. We will assume that the anticipated scrap value at the end of its life will be £5,000. Thus, we are expecting a loss of £35,000 over the life of this particular piece of machinery. To account for this we might decide to charge £7,000 each year as an expense called depreciation. The effect of this will be to reduce the profit shown by £7,000 each year over this five-year period.

Depreciation and cash

At this point, however, we must note the very real difference between depreciation and all the other expenses – from a cash point of view. In the case of materials, labour and all the other expenses shown in the profit and loss account, cash is or will be directly affected. However, although depreciation reduces profit or increases loss, it has no effect upon the cash – or, as we say, the cash flow. In fact the cash circle (2) in the model in Illustrations 1.4, 1.5 and 1.6 will be increased by the profit made for a period plus any depreciation charged before calculating that profit.

Depreciation therefore has the effect of reducing the profit or increasing the loss shown while at the same time conserving the investment within the business. What is happening is that that total business investment is not being increased, it is being conserved or, as accountants sometimes say, equalised. The amount being held back as depreciation is equalising what is being lost – what is secretly shrinking away – through the wearing out and/or the gradual obsolescence of the fixed assets.

Purpose of depreciation

Perhaps the most widely held fallacy of those who approach business finance with little if any understanding is that depreciation takes care of the replacement of the fixed assets to which it relates. Nothing could be further from the truth. The purpose of depreciation is to reduce the amount of profit shown and so reduce the amount available for distribution – in the case of limited companies the amount available to take out as dividends. Dividends are legally restricted to the profits shown after depreciation and taxation and, indeed, for limited companies the prime purpose of depreciation is to minimise the risk of over-distribution: taking out of the business more than it can afford to lose.

After all, if this adjustment were not made the profits shown would be that much larger and if these were distributed the total investment in the business would be reduced without it becoming evident until it was too late! This would be when the depreciated fixed assets were totally worn out or obsolete and nothing had been done to make up the value of the investment lost.

Depreciation and distribution

To help you understand this point, consider Illustration 2.5. Here we see the business model of a newly formed company called J Bloggs Ltd, a street trader (or barrow person if you prefer). It is a simple business that buys and sells everything for cash, carries no stock and has no accruals or prepayments.

We will assume that during its first year it buys its one fixed asset – a barrow – for £40,000 and involves itself in the following transactions. It buys merchandise – cabbages, lettuces and asparagus in season, etc. – for £40,000. It pays wages of £20,000 and incurs overheads – rent for the lock-up garage to house the barrow at night and candles for its headlamps, etc. – of £25,000, which includes £5,000 depreciation for the barrow. At the same time its sales for the year, again all for cash, amount to £100,000.

In Illustration 2.5 you can see that these figures show that J Bloggs Ltd has made a profit of £15,000. However, if you consider the cash situation you will see that cash has increased not by £15,000 but by £20,000 – the £15,000 profit plus the depreciation of £5,000. This is because although depreciation is deducted before arriving at the profit it does not reduce the cash in the business. No one has to write out a cheque for it! At the same time, when J Bloggs comes to decide how much she can distribute – take out as dividends for herself and her fellow shareholders – there is a limit of £15,000: the profit made for the period. This means that the company will have £5,000 more cash, which it can do anything it wants with, except take it out of the business as dividends.

You might also of course argue that it really represents the fact that the barrow is worth £5,000 less than at the beginning of the year. But it is still the same barrow and does the same work. It is just a bit older and perhaps looks it! However, whatever anyone may think about the barrow the business has £5,000 left in the till that it has to decide what to do with.

Illustration 2.5 J Bloggs Ltd, the street trader

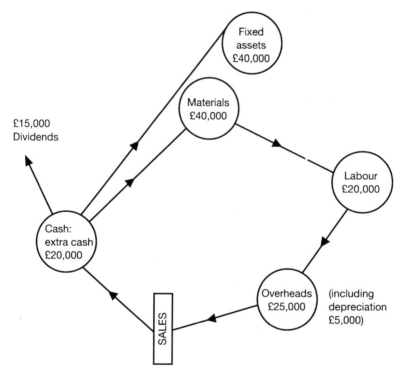

Profit = £15,000 (sales £100,000 less material £40,000
       plus labour £20,000 plus overheads £25,000).

Cash increase = £20,000 (profit £15,000 plus depreciation £5,000).

Note: It is assumed there are no debtors, no creditors,
       no accruals, no prepayments and no stocks.

Depreciation and investment

The surplus cash could be used to add to the fixed assets or to invest in another business as an outside investment or in carrying stocks (say, tinned carrots) to give the customers more choice or in allowing some of them credit – time –

before paying for their purchases. In other words, the money held back as depreciation can be used to do any of these things. However, whether the money will be available when it is needed to replace the barrow when it wears out or becomes obsolete will depend upon how well these investments turn out. For example, will people want to buy tinned carrots from a barrow, or will customers, given time, actually pay?

Depreciation is therefore a forced retention of profit and enables a business to reinvest the amount by which profits have been reduced by it. It must, however, be noted that deducting depreciation does not guarantee that the money will be there when it is needed for replacement. This will depend upon how and where the money held back is invested. It should also be noted that even if the money held back were placed into a totally safe investment and inflation were eliminated entirely, replacement would still not be guaranteed. Replacement is an investment decision and whether or not an investment is made is subject to considerations we shall deal with later in these studies.

Depreciation as a management judgement

This then is what depreciation is, its purpose and effect, but it must also be noted that the amount deducted in the profit and loss account will depend upon management judgement. The law requires a limited company to include a depreciation expense within its profit and loss account to provide for those of its fixed assets which wear out or become obsolete but the amount is left to the judgement of management. And, in the case of any fixed asset three judgements will be required: first, the asset's life; second, its scrap value; and, third, how the difference between cost and the scrap value should be deducted in the profit and loss account each year.

Methods of depreciation

Illustration 2.6 sets out the two best-known methods of depreciation, referred to as the straight-line and the reducing-balance methods, and these should be studied carefully. You will see that in the case of the straight-line method the depreciation is spread evenly over the life of the fixed asset, whereas by using the reducing-balance method more will be deducted in earlier than in later years over its life. The latter method is sometimes preferred as it means that as a fixed asset grows older and needs more repairs and maintenance the total deducted from the profit for depreciation plus repairs, etc. will be more evenly spread than under the straight-line method. Mind you, a separate calculation is required each year, which may be the reason the straight-line is used far more within business.

Illustration 2.6 Depreciation methods

Basic data:

Cost of fixed assets	£40,000
Life expectancy	5 years
Scrap value at end of life	£5,000

Depreciation methods:

1 *Straight line:* (£40,000 – £5,000) ÷ 5
  Annual depreciation charge   =   £7,000

2 *Reducing balance* (assuming depreciation to be
  written off at the rate of 20% per annum):

		Depreciation charge
Year 1 = £40,000 x 20%	=	£8,000
Year 2 = (£40,000 – £8,000) x 20%	=	£6,400
Year 3 = (£40,000 – [£8,000 + £6,400]) x 20%	=	£5,120

There is also a third method, rarely found, employed when 'usage' more than 'time' determines the life of a fixed asset. An example of this might be a cemetery with a limited number of grave plots available for burials – say 2,500. In such a case a method known as the 'diminution of units' basis might be applied (if you can spell or pronounce it!). The application of this method requires depreciation to be based on the units, in our example burial plots occupied/used annually. For example, if the cemetery cost £600,000 and 50 plots were filled this year, the depreciation calculation would be:

$$£600,000 \times \frac{50}{2,500} = £12,000$$

Other applications of this method would include such industries that own quarries or invest in very expensive equipment used in the distribution of electricity. Depreciation of their fixed assets might be based on the tonnes excavated or the kilowatts transmitted. (It is also perhaps of some relevance (especially for cemeteries) that depreciation calculated by this method is sometimes referred to as amortisation.)

Whichever depreciation method is applied, however, it must be noted that the amount calculated is a judgement and is only one of the judgements that may be necessary before measuring profit or loss.

Doubtful debt provision

It may be believed that certain sales included in the sales figure will not be paid for, perhaps where there are debtors who are suspected as being doubtful. In such situations a deduction from profit will need to be made to account for such doubtful debts and again the figure will be based upon the judgement of management.

For example, suppose that at the end of year 1 a company's debtors – amounts due from its customers – amounted to £30,000 and that £3,000 worth of them were considered doubtful. In such a situation a deduction – termed 'provision for doubtful debts' of £3,000 would need to be made before the profit or loss for the particular year was presented

You will see from this that the doubtful debt provision is unlike the provision for depreciation as it is not cumulative. We have seen how the charge for depreciation adds up year by year to a cumulative total, but this is not so in the case of the provision for doubtful debts. It will affect the profit and loss account if the amount required needs to be changed.

For example, suppose that, after providing £3,000 for doubtful debts in year 1, at the end of year 2 it was found a provision of £4,000 was required. The adjustment needed in year 2 would be to include a further provision for doubtful debts of £1,000. You can see in Illustration 2.7 how this adjustment is made over a series of years and how it affects the profit and loss account.

Bad debts and doubtful debts

It must also be appreciated that some doubtful debts may well become bad. In other words, no judgement is needed – there is proof that the customer cannot ever pay. In such a case the amount due will be 'written off', that is, included as an expense called a bad debt. This is also shown in Illustration 2.7.

Illustration 2.7 Provision for bad and doubtful debts
The following facts relate to the debtors of A Ltd over its first three years:

Year	Debtors at year end £	Provision for doubtful debts £	Bad debts £
1	60,000	3,000	1,500
2	75,000	4,000	1,700
3	90,000	3,500	2,400

Profit and loss account (extracts):

			£
Year 1	Deduct:	Provision for doubtful debts	3,000
		Bad debts	1,500
Year 2	Deduct:	Provision for doubtful debts (£4,000 – £3,000)	1,000
		Bad debts	1,700
Year 3	Add back:	Provision for doubtful debts (£3,500 – £4,000)	500
	Deduct:	Bad debts	2,400

Other judgements

Many more judgements might be necessary and these will be referred to as appropriate in our studies. However, the point to recognise is that the profit or loss presented in a profit and loss account is influenced by many judgements and can therefore never be claimed to be a precisely accurate measurement. This can prove confusing to those who view accounting as an exact science. It is, however, a combination of (it is hoped) accurate recordings with well-founded judgements and, like many well-founded judgements, they may at times be flavoured with bias and coloured by incompetence!

Provisions

Finally, before we leave 'the judgements' let me return to the word 'provision'. – used to describe the deductions from profit for depreciation and doubtful debts.

'Provision' describes an expense which it is certain will be incurred but which cannot be calculated exactly. For example, no one claims when £4,000 depreciation or £3,000 doubtful debt provisions are deducted as expenses in the profit and loss account that the fixed assets have lost precisely £4,000 through wear and tear and obsolescence this year or that £3,000 worth of the amount due from customers at the year end will not be paid. They are calculations based in the case of depreciation on the method used and in the case of doubtful debts on the evidence available at the time the figures were produced. We do, however, know for certain that things wear out and become obsolete and customers have been known not to pay!

UNDERSTANDING THE PROFIT AND LOSS ACCOUNT

So far we have seen that to use a profit and loss account as a measurement of the return on the business investment five points need to be understood:

(1) *Definition*   the definition of profit and loss – the growth in or shrinkage of the investment in a business over a period of time.
(2) *Bias*   that the measurement of profit or loss is biased towards the working capital area of investment because of the need to concentrate upon the trading or operating profit. After all, there is only one purpose in putting money into things a business intends to sell: to sell the saleable merchandise, products and services produced for more than they cost.
(3) *Period*   the period covered by the profit and loss account – the year – which has not been chosen accidentally but because most businesses operate seasonally.
(4) *Profit and cash*   the difference between profit and loss and cash is caused by the need to match expense with income within the profit and loss account, while cash is concerned simply with reality – the clink of the coin,

the rustle of the banknote and the flutter of the cheque. It is because of this difference that a business can be making a profit and yet be short of money or making a loss yet have money in the bank.

(5) *Judgements*   Fifth, the judgements which go into the calculation of profit or loss prevent these measurements from being precisely calculated – the judgement of stock, depreciation and doubtful debts for instance.

ORGANISATION OF DATA

Now let us consider the second stage in using financial information. Whereas the first is to understand what is presented, the second is to organise the data so that it can be used effectively. To help us do this let us examine the relationship of expense to income. By this I mean that, broadly speaking, business expenses relate to sales in two very different ways.

(1) *Variable expenses*   First, we have those expenses that move in direct sympathy with sales income, which are referred to as variable expenses. Examples are the material and manufacturing labour costs in the goods we sell and produce or the sales staff commission based on the sales made during the period. In these cases it might be said that if sales increase or decrease such expenses should move in direct proportion to such changes. I emphasise the word 'should' as there may be reasons, discussed later, that this assumption may not be valid.

(2) *Fixed expenses*   Second, we have expenses which have no such relationship. In fact this second group of expenses relates largely to time: for example, insurance for the year, administrative salaries for the month, rent for the quarter.These expenses are often termed the fixed expenses for the period and the assumption is that they should remain constant whatever the sales activity may be – again, an assumption subject to question as we shall see!

The breakeven chart

We can illustrate this relationship of expense to sales income by looking at the chart set in Illustration 2.8. Here we show a vertical axis (AB) measuring money values and a horizontal axis (AC) measuring units produced and sold for the year. Line AD describes the variable expenses which move in sympathy with what is produced and sold, while fixed expenses for the year are shown as the distance AE on the vertical axis AB. So EF is the line describing the total cost for the year depending upon the units sold.

Illustration 2.8 Breakeven chart: stage 1

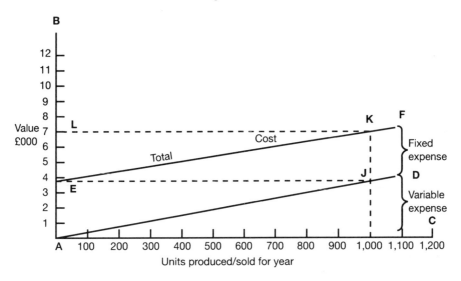

We can see from the chart that if we produce and sell nothing the total cost will be AE, the fixed cost for the period. It also shows that if we produce and sell 1,000 units the cost would be 1,000 units' worth of the variable expense, point J, plus AE, which is shown as point K. This we can trace to the vertical axis at point L.

The breakeven point

We can also expand the picture by drawing in the cumulative sales value line, shown in Illustration 2.9 as line AG. This shows that as we sell we reach the point H when line AG intersects with the total cost line EF. This is known as the breakeven point (BEP): the point where the difference between the sales income and the variable expenses equals the fixed expenses for the period – in this case the year – under review. This difference between the total variable expenses and the sales income is referred to as the contribution. Illustration 2.10 sets out the arithmetical calculation of the breakeven point for your interest. However, this calculation and its uses will be dealt with in more detail when dealing with marginal costing in chapter 7.

Illustration 2.9 Breakeven chart: stage II

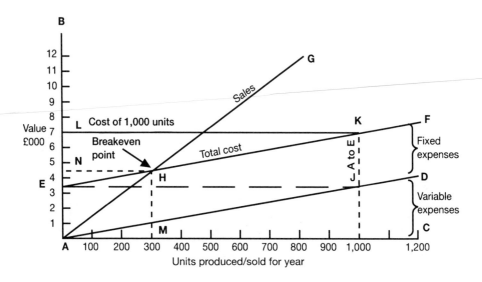

Illustration 2.10 Breakeven calculations

Assume the following facts for B Ltd, which produces one particular service:

	£
Sales price per unit	10
Variable cost per unit	6
Difference or contribution	4

If fixed expenses for the year are £720,000 the breakeven point calculation is:

$$\frac{£720,000}{£4} = 180,000 \text{ units}$$

or a sales value of £1,800,000 (180,000 units x £10 per unit).

Variable and fixed expenses

An understanding of the relationship of expense to income is vital if you are to
be able to read, understand and – most important of all – use a profit and loss
account. To appreciate how this division of expenses in relationship to sales
helps us use the information contained in the profit and loss account let us examine Illustration 2.11. This sets out the results of A Ltd over the last three years.
In (a) no division is made between the fixed and variable expenses; in (b) such a
division is made.

Illustration 2.11 A Ltd: profit summaries

a) Profit summary:

	Years					
	1		2		3	
	£	%	£	%	£	%
Sales	10,000	100	12,000	100	15,000	100
Material costs	4,000	40	5,600	47	7,000	47
Labour costs	2,000	20	2,400	20	3,000	20
Administration costs	500	5	700	6	800	5
Selling costs	1,500	15	1,800	15	3,000	20
Subtotal	8,000	80	10,500	88	13,800	92
Trading profit	2,000	20	1,500	12	1,200	8
	10,000	100	12,000	100	15,000	100

b) Re-analysis of profit summary:

		Years					
		1		2		3	
		£	%	£	%	£	%
Sales		10,000	100	12,000	100	15,000	100
Material costs	– Variable	4,000	40	5,600	47	7,000	46
Labour costs	– Variable	2,000	20	2,400	20	3,000	20
Administration costs	– Fixed	500	5	700	6	800	5
Selling costs	– Fixed	500	5	500	4	500	3
	– Variable	1,000	10	1,300	11	2,500	17
Subtotal		8,000	80	10,500	88	13,800	91
Trading profit		2,000	20	1,500	12	1,200	9
		10,000	100	12,000	100	15,200	100

In (a), where no division is made, the percentage of each expense to sales is only partially of use as both fixed and variable expenses are mixed together under each heading, with the exception of materials and labour costs. However, once the division is made, significant facts are revealed, such as:

- Material costs – which should be variable – do not vary in proportion to sales as they should, and we need to know why.
- Administration fixed costs do not remain fixed – again we need to know why.
- Sales variable expenses do not vary with sales – again why?

CONTROL OF EXPENSES

From this it can be seen that by reorganising the information so as to divide expenses between those which vary with sales as opposed to those which are fixed for the period we discover the two golden rules of expense control:

(1) *Golden Rule Number One:* Variable expenses should be controlled as a percentage of activity. In other words, if sales double variable expenses should also double and vice versa.

(2) *Golden Rule Number Two:* Fixed expenses should be controlled as an amount not as a percentage of sales – they should not move in sympathy with activity. Just because sales rise or fall this should not necessarily affect the fixed expenses. They should remain the same.

Mind you, we must never forget Golden Rule Number Three, which is that differences from the norm require in the first place explanations not vilifications or compliments. For instance, if the rent is increased the fixed expenses will increase but apart from negotiating a different rental – perhaps involving a move to different premises – little can be done. Or, again, if world prices for a key raw material fall the percentage of material – a variable cost – to sales will reduce although this certainly does not reflect management efficiency.

The profit and loss division – the gross profit

The need to strike relationships between expenses and sales income is responsible for the development over the years of profit and loss accounts which divide profits before and after administrative, selling and distribution expenses.

Profit before such expenses is often termed the 'gross profit', which is a very similar measurement to the contribution referred to earlier. It is calculated by deducting from sales, in the main, those expenses like materials or merchandise and manufacturing labour which will be of a variable nature. However, the gross profit of a manufacturing business will also be after deduction of manufacturing overheads some of which will be of a fixed nature. Nevertheless, gross profit as a percentage of sales should remain reasonably constant from one period to another because gross profit is calculated after having deducted from sales largely variable expenses. If this is not the case you need to ask why. Have sales prices changed and/or have variable costs per unit sold altered? The percentage should also be comparable between businesses in the same industry as sales prices and variable costs per unit sold should be similar.

Trading and profit and loss account

Where it is felt useful to set out the gross profit businesses will sometimes produce internally for management information what is termed a Trading and Profit and Loss Account. An example of this is set out in Illustration 2.12.

Illustration 2.12 A Ltd: trading and profit and loss account for the year ended 31 March

		£	£
Sales			10,000,000
Less:	Material costs	4,000,000	
	Manufacturing labour costs	2,000,000	
			6,000,000
Gross profit			4,000,000
Less:	Administration expenses	1,500,000	
	Selling expenses	1,000,000	
	Other expenses	500,000	
			3,000,000
Net* profit			1,000,000

* The term 'net' is used to indicate that profit is not an average but a net amount for the period involved, having been calculated after deducting both variable costs and fixed expenses from the sales achieved.

It must be noted, however, that we are at the beginning of our studies of this subject and we shall be developing each area in greater depth at a later stage. However, even at this initial stage it can be seen that in the control of expenses – and therefore profits – it is necessary to take 'two bites at the cherry'. First, variable expenses and therefore the contribution or gross profit, when this is presented, should be controlled as a percentage of sales. If this percentage changes we need to know why. Second, fixed expenses should be controlled as an amount and any changes should be justified. Remember that here no justification will lie simply in changes in the level of activity. Just because sales increase, for instance, administrative overheads do not necessarily need to increase in proportion.

Manufacturing trading and profit and loss account

With a manufacturing business it is possible to extend the profit and loss account into three sections: the first concerning itself with the cost of manufactured products for the period – termed the manufacturing account; the second with establishing the gross profit – defined as sales less the matched manufacturing costs of the goods sold plus the warehousing cost and termed the trading account; and finally, a third section revealing the net profit for the period – which is the purpose of the profit and loss account. Illustration 2.13 sets out an example of such a presentation which you should study with the following comments.

First, it should be noted how the work in progress stock is adjusted as a net amount against the total cost of manufacture for the period. By this presentation the fact that the value of the work in progress stocks are rising or falling is highlighted. Closing work in progress stock being higher than at the beginning of the period indicates that questions need to be asked regarding whether or not production is flowing through into finished goods as required. Are bottlenecks or increases in production the cause of the increased stock value?

Again, the same presentation is adopted with finished goods stock. The difference indicates whether or not finished goods are being sold as rapidly as before.

Illustration 2.13 Manufacturing, trading, profit and loss account for the year ended 31 December

	£000	£000
Raw material		
Opening stock	10,000	
Purchases	120,000	
	130,000	
Less: Closing stock	15,000	115,000
Direct wages		35,000
Direct expenses		5,000
Prime cost		155,000
Factory overheads		14,000
		169,000
Add: Work in progress stock		
Opening stock	10,000	
Less: Closing stock	12,000	2,000
Cost of manufacture carried down		167,000
Sales/turnover		250,000
Cost of manufacture brought down	167,000	
Add: Warehouse costs and overheads	20,000	
Add: Finished goods stock	£000	
Opening stock	15,000	
Less: Closing stock	12,000	3,000
Cost of manufactured goods sold		190,000
Gross profit carried forward		60,000
Gross profit brought forward		60,000
Administrative overheads	10,000	
Sales and distribution overheads	30,000	40,000
Net profit before interest and taxation		20,000

THE FULL PROFIT AND LOSS ACCOUNT

'Below the line' items

As well as trading or operating items a full profit and loss account will also include income and expenses unconnected with the sale of goods, merchandise or services. Examples of these items are investment income such as interest or dividends received, the profit or the loss on the sale of fixed assets or outside investments, and the payment of interest on loans. These are often termed 'below the line' items and are shown in the more detailed profit and loss account set out in Illustration 2.14. Here you will see a profit and loss account set out for presentation to the shareholders of a limited liability company.

Illustration 2.14 C Ltd: profit and loss account for the year ended 30 September (layout in accordance with Companies Act 1985, format 1)

	£000	£000
Turnover		170,000
Less: Cost of sales*		100,000
Gross profit		70,000
Less: Distribution costs (these include sales expenses)	12,000	
Administration costs	18,000	30,000
Trading or operating profit:		40,000
Add: Non-trading income	5,000	
Investment income	500	5,500
Profit on sale of machinery		45,500
Less: Non-trading expenses:		
Interest on loans	7,000	
Loss on sale of equipment	1,000	8,000
Profit on ordinary activities before taxation		37,500
Less: Taxation		12,500
Profit on ordinary activities after taxation		25,000
Less: Proposed dividend		5,000
Retained profit		20,000

* Includes the cost of manufacturing labour and and manufacturing expenses, i.e. factory rent, rates, depreciation of plant and machinery, etc.

If a retail operation, the cost of sales figure would include merchandise cost only. In the case of most service industries there is no direct cost of sales and so no gross profit is shown.

(If shares issued numbered 100,000,000, earnings per share = 25p, i.e. profit after taxation £25m divided by shares issued 100m.)

Terminology and layout

You will note how the term 'turnover' is used in place of 'sales' – another case of duplicate jargon as they mean precisely the same thing: sales invoiced during the year. It may also be worth noting that sales recorded for some activities, such as the sale of postage stamps or the copies run off on Xerox machines, are termed revenues by the organisations concerned, Post Office Counters and Xerox Plc. So in this area we can even claim triple jargon!

You will also note from the illustration that investment income is added in 'below the line'. This would include dividends on outside investments. There are also two items referring to a profit and a loss on the sale of machinery and equipment. These would be the difference between the cost of the particular item less the accumulated depreciation and the amount received on its sale. For example, a machine costing £40,000 with depreciation to date amounting to £35,000 (giving a book or written-down value of £5,000) is sold for £6,000. The profit of £1,000 on the sale would be shown in the profit and loss account.

Taxation

It will also be seen that this illustration includes the corporation tax calculated on the profit for the year as a deduction headed 'Taxation'. This taxation expense will not have been paid by the year end and in fact the precise amount payable will be subject to agreement and even at times argument with the Inland Revenue!

Dividends

From the figure for profit after taxation the dividends for the year are deducted, leaving the profits retained; in other words, remembering what we learned in chapter 1, the growth created by the business which is left in for reinvestment. The dividends referred to will include both interim dividends paid during the year and any final dividends declared but unpaid at the year end.

In many cases limited companies will declare and pay an interim dividend before the year end based on the expectation of sufficient profits for the year to cover such a distribution. It is, however, only the final dividend which reflects the known profit situation at the year-end. The final dividend is therefore declared but not paid until after the profit and loss account has been presented.

Earnings per share

The profit after taxation is often referred to as 'the bottom line figure', and in Illustration 2.14 this amounts to £25,000,000. It is this figure divided by the number of shares issued to the shareholders which is the basis of the earnings per share calculation. Again, this calculation is shown in Illustration 2.14 and shows earnings per share of 25p.

Once again, the importance of this measurement, as is so often the case in finance, is in its comparison rather than its amount. To improve the earnings per share might be said to be the ultimate ambition of a limited company, proving as it does that profits per share are continually rising. However, such simplicity of ambition might well be challenged on the grounds of 'short termism' if such improvement were sought annually. There may well be times for consolidation or even readjustment during which profits may not increase, or even reduce, pending significant future increases.

The importance of this measurement is therefore in comparison over years rather than the immediate year's figure. The trend over years is more important than any immediate comparison.

Exceptional items

Finally, there is a category of expenditure or income set out within the profit and loss account, which goes under the all-embracing title, 'exceptional'. This refers to expenses or income which due to their nature and their materiality are considered unusual or exceptional. A typical example might be losses on long-term contracts or a settlement of insurance claims. Both these items are unusual from the point of view of the normal activities of a business and, coupled with the fact that the amount concerned was large in relation to the business (in other words it was, as accountants say, material), the items would be classified as exceptional.

Consolidation

Much of what we have discussed in this chapter will be expanded upon in more detail later in the book but for the present we have completed our initial view of the profit and loss account. Now to consolidate your understanding of the measurement of profit and loss, turn to Illustration 2.15. Here you will see a list of items of expense and income and your task is to list these in the form of a trading and profit and loss account. When you have completed this compare your answer with that shown in Illustration 2.16.

Those with a particular interest in manufacturing industries should now consider the content of Illustration 2.17. Here you will find the summarised financial transactions for the year ended 31 March of B Ltd, a manufacturing company. Present this information in the form of a manufacturing, trading and profit and loss account for the year (in the form of that in Illustration 2.13) and once completed (and only then) compare your answer with Illustration 2.18.

Illustration 2.15 A Ltd: transactions for year ended 30 June

	£
Materials – opening stock	10,000
Labour for year – manufacturing	60,000
Administration overheads recorded for year	40,000
Cash paid to suppliers of material	110,000
Purchases recorded for year	130,000
Closing material stock	15,000
Depreciation for the year	5,000
Materials delivered but no invoiced received	1,000
Cash received from debtors	210,000
Insurance paid for period after year end	500
Interest on loans to business for year	150
Dividends received for year	100
Sales for year	260,000

Illustration 2.16 A Ltd: trading and profit and loss account for the year ended 30 June

	£	£	£
Sales	260,000		
Less: Materials			
Opening stock	10,000		
Add: Purchases	131,000	141,000	
Less: Closing stock		15,000	
		126,000	
Manufacturing labour		60,000	
			186,000
Gross profit			74,000
Less: Overheads		39,500	
Depreciation		5,000	45,000
Trading profit			29,500
Add: Dividends received			100
Less: Interest paid on loans			150
Net profit			29,450

Illustration 2.17 B Ltd: transactions for year ended 31 March

	£
Direct expenses	10,000
Administrative overheads	25,000
Turnover/sales	390,000
Closing raw material stock	15,000
Factory overheads	22,000
Sales and distribution overheads	35,000
Opening work in progress stock	14,000
Opening raw material stock	18,000
Warehouse cost and overheads	15,000
Purchases	220,000
Closing finished goods stock	15,000
Direct wages	42,000
Closing work in progress stock	11,000
Opening finished goods stock	13,000

Illustration 2.18 B Ltd: manufacturing, trading and profit and loss account for the year ended 31 March.

	£000	£000	£000
Raw material			
Opening stock		18,000	
Purchases		220,000	
		238,000	
Less: Closing stock		15,000	223,000
Direct wages			42,000
Direct expenses			10,000
Prime cost			275,000
Factory overheads			22,000
			297,000
Add: Work-in-progress stock			
Opening stock		14,000	
Less: Closing stock		11,000	3,000
Cost of manufacture carried down			300,000
Stock/turnover			390,000
Cost of manufacture brought down		300,000	
Add: Warehouse costs and overheads		15,000	
		315,000	
Add: Finished goods stock			
Opening stock	13,000		
Less: Closing stock	15,000	2,000	
Cost of manufactured goods sold			313,000
Gross profit carried forward			77,000
Gross profit brought forward			77,000
Administrative overheads		25,000	
Sales and distribution overheads		35,000	60,000
Net profit before interest and taxation			17,000

CONCLUSION

We have now completed our studies of the profit and loss account – the measurement of the return on the business investment or, if you prefer, the score line of business. But what about the risk or the chances of the profit or the loss being made? To answer this question we need to go on to chapter 3, which deals with the balance sheet. This statement continues our initial view of match-fitness that we discussed in chapter 1: a view which considers the position money takes – its sources and uses – once the business game is played.

3

THE BALANCE SHEET

Laurel and Hardy, Rolls and Royce, Return and Risk – partners in their respective fields, each proving the whole far exceeds the sum of the two parts. In business finance return and risk concern themselves with the measurement of profit and investment. The importance of what they individually present is, however, far exceeded by the importance of their relationship to each other – the return on the capital employed.

In the last chapter we looked at the return on the business investment measured in the profit and loss account – the score line of business. Now is the time to consider the position of the financial players – where the money is invested and how this has been financed – set out in the balance sheet, a statement produced to address the second primary investment question of risk: the chances a business has of making a profit. And here we have a very different situation because, unlike the question of return which is set out for all to see in the profit and loss account, risk is something you have to work out for yourself. No one can measure the risk for you. (They can, but would you believe them? And the answer to this question is in all cases 'No!' – especially when it is your own money you are risking.) This then is the problem of posing the question of risk. You want to know the answer – the risk or chances of making a profit – but you need to work it out for yourself.

RISK – THE STARTING POINT

Having posed the dilemma you have to seek the solution. As I pointed out previously, in the case of a horse, you start with its name because from that you can begin 'doing your own homework' – work out for yourself the risk of the horse winning. And that is precisely what everyone concerned with investment needs to do so far as risk is concerned: work it out for themselves. As in horse racing, however, you need a starting point. With a horse it is its name; in the case of a business it is the balance sheet: a summary of the business model which we described in chapter 1.

The model and the balance sheet

To illustrate the balance sheet in these terms, turn to Illustration 3.1 which sets out the business model of a company called A Ltd. The model of this company shows the investments within each circle as at the date selected – in this case 31 December. However, it does more than that, because it also tells us from where this money came. It defines the capital circle.

Illustration 3.1 A Ltd: model as at 31 December

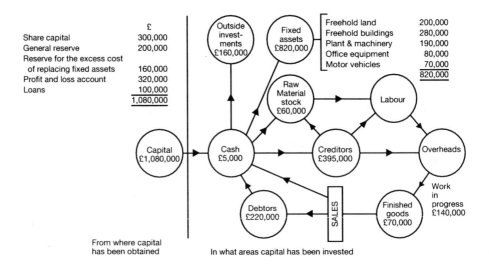

	£
Share capital	300,000
General reserve	200,000
Reserve for the excess cost of replacing fixed assets	160,000
Profit and loss account	320,000
Loans	100,000
	1,080,000

Outside investments £160,000

Fixed assets £820,000

Freehold land	200,000
Freehold buildings	280,000
Plant & machinery	190,000
Office equipment	80,000
Motor vehicles	70,000
	820,000

Raw Material stock £60,000

Labour

Capital £1,080,000

Cash £5,000

Creditors £395,000

Overheads

Debtors £220,000

SALES

Finished goods £70,000

Work in progress £140,000

From where capital has been obtained

In what areas capital has been invested

In our likening of business to a game, the balance sheet might be described as the position of the business players as at a particular point in time. The position continually moves, of course, and so comparisons with 'snapshots' and 'a movie clip' are also not inappropriate. However it may be described, the fundamental nature of the balance sheet being a summary of the money model of the business – its sources and uses – must always be kept in mind.

It is indeed this model which is presented in the statement referred to as the balance sheet. And just like the model, the statement is divided into two, describing where the money is invested in the business in one half and from where that same money has been obtained in the other, at a particular point in time. It is this statement which provides the starting point for anyone wishing to question the chances (the risk) of a business making a profit (a return).

The balance sheet as an agenda

After all, if profit is to be made the business must invest its capital in the right places, but, equally important, it must obtain its funds – its money – from the right sources. This therefore is the purpose of a balance sheet – to serve as an agenda from which questions can be raised regarding the uses and sources of money invested in a business.

However, before we examine these questions, let us first see how a balance sheet is read.

Reading the balance sheet

As already stated a balance sheet summarises the financial model that we studied in chapter 1. In this we saw how a business invests its cash into two main areas: in those things it has no intention of selling, called 'fixed assets' and in those things it has every intention of selling – its 'working capital'. We also have a third area which might apply to a business once it has been established. Money can be put into outside investments which, if they are not intended for sale, are included by accountants as one of the fixed assets. However, they do require separate consideration from the other items included under this head.

Now turn to Illustration 3.1 again and look at the model in more detail. Here we see amounts placed in each circle and if we then turn to Illustration 3.2 we see these same amounts set out in balance sheet form.

Illustration 3.2 A Ltd: balance sheet as at 31 December

	£	£	
Fixed assets			
Freehold land	200,000		
Freehold buildings	280,000		
Plant and machinery	190,000		
Office equipment	80,000		
Motor vehicles	70,000		820,000
Outside investment in C Ltd			160,000
Working capital			980,000
Current assets	£	£	
Stocks: Raw material	60,000		
Work in progress	140,000		
Finished goods	70,000		
Debtors	220,000		
Cash balances	5,000	495,000	
Less: Current liabilities			
Creditors		395,000	100,000
			1,080,000
Financed by:		£	£
Share capital			300,000
Reserves: General reserve		200,000	
Reserve for the excess cost of replacing fixed assets		160,000	
Profit and loss account		320,000	680,000
Long-term loans			100,000
			1,080,000

COMPONENTS OF A BALANCE SHEET

Fixed assets

In the first place we find that on 31 December A Ltd owns the following fixed assets: freehold land £200,000, freehold buildings £280,000, plant and machinery £190,000, office equipment £80,000 and motor vehicles £70,000, giving a total of £820,000.

Valuation of fixed assets

At this stage we must also be aware of the conventions of valuation which we use in the balance sheet. It is important to understand these conventions to avoid gaining the wrong impression as to the value of the items that we are looking at.

The convention in the case of the fixed assets is to value them at cost or revaluation value less depreciation to date. So in the case of a machine bought for £40,000 and depreciated at £7,000 per annum, the value on the balance sheet at the end of the third year of owning it would be: cost £40,000 less depreciation to date £7,000 x 3 (years) equalling £21,000 – giving a net figure of £19,000.

It must be recognised that this will not necessarily be the value of such items if they were to be sold beneath an auctioneer's hammer. It is this 'convention' value which is often referred to as the 'written-down', 'book' value or 'the going concern valuation'. It is the value based on the assumption that the item will not be sold but will be kept during its working life by the business. We will discuss revaluation value later in this chapter.

Outside investments

So we have arrived at the total of the fixed assets of £820,000. We can see from Illustration 3.2 that A Ltd also has an outside investment in C Ltd valued at £160,000. This value is again based on the convention of cost or revaluation value. Nowadays it is listed under the title fixed assets, as you will see when we consider presentation formats. However, I have kept it on its own so that when we consider the 'risk questions', later in this chapter, we can deal with this item separately from the other fixed assets.

Current assets

At the same time A Ltd also owns current assets. The word 'asset' is a financial term which refers to things of value. A fixed asset is something of value which the business has no intention of selling whereas current assets are things of value which either are cash or which the business has every intention of converting back into cash. These include such things as stocks, debtors (that is, people and businesses that owe money for sales made to them) and of course the cash and bank balances the company owns at the balance sheet date. Current assets could also include any investments held temporarily by a business, sometimes referred to as short-term investments, for example money placed in an investment for use within the next twelve months.

If we look again at the model in Illustration 3.1, these items included under the heading current assets are found mainly in the outside circles which make up the working capital investment. They are, in the case of A Ltd, stocks of raw materials £60,000, stocks of work in progress £140,000 (this is the stock partly completed and will include the material, labour and the overhead costs incurred up to the point of production reached), finished goods stock at the value of £70,000 (again made up of the appropriate materials, labour and overhead costs which have gone into these items once they have been manufactured) and the debtors (people or businesses who owe money at the balance sheet date for goods or services sold to them for which they have not yet paid), which amount to £20,000. However, we also include cash and bank balances of £5,000 and (if there were any), any short-term investments, making a total of £495,000.

This means that the current assets include items which are not strictly part of the working capital investment as we have previously defined it. Cash and bank balances are in fact neither one thing nor the other as they might become fixed assets or working capital. However, for balance sheet purposes they are included under current assets. The reason for this will become clearer later when we consider the question of liquidity.

In the case of current assets we again have to consider the financial conventions for valuation of these items, especially those applying to stocks, which are valued in the following ways.

Valuation of raw material stock

The value of the raw material stock is based on what the materials cost when they were bought, or their net realisable value at balance sheet date if that is lower. An example of this is set out in Illustration 3.3(a).

Valuation of work in progress and finished goods stocks

For work in progress and finished goods the convention is that, before we value these items at all, we must be satisfied with the answers to two questions:

(1) Are the items, which are in the process of production or which are at present produced and are included as work in progress or finished goods stocks, saleable or will they become saleable? Have they passed the necessary technical inspections?
(2) If the answer to the first question is 'yes', the second question is : when these items are sold will they be sold at their 'normal sale prices'?

If it is considered that both these questions can be answered in the affirmative, then the value of such items will be based upon the material and labour costs that have gone into their manufacture, plus the manufacturing and administrative overheads which are felt applicable up to the point of production reached.

However, if we are unable to give affirmative answers to these two questions, then the value must be based on what we believe is a reasonable valuation in the light of the condition of the stocks concerned. Again, an example of how work in progress and finished goods stocks are valued is set out in Illustration 3.3 (b).

Valuation of debtors and cash

Having considered the conventions for valuing stock, we come to those which we use for debtors (or accounts receivable) and cash. In the case of cash this will be the amount owned either as cash in hand and/or in the company's bank account(s) at the balance sheet date. However, the value of debtors would be based on what is due to be paid by those people and businesses who owe the money for goods, services or merchandise sold to them, less any adjustment for doubtful debts.

Illustration 3.3 stock valuation

(a) Raw material stock valuation:
   Cost when purchased   50p per kilo
   Cost at Balance Sheet 40p per kilo

For balance sheet purposes raw material stock value is taken as 40p per kilo – the lower of cost or net realisable value (assumed to be value at the balance sheet date).

(b) Work in progress and finished goods value:

	Material	Labour	Manufacturing and admin. overheads	Total stock value
	£	£	£	£
Finished goods stock value calculated per unit as	40	10	8	58
Work in progress stock (assume half-completed)	40*	5*	4*	49*

* These figures assume that all material costs are incurred at the beginning of the manufacturing process and that labour and overheads are incurred in direct proportion with manufacturing progress.

This means that if on the balance sheet date debtors outstanding amounted to £40,000 but £20,000 were considered doubtful we would value them at £20,000. The £20,000 would have been charged through the profit and loss account, as you will remember from the last chapter, as a 'provision for doubtful debts' and it would then be deducted before arriving at the debtors or 'receivables' figure shown on the balance sheet.

Valuation of temporary investments

If a business holds investments it does not intend to keep – amounts invested for periods of less than a year – they would, as previously mentioned, be summarised under the current assets heading and their value would be based on their cost at the balance sheet date.

Current liabilities

We have now considered A Ltd's current assets, which total £495,000. However, to complete the presentation of the working capital investment including cash we need to discover what is owing to creditors (or accounts payable) or the amounts due within twelve months from the balance sheet date. This comprises the inside circle of the working capital cycle, set out in Illustration 3.1, which will be made up of items which are listed under the collective name of 'current liabilities'. A liability is a financial term for sums of money which are owed by a business. A loan with more than one year before it is due for repayment is a liability and so is a creditor for materials payable next month. However, such a loan is a long-term liability as it is not repayable for at least twelve months, whereas the material creditor is termed a current liability as it is payable within the next twelve months.

In the case of A Ltd the current liabilities include creditors for materials, labour and overheads. They might also include amounts owing for corporation tax or dividends declared but not yet paid, and indeed any other items payable within twelve months from the date of the balance sheet. In this particular case they amount to £395,000.

So we have a picture of investment in A Ltd as follows: fixed assets £820,000, outside investments £160,000 and net current assets of £100,000 (that is, current assets £495,000 less current liabilities or, as they might be described, 'amounts falling due within a year' £395,000). All this brings the total for the 'top half' of the balance sheet to £1,080,000.

THE RISK QUESTIONS

This half of the balance sheet thus sets out where the money is invested, and from this we can pose several 'risk questions' relating to the possibility of the business making a profit.

Fixed asset questions

In the case of the fixed assets, for example, are they the right ones? If they are not, the possibility of profit will be that much less. And second, does the business seem able to replace its fixed assets as and when this becomes necessary? Of course these questions cannot be answered simply by reading the balance sheet. The question whether or not a business has the right fixed assets will require technical more than financial knowledge, and a physical inspection of the land, buildings and plant and machinery would be necessary before any conclusions could be drawn. However, a balance sheet provides a starting point for such questions. It tells you what the business owns and how much it has invested in each area. It might be said to 'point you in the right direction'.

Again, in the case of the ability of a business to replace its fixed assets, further information will be required, and certainly an examination of the pattern of replacement over past years will be useful in answering this question. In fact an examination of a series of past balance sheets will often provide much evidence of value when examining whether or not the business has a record of fixed asset replacement. It will reveal the pattern of such replacement. For instance, in the case of a limited company information must be attached to its balance sheet showing the value of replacements to fixed assets made during the year. This figure can then be compared with those for previous years and to the amount held back for depreciation over the same period. If such a review shows that the funds invested over, say, three or more years in the working fixed assets like plant and machinery in a manufacturing business or fixtures and fittings in a retailer were less than those held back as depreciation it would raise questions as to the adequacy of the replacement policies of the business. After all, depreciation is based upon a fixed asset's historical cost and so you would expect, with the incidence of inflation and new technology, that replacement costs would exceed the accumulated depreciation.

Outside investments

In the case of outside investments the question of suitability needs to be raised. What is the thinking behind the investment decision – why invest outside the business – is there a clear logic in this and, if so, what?

It must always be remembered that sizeable outside investments will in most cases be inspired and invariably agreed by the top management – the main board in the case of limited companies. It therefore follows that illogical or, dare we say, lousy investments indicate the level of thinking within the top echelons of command.

Net asset questions

In the same way questions need to be raised when considering current assets and current liabilities. For instance, in this area perhaps the first concern will be liquidity – the ability of the business to pay its creditors as and when they are due. You will remember we discussed this in chapter 1 when we saw that the creditors – the current liabilities – look to the cash flowing from the working capital – the current assets – to meet their bills.

The liquidity ratio

Indeed liquidity is such a central question that when balance sheets are studied the relationship of current assets to current liabilities is often expressed as a ratio. It is also the reason that cash and bank balances are included with the working capital items under the heading current assets so as to provide a complete view of liquidity. The word 'ratio' in finance refers to an index used to establish comparisons. So in our example in Illustration 3.2 the ratio would be set out as £495,000, the current assets, divided by £395,000, the current liabilities, giving an index of 1.25. We have, however, to be aware that few ratios have any importance taken in isolation. They need to be compared and for this reason it is the trend more than the individual ratio that needs to be observed.

In Illustration 3.4 you will see this ratio compared with the same ratio for the last four years. And it is this trend which can then be examined. This shows that current assets are not covering the current liabilities as much as they did, so the question is why? Was it planned or does it indicate a liquidity problem – that bills are getting harder to pay? Notice the questions that are then posed: is the overdraft increasing or bank balance in hand reducing, and/or is there a delay in the time being taken to pay creditors?

Illustration 3.4 Current ratio

		Years			
	1	2	3	4	5
$\dfrac{\text{Current assets}}{\text{Current liabilities}}$	2.11	1.86	1.64	1.42	1.25*

*Calculation = $\dfrac{£495,000}{£395,000}$

Question arising:
1. Was the change planned?
2. Does it indicate a growing inability to meet the current liabilities out of the current assets? Are there signs of an increasing overdraft or falling cash/bank balances, customers being chased more rigourously, and/or a delay in the payment of creditors?

We shall be looking at these and other interpretation questions later but at the present time all you need to understand is the fact that questions stem from financial information and these follow a logical progression: a progression we have been introducing throughout our studies so far.

Minimising investment in working capital

Of course liquidity is only one question that concerns us in this area. You will remember from chapter 1 that there is also the need to minimise the investment in working capital which forms the major part of the net current assets.

So the second question is the one regarding minimising the investment. Can the business reduce its stocks, shorten the credit time taken by its customers or lengthen the credit obtained from its suppliers? After all, if the investment in working capital can be reduced the money saved can perhaps be invested in better fixed assets and so improve profitability. It could even be taken out of the business altogether, which, if profits can be maintained with less capital, will improve the overall measurement of profits in relation to the total capital employed. Again this was discussed in chapter 1 and an example provided in Illustration 1.3.

THE SOURCES OF FUNDS

This then is how one half of the balance sheet should be read but how about the other – the one which sets out from where the business obtained the money which it has invested?

In our first look at the sources of capital, when we examined the money model at a business's birth, we considered only two: the owners' funds or capital which, in the case of a limited company, are termed the share capital, and borrowed or loan capital.

Profits retained

Of course at that time we were looking at an initial investment in a business. However, as a business continues we find that these two original sources of capital – owners' capital and loan capital – will be increased in the years ahead by a third source. The one which arises from the retention of profits, which is sometimes called in the case of limited companies, the 'reserves'.

Profit and cash

To understand this third source let us go back to the business model in Illustrations 1.4, 1.5 and 1.6. The trading or operating profit of a business can be traced on this model as the difference between what goes into the working capital cycle and what comes out from selling the products, services or merchandise of the particular business. If more comes out than goes in we have a profit; if more goes in than comes out we have a loss. This means that if we look at the model shown in Illustration 3.5, the profit will be represented by the cash circle growing larger. Note the broken lines in the illustration: a loss will be represented by the cash circle growing smaller, thus the smaller broken circle would represent a loss.

We are of course oversimplifying the situation because, as we have discussed, investment in a business is always moving, and from our profit and loss account studies you will remember there is often a time gap between profit and cash. However, if we could leave our working capital and fixed asset investments in all areas except cash at precisely the same level, eventually profit would be reflected by more cash and loss by less cash in the business.

The destination of profits and losses

Having examined the nature of profit and loss let us look at what happens to such profits or inflated cash or such losses or deflated cash.

First, in the case of profits, some will have to be paid out as taxation and in the case of limited companies some will also have to be paid out as dividends to the shareholders. However, any profits left over (retained) will go to increase the fixed assets and/or outside investments and/or working capital. In other words, retained profits will be represented by more cash and this will be used in precisely the same ways as additional cash introduced by owners as share capital or lenders as loan capital.

Illustration 3.5 Effect of profit/loss on cash

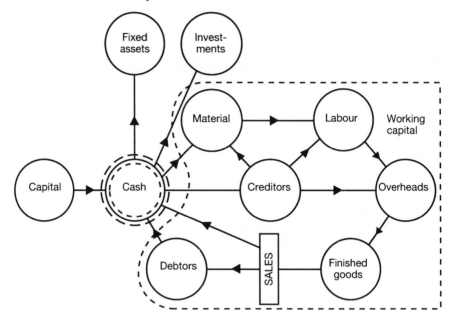

No one wants losses, so they *have* to be retained! This means that a loss will lead to less cash being invested in fixed assets and/or outside investments and/or working capital.

Profit as a source of capital

Retained profits are perhaps the most important source of capital within any enterprise once it has been established, and are for most businesses the major source of capital used for expansion. If you think of yourself starting a business, once you have invested all your own capital and what you can borrow from other people, from where else would you obtain permanent capital? And the answer is from retained profits.

It must, however, be noted that this source of money does not happen at the close of the year – it is happening all through the period profits are being made. For this reason it is not necessary to plan simply to make profits, it is just as necessary to plan the continual investment of the additional funds such profits are creating within the business, as they arise.

It is equally necessary to plan carefully the investments we reduce when losses are being made. This will ensure that we do the least possible harm to the future potential of the business.

'Reserves'

It is unfortunate that in this area of capital source we find confusion caused by the term used. The word 'reserves' seems to provide a particular mystery to many people and it is necessary to rid ourselves of this if we are to appreciate this vital source of money. It must be understood that the word 'reserve' in finance is simply a term used to describe retained profits, the third source of capital, not how they are applied or spent.

'Reserve' therefore does not have its military meaning of referring to unused resources. In fact retained profits – the reserves – are fully used within the enterprise, in fixed assets, outside investments and/or net current assets which include the working capital, in the same way as share or loan capital. This means that statements such as 'we shall pay for it out of our reserves' are the mark of financial illiteracy – worse than dropping aitches!

Profit/reserves and cash

In other words, when reserves are shown in a balance sheet it does not mean that this amount of money is lying idle within the business, available for investment in any new project that may come to mind. The location of the funds represented by the retained profits – the reserves – will be in the three main areas: in fixed assets, outside investments and/or working capital. To determine whether or not there are some sources available to finance any particular project or to meet any future contingency, the investments in fixed assets, outside investments and working capital must be individually studied. This will enable one to see whether there is any cash available or any assets which the business could borrow money on or convert into cash if that is felt appropriate.

Named reserves

In the past it was the practice to 'name' the reserves, although recently this has become less 'fashionable'. However, you may still come across examples such as the 'general reserve' or the 'reserve for the excess cost of replacing fixed assets'. In such cases it must be particularly noted that such names refer to the rationale behind the retention of the profit, and not where the money is invested. For example, a general reserve refers to the general need to retain profit so as to increase the overall capital invested in the business, while the reserve for the excess cost of replacing fixed assets refers to the need to retain profits and increase the capital in the business to keep pace with the forecast additional cost of replacing fixed assets. From chapter 2 you may recall that depreciation takes care of only the original or, as they say, historical cost of fixed assets. However, when fixed assets require replacing some may cost more to replace as a result of new technology or inflation. When such 'reserves' are created the amount that otherwise would have been shown under the heading profit and loss account is reduced by the appropriate amount and this sum will then be referred to by selected nomenclature. For example, if profits for the year to be retained (after taxation and dividends) are, say £250,000 of which £60,000 is to be termed general reserve, they will be shown in the balance sheet under two heads:

	£	£
Profit and loss account	190,000	
General reserve	60,000	250,000

The building up of reserves

Reserves are cumulative and they grow or are reduced depending upon the profit or loss retained at the close of each period. To illustrate this situation turn to Illustration 3.6, where we see a series of profits and losses for A Ltd over its first three years. We see that in year 1 the profit retained is £60,000 and the balance sheet for that year would show profit and loss account £60,000. In the second year the retained profit figure is £50,000 and in the corresponding balance sheet the profit and loss account figure will stand at £110,000, (£60,000 plus £50,000 from year 2)

Illustration 3.6 A Ltd: summary of profit and loss

Years	1	2	3
	£	£	£
Before taxation			
Profits	120,000	130,000	
Losses			40,000
Less: Taxation	40,000	60,000	–
After taxation			
Profit	80,000	70,000	
Loss			40,000
Less: Dividends	20,000	20,000	–
Profits retained	60,000	50,000	
Losses retained			40,000
Balance sheet:			
Profit and loss account	60,000	110,000	70,000

In the third year A Ltd suffers a loss of £40,000 so the profit and loss account figure on the balance sheet now reads £70,000, that is, £110,000 less the £40,000 loss for year 3.

THE SOURCES OF CAPITAL DEFINED

The need to separate the sources of capital from their specific location is funda-mental in understanding a balance sheet. The sources of capital for A Ltd are those shown in Illustration 3.2. These are share capital £300,000, the reserves and profit and loss account £680,000 and loans of £110,000, a total of £1,080,000.

In Illustration 3.2 you will note that two reserves ('General' and excess cost of replacing fixed assets') are shown together with the profit and loss account. It is becoming more and more common to find retained profits are left without any set names such as these and simply to refer to them as profit and loss account. There is, however, one other profit which we have not mentioned which may appear on a balance sheet: the one referred to as the revaluation reserve.

Revaluation of fixed assets

The revaluation reserve refers to the adjustment required when a revaluation of fixed assets takes place. For instance in the case of land and buildings it is recommended that limited companies should revalue these frequently and when this happens a further profit may appear on the balance sheet. An example of this is shown in Illustration 3.7, in which the figures before and after revaluation are set out and the profit on revaluation of £150,000 is shown among the sources of capital.

Illustration 3.7 A Ltd: balance sheet as at 31 December

	Before revaluation £	After revaluation £
Fixed assets	600,000	750,000
Investment	40,000	40,000
Working capital	20,000	20,000
	660,000	810,000
	£	£
Share capital	400,000	400,000
Profit and loss account	260,000	260,000
Revaluation reserve		150,000
	660,000	810,000

The purpose of such revaluation is to provide investors and managers with a more up-to-date value of the capital employed against which profits can be compared and the value and progress of the business may be more correctly assessed. This once again is a matter to which we shall return in later studies.

Shareholders' funds and gearing

Finally, it must be noted that retained profits, including profits on revaluation, increase the value of the shareholders – the owners – investment in the business. After all, profits retained in a business represent the sacrifice of the shareholders. These are profits which could have been taken out by, or as we say distributed, as dividends to, the shareholders. In the same way, profits on revaluation represent a growth in the assets owned by the shareholders, although unlike other profits they may not be distributed as dividends. This therefore means that when gearing is calculated (as in Illustration 3.8) the proportion of the total capital provided by shareholders will be made up of the retained profits and all the other reserves, including the profits calculated on revaluation, plus the share capital. To this is then added the loan capital of £300,000, making a total sources of capital figure of £1,200,000. At this point the gearing – proportion of loan capital to this total – can then be calculated as set out in the illustration. Again, you will recall the importance of this ratio the discussion of this topic in chapter 1 when we considered the 'pressure' borrowing funds puts upon those running a business.

Illustration 3.8 A Ltd: balance sheet as at 31 December (layout in accordance with Companies Act 1985 recommendation)

Balance sheet extract:

	£	£
Share capital		300,000
Revaluation reserve	200,000	
General reserve	100,000	
Profit and loss account	300,000	600,000
Shareholders' funds		900,000
Loan capital		300,000
		1,200,000

Gearing = 300,000 : 1,200,000
= 1 to 4

BALANCE SHEET REVIEW

Having examined the balance sheet of A Ltd in detail we can now review the complete statement set out in Illustration 3.2. Here we see that the heading reads 'A Ltd: balance sheet as at 31 December'. This 'as at' emphasises the fact that the balance sheet is not presented for a period of time but as at a point in time. It is in some cases – the fixed assets and profits retained – cumulative, but the accent throughout is upon the picture – the snapshot (a movie clip perhaps better describes it) – here and now. The contents are then divided into two sections.

First, we see where the investments have been made: in fixed assets £820,000, outside investments £160,000, and net current assets (made up of current assets £495,000 less current liabilities £395,000) £100,000, adding up to a total of £1,080,000. The statement then goes on to tell us how this total investment has been financed: by issuing shares of £300,000, retaining profits/reserves £680,000 and by means of borrowing £100,000, again equalling the same total of £1,080,000.

The use of the balance sheet

By examining this statement we can, first, assess the relative risk or chances of each investment we have made in helping the business to make profits and, second, discover the proportion of borrowed to owners' funds – 'the gearing' of the business. We can find out the terms on which such capital is provided – interest rates and repayment dates in the case of loans, i.e. the extent of the pressure. After all, it is all very well investing funds in the right places to make profits but we must remember that funds must be obtained from the right sources. However well money is invested, if it is obtained from the most expensive sources much of the profit obtained will be lost.

Present balance sheet format

Balance sheet layout is a continually changing feature of financial communication. Indeed there is a different layout within nearly every advanced economy. This means that American, Japanese and United Kingdom balance sheets vary in their presentation. Although the same facts are being presented their order changes and their terminology may well be different.

It is not felt appropriate to set out these variations here but simply to refer to them, drawing your attention to the fact that however the balance sheet is presented it still deals with where the money is invested and from where that same money has been funded. For information, Illustration 3.9 shows the balance sheet format recommended at the present time, which varies slightly from the earlier example. The figures are unchanged from those shown in Illustration 3.2 save for the inclusion of the revaluation value of fixed assets to include a profit of £150,000, and the reserves, other than the revaluation reserve, have been combined into profit and loss account, thus avoiding their division into different headings.

**Illustration 3.9 A Ltd: balance sheet as at 31 December 19—
(layout in accordance with Companies Act 1985 recommendation)**

Fixed assets

		£	£
Tangibles (at revaluation value)		970,000	
Investments		160,000	1,130,000

Current assets	£		
Stock: Raw material	60,000		
Work in progress	140,000		
Finished goods	70,000		
Debtors	220,000		
Cash	5,000	495,000	

Less: Creditors – amounts falling due within one year		395,000	
Net current assets			100,000
Total assets *less* current liabilities			1,230,000
Less: Creditors – amounts falling due in more than a year			100,000
			1,130,000

Capital and reserves			£
Share capital			300,000
Revaluation reserve			150,000
profit and loss account			680,000
			1,130,000

Notes:
The totals above differ from those in Illustration 3.2 for the following reasons:
1. Buildings of £80,000 included in fixed assets have been revalued at £430,000, resulting in a revaluation reserve of £150,000.
2. The long-term loans of £100,000 are, under this recommended layout, deducted – as 'Creditors – amounts falling due in more than a year' – from 'Total assets less current liabilities'.
3. All reserves and the profit and loss account amounts are added up to a total of £680,000 and presented under the latter title.

However, in the new format there are some new terms. For instance, current liabilities are referred to as 'amounts falling due within one year' as already mentioned, and loans and other long-term liabilities as 'amounts falling due in more than a year', and their position is changed. They are also deducted from the total assets less current liabilities of the business instead of being included with share capital and retained profits as previously.

It should also be noted that outside investments are included under the general heading of fixed assets together with those items which previously went under this heading. (We have, despite protest, come into line in this example!)

Intangible assets

Illustration 3.9 also introduces the term 'tangible' fixed assets. So you might ask what are intangible fixed assets? These are fixed assets whose value is determined at a point in time by means of market forces or cost but where their continuing value is beyond the control or prediction of the owners or managers of a business. Examples of these are copyrights, goodwill, brand names and research and development costs. Each in turn has a value or cost at the time it is created but this can in no way be guaranteed to continue.

Valuation of intangible assets

The copyrights of the best-selling author may be of great value today but if fashion changes and no one wishes to read his or her books what then is their value? A business's name and reputation may create goodwill of real value, but once these are lost so is the value of its goodwill. In other words, if we return to Illustration 3.9 it shows A Ltd to have a total value – sometimes referred to as a total net asset value – of £1,130,000. However, if because of its reputation, business connections, etc., people are willing to value it at £1,500,000 without disputing any values contained within the balance sheet as shown, it will be assumed that they are willing to pay £370,000 – the difference between £1,130,000 and £1,500,000 – for the value of its goodwill.

Again, the value of a brand name rises and falls with the public's opinion of the business's products – fickle at the best of times – and research and development costs would have value only if they translate themselves into a saleable product, service or merchandise.

It is because of the uncertainty over the continuing value of intangible assets that accountants recommend that they should be separately shown on the balance sheet and written off against profits as soon as possible. You will see an example of this being done in Illustration 3.10, where the position before and after such adjustment is shown.

Illustration 3.10 A Ltd: balance sheets

	Before £000s	After £000s
Fixed assets:		
Tangible	500	800
Intangible	90	–
Investments	40	40
	930	930
Net current assets	80	80
Total assets *less* current liabilities	1010	920
Less: Creditors – amounts falling due in more than a year	200	200
	£810	£720
Capital and reserves:	£000s	£000s
Share capital	350	350
Profit and loss account	460	370 (460–90)
	£810	£720

Cumulative nature of balance sheets

Finally – and perhaps most importantly – it must be noted that, unlike a profit and loss account, which is a summary of financial data for a period of time, a balance sheet is a statement of financial information at a single point in time. In respect of the fixed assets it is showing a cumulative picture and therefore does not tell us what a business has done over the preceding year unless it is its first year of existence.

For this reason, if we want to examine what has happened over, say, the preceding year, we would need to extract the difference between the balance sheets as at the end of that year and the end of this. This indeed is what is set out in the cash flow statement discussed in the next chapter.

Balance sheet date

It must also be remembered that because a balance sheet is presented as at a set date figures may be affected by the date selected. For example, stock or inventory levels, or amounts owed by debtors (or receivables) or to creditors or (payables) may vary throughout the year. However, because a balance sheet is taken out at one date, it may, and indeed in most cases will, give different values for such items than if another date had been chosen. Indeed, year-ends, and therefore balance sheet dates, are sometimes selected so as to coincide with when such values will provide the best possible view of the business. This step is most often taken so as to present the most favourable liquidity position, but again this matter will be dealt with in more detail in later discussions of interpretation.

CONCLUSION AND CONSOLIDATION

To test your understanding of balance sheets, turn to Illustration 3.11. Here you will find examples of the investments and sources of capital of A Ltd and B Ltd. Arrange these two lists of items as balance sheets for each of the two businesses in the recommended format set out in Illustration 3.9. When you have done this (and only then!) check your answers with Illustrations 3.12 and 3.13.

Illustration 3.11 A and B Ltd: investments and sources of capital

Business investment of A Ltd as at 31 December 19—

	£
Outside investments	50,000
Freehold land	60,000
Merchandise stock	50,000
Fixtures and fittings	30,000
Share capital	200,000
Motor vehicles	20,000
Creditors	60,000
Bank and cash balances	45,000
Debtors	5,000
Buildings	60,000
Profit and loss account	60,000

Business investment of B Ltd as at 31 March 19—

	£
Work in progress	60,000
Plant and machinery	40,000
Creditors	140,000
Share capital	200,000
Debtors	160,000
Raw material stock	10,000
Outside investments	30,000
Bank overdraft	60,000
Land and buildings	230,000
General reserve	30,000
Finished goods stock	30,000
Profit and loss account	60,000
Loans repayable in three years	50,000
Depreciation to date on plant and machinery	20,000

We have now completed our initial study of the balance sheet: the agenda we use to consider the risk, the chances a business has of making profit. It is of course incomplete because in many areas it provides, as we have seen, merely a starting point, and there is much 'homework' still to be done. Neither does it mention many aspects of a business which are crucial to its future profitability – the skill of its workforce and the calibre of its management, for instance. However, despite all these deficiencies it remains the only agenda we have and needs to be understood and used within its obvious limitations.

You have now completed this stage in your understanding of business finance so you are in a position to proceed to the next chapter, which is concerned with a very familiar topic for every one of us: having the 'ready' to arrive – the cash flow forecast.

Illustration 3.12 A Ltd: balance sheet as at 31 December 19—

	£	£
Fixed assets:		
Freehold land	60,000	
Buildings	60,000	
Fixtures and fittings	30,000	
Motor vehicles	20,000	
	170,000	
Investments	50,000	220,000

	£		
Current assets:			
Merchandise stock	50,000		
Debtors	5,000		
Bank and cash balances	45,000	100,000	
Less: Creditors – amounts falling due within one year		60,000	
Net current assets			40,000
			260,000

	£
Capital and reserves	
Share capital	200,000
Profit and loss account	60,000
	260,000

Illustration 3.13 B Ltd: balance sheet as at 31 March 19—

	£	£
Fixed assets:		
Land and buildings	230,000	
Plant and machinery	20,000	
	250,000	
Investments	30,000	280,000

	£		
Current assets:			
Stocks: Raw material	10,000		
Work in progress	60,000		
Finished goods	30,000		
Debtors	160,000	260,000	
Less: Creditors – amounts falling due within one year		200,000	
Net current assets			60,000
Total assets *less* current liabilities			340,000
Less: Creditors – amounts falling due in more than a year			50,000
			290,000

	£
Capital and reserves	
Share capital	200,000
General reserve	30,000
Profit and loss account	60,000
	290,000

4

THE CASH FLOW FORECAST

CASH AND CHOICE

We began our study of money measurement in business by listing three questions to which investors and managers seek answers. What is the return? – which we have seen is calculated in the profit and loss account. What is the risk? – which we saw approached through the balance sheet. So what of the ready – the availability of cash?

Cash provides choice for decision-makers. Without it managers find their options closed and their decisions influenced more by immediate cash positions than by long-term needs of the business. After all, if you are without money you have no choice as to whether or not, say, to pay bills, chase debts or replace fixed assets.

MONEY MOVEMENT – THE CASH FLOW

In our study of profit and investment – the return and the risk – we made a direct comparison with all other types of investment – the bet on the horse, the purchase of jewellery, the speculation on property. However, something unique happens to cash in a business: it moves. As we have already mentioned, when you place money on a horse the one thing you do not want is for the money to move. You prefer all movement to be confined to the horse and the money to stand absolutely still!

In business the movement of money is crucial to its progress and to its success. We refer to this as the cash flow, which means the continual movement of money throughout the enterprise during any period of time. A cash-flow problem signifies therefore that the cash is not moving as is required. In most cases this means there is insufficient cash to meet the business's needs. In vulgar parlance, the business is skint or strapped for cash.

THE CASH FLOW FORECAST

An understanding of the movement of cash is essential to those running a business, because they have to realise that unless they have money as and when it is needed the business could collapse. Decisions are motivated more by cash requirements sooner than the real needs of the business.

The basic method of controlling cash – to determine its availability – is simply to forecast over the period ahead the cash which it is anticipated will arrive and to deduct from this the cash which it is expected will be spent. It is this forecast which enables those managing the business to examine its cash position over the period ahead. The statement setting out this situation is termed the cash flow forecast and it is divided into monthly, weekly or even daily intervals depending upon the particular needs of the business.

Construction

To illustrate this, refer to Illustration 4.1. Here we see a statement headed 'A Ltd cash flow forecast' and if you look at its contents you will see that in month 1 A Ltd is planning to receive £322,000: £260,000 from cash sales, £60,000 from credit sales – that is, cash from people or businesses who have bought goods on credit (the debtors, or receivables, remember) – and £2,000 from interest on outside investments the company has made. We also see that during the month A Ltd is planning to spend £260,000: £90,000 to the suppliers of materials who were not paid immediately for them (the creditors, or accounts payable, remember), £70,000 on wages, £60,000 on overheads and £40,000 which will be paid out to shareholders as dividends.

Illustration 4.1   A Ltd: cash flow forecast

	Month 1	Month 2	Month 3
	£	£	£
Receipts			
Cash sales	260,000	200,000	
Credit sales	60,000	40,000	
Interest received	2,000	–	
Subtotal A	322,000	240,000	
Payments			
Credit purchases of materials	90,000	160,000	
Wages	70,000	70,000	
Overheads	60,000	75,000	
Dividends paid	40,000	–	
Machine purchased	–	50,000	
Subtotal B	260,000	355,000	
Balance brought forward C	15,000	77,000	(38,000)
Balance carried forward D	77,000	(38,000)	
D = (A + C) – B			
Brackets = overdraft			

However, at the close of the previous month A Ltd had cash balances to bring forward of £15,000 – what is termed a positive cash-flow position or a balance in hand (duplicate jargon rears its head again). The final balance carried forward at the end of month 1 is therefore arrived at by adding the receipts, subtotal A, of £322,000 to the balance brought forward, subtotal C, of £15,000, making a total of £337,000, and deducting from this subtotal B, the total expenditure for the month of £260,000. This gives the balance to be carried forward of £77,000 – again a positive cash-flow position.

In month 2 we continue in the same manner with just a few variations: first, we do not receive any interest on investments; second, we buy a new machine for £50,000 and the final balance carried forward becomes a minus of £38,000 – known as a negative cash flow position. You will also note the use of brackets when a negative figure is presented, as in this case. It is customary for those presenting financial data to use brackets (when perhaps they run out of red ink) to surround figures which are negative or different from what is normally expected.

Cash, sales and debtors

In looking at this cash flow forecast it must be emphasised that our concern is entirely and exclusively with cash. For instance, we are not concerned with the sales we invoice, only with the cash we receive from those we sell to, and the two figures can of course be very different – remember debtors, or receivables. You will remember from chapter 2, when we were dealing with the profit and loss account, that the sales figure, or turnover as it is often called, is based on what the business has invoiced irrespective of cash receipts. In the cash flow forecast, however, it is only the cash we receive from the customers which is of interest to us.

Cash, purchasers and creditors

This is also true of payments for materials, wages, overheads, dividends, and machines and other fixed assets purchased. These refer in each case entirely to the cash the business pays out, not the costs in the profit and loss account or valuations in the balance sheet – remember creditors, or payables. We have therefore a timing and blurring difference to take into account when comparing the balances in the cash flow forecast with the profit or loss in the profit and loss account and investment values in the balance sheet.

Timing difference

First, so far as time is concerned, the profit and loss account is a measurement of growth or shrinkage in relationship to invoiced sales for the period for which it is produced. It concerns itself solely with those expenses which directly refer to the same period of time as the sales to which they are matched. However, cash is only concerned with the 'pragmatic doctrine'. Has the cash been spent or received during the period covered by the cash flow forecast? If it has, it must be included; if not, it must be excluded.

Revenue/capital and cash

The second consideration is that cash does not recognise any difference between fixed assets (capital expenditure) and items of profit and loss expense (revenue expenditure). It blurs or mixes them together. From a cash point of view there is no division, for example, in Illustration 4.1 between the purchase of a machine shown as a payment in month 2 and money spent on materials, wages and overheads during the same period. Money is spent in both situations whether it is capital or revenue expenditure.

Profit and loss and cash

All this means that the cash-flow position, whether negative or positive, will not necessarily reflect the profit or loss of the business during the same period. The business could be making a profit and yet be 'broke' in cash terms – that is, short of money. Or it could be making a loss and yet be 'flush' – showing a healthy cash balance. This fact must be firmly understood by all those concerned with business. It was a point we also covered in chapter 2 when discussing the profit and loss account, and if you have any difficulty in understanding this you should refer back to that chapter.

Depreciation and cash

Finally, in comparing the measurement of cash flow with profit or loss, we must remember that we have one major expense recorded in the profit and loss account which does not directly affect cash expenditure – depreciation.

Again, you will recall from chapter 2 that depreciation is an assessment of the loss – the secret shrinkage we called it – that goes on during the life of any fixed asset which is subject to obsolescence and/or wear and tear. It is this calculated loss or shrinkage which is included as an expense in the profit and loss account and by doing this the profit is correspondingly reduced or the loss increased.

But let us stop and think about this expense and compare it with all the others, like those relating to labour and materials and other expenses like advertising, rent and insurance. There is a major difference, and it is of course that depreciation, unlike all the other expenses, does not reduce the cash in the business. In a business we do not take out our cheque book and write a cheque for depreciation, as we will certainly have to do in the end to meet the costs of materials, wages, rent, advertising and insurance.

Depreciation, from a cash point of view, is therefore not an expense. It reduces the profit or increases the loss but it does not reduce the cash the business has and therefore once again we have a major difference between the assessment of profit or loss and the cash position. It might be said that from a cash point of view depreciation is a 'phoney' item.

Reading a cash flow forecast

So let us now stand back and see what this cash flow forecast tells us. First, we must understand why cash is so important within a business. As we have already said, it is the lubrication needed to make decisions for the benefit of the business as a whole and because of this its availability enables a business to create the profits and acquire the investments it requires. Again, it might be said that cash is the bus fare needed for the business's journey – it enables it to arrive! If we run out of cash we may never reach our destination, however attractive it may be. For instance, if we examine the cash flow forecast for A Ltd in Illustration 4.1, we see that A Ltd could be heading for a substantial profit at the close of the year, but if it has not negotiated an overdraft or a loan of at least £38,000 to become available during months 2 and 3, it may never arrive. Or again, if it avoids the need to seek such help by cancelling its purchase of the machine its fixed assets will be that much less able to meet its future production needs and so profit-making targets.

This is the fundamental reason for cash planning and control. It provides a view over the period ahead so that we can take appropriate action. In cash planning you need time – engineers might call it lead time – to arrange the necessary loan facility or curtail expenditure plans if these are felt to be more than can be afforded.

Managers must also recognise that cash directly influences all their decisions. As we have seen, cash might be described as the lubrication which is needed to make every major decision. Without it, just like an engine without oil, the businesses seizes up. For example, if a business has no cash, its managers no longer make decisions – they are made for them. The bills cannot be paid and if this continues people and businesses owed money will take remedial action. Or managers might be tempted to buy inferior materials at a lower cost, thus affecting the quality of what is produced.

The lack of cash when it is needed reduces the options open to the decision-makers of a business. It should therefore be no surprise that perhaps the major cause of business failure is inadequate cash planning and control.

CASH PLANNING AND PROGRESSING

Having set out the cash flow forecast it will then be necessary to compare it with events as they occur – to progress the position as time goes by.

As a result of this comparison, if differences are found between actual and comparative figures, we will need to check the impact this will have on the period ahead. In month 1 in Illustration 4.1 for example, if when we compare the actual credit sales receipts against the forecast £60,000 we found them to be only £50,000, there is a difference of £10,000. This might well indicate slow payment of certain amounts which will be corrected in month 2, and the figure for month 2 for credit sales would then read £50,000 – that is, £40,000 plus the extra £10,000. However, it might also mean that the forecast figures were over-optimistic and a recalculation of the future cash-flow position would need to be made. Continual revision of the cash flow forecast is a vital part of cash control as early warning of the effects of such changes will provide more time to take the necessary corrective action.

We must also appreciate that effective cash-flow forecasting and control require joint action by all managers – and indeed employees – at all levels of a business. Anyone concerned with cash planning must enlist the help of every person employed within the business to ensure that the greatest possible warning or lead time is given whenever any changes occur to the cash plan. For example, sales staff need to warn the business when they suspect customers will not be able to pay amounts due.

To illustrate this comparison the first three months of a cash flow forecast setting out columns for both budgeted and actual figures are shown in Illustration 4.2. In this you will see that the budgeted figures have been included and these await comparison with the actual data as it becomes available. It will be necessary then, if differences occur, to calculate their impact on the future net cash-flow positions over the period ahead. In other words, the business will be able to recalculate the future budgeted figures.

Illustration 4.2 cash flow forecast

	Month 1		Month 2		Month 3	
Receipts	Budget £	Actual £	Budget £	Actual £	Budget £	Actual £
Sale of goods – debtors	50,000		60,000		40,000	
Sale of fixed assets	5,000		–		–	
Dividends/interest received	1,000		500		2,000	
Subtotal A	56,000		60,500		42,000	
Payments						
Material – creditors	30,000		40,000		41,000	
Wages/salaries	10,000		12,000		12,000	
Overheads	5,000		6,500		7,000	
Fixed assets purchases	4,000		10,000		12,000	
Subtotal B	49,000		68,500		72,000	
Balance (A – B)	7,000		(8,000)		(30,000)	
Balance b/fwd	2,000		9,000		1,000	
Balance c/fwd	9,000		1,000		(29,000)	

CASH FLOW – THE TOTAL VIEW

So far we have examined the cash flow on a day-by-day, month-by-month basis for the purpose of forecasting the availability or otherwise of cash through the cash flow forecast. However there is perhaps a more fundamental way of observing and managing cash. The way so aptly described by Micawber in *David Copperfield* as living within or beyond one's means. This of course avoids the detailed analysis of cash over the period ahead divided into weeks or months, etc.; instead it takes on a more total view.

To illustrate this in a business context let us go back to our model set out in Illustration 1.2. Here we can see that everything is flowing into or out of cash. Cash is the centre point – the fulcrum of business investment. Whatever is done within a business will eventually have an effect upon its cash position. It therefore becomes a very convenient measurement around which to examine the financial effects of business decisions, policies and plans. It is because of this fact that managers and investors have increasingly turned to an examination of cash movement in total to trace the progress of the business investment.

In other words, managers have converted their plans into an examination of their impact upon what cash in total will come into the business and precisely what will happen to it if we follow the policies agreed for the business over the period under review.

Investment review and analysis

To illustrate this, look at the business investment of an enterprise at two points in time shown in Illustration 4.3. Here you will see the balance sheets of a company setting out its position at both the beginning and end of a year. It will be remembered from chapter 3 that in each situation we are looking in certain areas at a cumulative position. The fixed assets for instance are those A Ltd owns as at that point in time and they may well include items which have been owned for many years.

The cumulative aspect

It is this cumulative aspect of the figures included in the balance sheet which prevents us examining precisely the changes that have occurred in the short term. We can, however overcome this problem by concentrating the changes between the figures shown as at two points in time. We can then present the picture in cash terms, first, as regards what additional cash has come into the business and from what sources, and, second, in which areas such funds have been invested during the period at which we are looking.

We can apply this approach either to a historical or to a forecasted situation. However, in whatever way it is viewed, it will have the effect of concentrating attention upon the changes which have taken or are planned to take place within the particular business. It will take us away from the long term cumulative view.

THE SOURCE AND APPLICATION OR USE OF FUNDS STATEMENT

To demonstrate this let us turn to Illustration 4.4 while at the same time keeping an eye on Illustration 4.3.

Illustration 4.3   A Ltd: balance sheets

Last year			This year	
£	£		£	£
		Fixed assets		
100,000		Land and buildings		200,000
50,000		Plant and machinery		40,000
150,000				240,000
60,000		Investments		60,000
		Working capital		
		Current assets		
	120,000	Stock	170,000	
	200,000	Debtors	320,000	
	320,000		490,000	
		Less:		
		Current liabilities		
140,000	180,000	Creditors	120,000	370,000
350,000				670,000
£		Financed by:		£
250,000		Share capital		400,000
100,000		Profit and loss account		270,000
350,000				670,000

In Illustration 4.4 we have a summary or statement of the differences between this and last year's figures set out in the balance sheets shown in Illustration 4.3. This is called a source and application or use of funds statement.

Sources

In this particular example it tells us that during the year £150,000 has come into A Ltd from additional share capital and £170,000 from retained profits, a total of £320,000 from these two sources. These figures have been calculated by deducting last from this year's figures in each case.

Applications

The statement then goes on to describe, based on similar calculations, how during this same period £90,000 has been invested in fixed assets, nothing in outside investments and £230,000 in working capital. Again the total of all these applications comes to £320,000. This is why it is called a source and application of funds or use statement. It describes where we have invested our money and the sources from which it came over a selected period of time. We can of course express this statement in much more detail depending upon our needs, and certainly if we were planning future investments, it would be necessary to obtain the fullest possible picture.

Illustration 4.4 A Ltd: source and application or use of funds statement for the year 19 —

Source of funds		£		£
Share capital		150,000		
Profits retained		170,000		320,000
Application of funds	Increase	Decrease		
	£	£		£
Fixed assets				
Land and buildings	100,000			
Plant and machinery		10,000	=	90,000
Working capital	Increase	Decrease		
	£	£		
Stock	50,000			
Debtors	120,000			
	170,000			
Creditors		60,000	=	230,000
				320,000

Note:
A reduction in credit taken (creditors) is an application of funds (or an increase to the investment made in the business).

Sources and depreciation

We have also oversimplified the picture by ignoring the effect of depreciation. What I mean is that, as we have already explained, depreciation is not a cash expense. It reduces a business's profits but not its cash balances.

We can demonstrate this if we set out Illustration 4.3 in more detail, as in Illustration 4.5. Here we are assuming that the depreciation deducted during year 2 amounted to £60,000, and this means that we would have a further source of cash for investment, a source that, if we wish to have a full view of the increase in money invested, must be included. For these purposes, therefore, the sources must be increased by the amount held back as depreciation for the year.

If this is done, however, we must also adjust the fixed assets figure. This is because the difference of £90,000 (shown in Illustration 4.4) between the fixed assets at the beginning and end of the year, is given after deducting this additional depreciation of £60,000 in arriving at the figure for the second year for the fixed assets.

For this reason the true investment in fixed assets during the year should have read £150,000. This is the £90,000 already calculated plus the £60,000 depreciation deducted for this year. The revised balance sheet for A Ltd, which includes this adjustment, is set out in Illustration 4.5, and a revised source and application or use of funds statement based on this is set out in Illustration 4.6. Here you will see that in addition to the source of funds during the year from share capital £150,000 and profits retained £170,000 we have included – added back, in fact – £60,000 for depreciation, making a total of £380,000. You will also see that the fixed asset increase is shown as £150,000 as we have just explained, and everything that would fall under current assets *less* current liabilities in the balance sheet is lumped together as one figure, namely £230,000, described as working capital.

Illustration 4.5 A Ltd: this year and last year's figures (including depreciation)

£			Cost	£	£ Less depreciation to date	£
			Fixed assets			
100,000			Land and buildings	200,000	–	200,000
50,000*			Plant and machinery	180,000	140,000	40,000
150,000						240,000
60,000			Investments			60,000
			Working capital			
	£		Current assets			
	120,000		Stock	170,000		
	200,000		Debtors	320,000		
	320,000				490,000	
			Less:			
			Current liabilities			
140,000	180,000		Creditors		120,000	370,000
350,000						670,000
			Financed by:			
250,000			Share capital			400,000
100,000			Profit and loss account			270,000
350,000						670,000

* Made up as follows	£
Cost	130,000
Less: depreciation to date	80,000
	50,000

Illustration 4.6 A Ltd: source and application or use of funds statement (after inclusion of depreciation (£60,000))

Source of funds	£
Share capital	150,000
Profits retained	170,000
Depreciation	60,000
	380,000

Application of funds	£
Fixed assets	150,000
Working capital	230,000
	380,000

Working capital detailed

A more detailed example of a source and application or use of funds statement, prepared from the balance sheet of B Ltd in Illustration 4.7, appears in Illustration 4.8. In this case the working capital changes are set out in detail as are those that apply to the fixed assets.

You will also notice that in this illustration the company concerned, B Ltd, has made a loss in the year which involves a deduction of £110,000 – note the use of brackets again – from the sources for the period. Remember what we previously described as profit being growth and loss being shrinkage of the investment in a business? If not, revise chapters 1 and 2.

Illustration 4.7 B Ltd: balance sheets as at 31 December 19—

Last year £	£		This year £	£
		Fixed assets		
	120,000	Land and buildings	170,000	
210,000	90,000	Plant and machinery	110,000	280,000
170,000		Working capital investments		160,000
		Current assets		
	90,000	Stock	150,000	
	160,000	Debtors	140,000	
	250,000		290,000	
		Less:		
		Current liabilities		
150,000	110,000	Creditors	90,000	200,000
530,000				640,000
		Financed by:		
300,000		Share capital		500,000
160,000		Profit and loss account		50,000
70,000				90,000
530,000				640,000

Note:
Depreciation on plant and machinery for the year is £50,000.

Illustration 4.8 B Ltd: source and application of funds statement

Source of funds			£
Profit and loss account			(110,000)
Depreciation			50,000
From operations			60,000
Share capital			200,000
Loans			20,000
			160,000

Application of funds	Increase	Decrease	
Fixed assets	£	£	£
Land and buildings	50,000		
Plant and machinery	70,000		
Investments		10,000	= 110,000
	Increase	Decrease	
Working capital	£	£	
Stocks	60,000		
Debtors		20,000	
Less: Creditors		10,000	= 50,000
			160,000

Note:
A reduction in credit taken (creditors) is an application of funds or an increase to the investment made in the business.

Cash balance change

In all the examples we have so far seen, references to the cash and bank balances have been omitted but it is changes to these which are a specific concern of managers and investors (as they were to Micawber).

Because of the importance of the measurement of cash and the effect that the sources and uses of money within a business have upon it, a statement known as the cash flow statement has been designed. In many ways this cash flow statement might be described as a source and use of funds summary which concentrates upon the result of the changes described upon a business's cash position.

Its purpose is therefore not just to dissect differences but to highlight whether the sources for investment are equal to or less than the investments made during the selected period of time. After all, if the investments made are less than the sources, more cash will have been created than used and the cash and bank balances should reflect this fact. In the same way, if the sources of funds are less than what has been invested, the bank and cash balances will have been reduced. The format suggested for the cash flow statement is aimed at presenting this view of the business. Illustrations 4.9 to 4.12 provide you with two examples of how these statements are compiled and presented so as to highlight the changes in the cash/bank position. From the layout of the cash flow statements in these illustrations you can see whether or not the business has, as it were, 'lived within its means'. Illustration 4.11 shows that sources of £105,000 exceed C Ltd's applications of £97,000 by £8,000. C Ltd has therefore lived within its means by this amount. On the other hand, Illustration 4.12 shows that sources of £390,000 are less than D Ltd's investments of £405,000 during the period. In this case, therefore, D Ltd has 'lived beyond its means' by £15,000.

llustration 4.9 C Ltd: balance sheets as at 31 March

Last year			This year	
£	£		£	£
		Fixed assets		
100,000		Land and buildings		130,000
70,000		Plant and machinery		90,000
170,000				220,000
20,000		Investments		25,000
		Working capital		
		Current assets		
	10,000	Stocks	20,000	
	110,000	Debtors	120,000	
	20,000	Cash/bank	28,000	
	140,000		168,000	
		Less: Creditors – amounts		
	60,000	falling due within one year	78,000	
80,000		Net current assets		90,000
270,000		Total assets less current liabilities		335,000
30,000		Less: Loans		65,000
240,000				270,000
£		Capital and reserves		£
140,000		Share capital		140,000
100,000		Profit and loss account		130,000
240,000				270,000

Illlustration 4.10 D Ltd: balance sheets as at 30 September

Last year			This year	
£	£		£	£
		Fixed assets		
	500,000	Land and buildings	750,000	
	60,000	Fixtures and fittings	120,000	
580,000	20,000	Investments	40,000	910,000
		Current assets		
	40,000	Stocks	75,000	
	5,000	Cash/bank	–	
	45,000	Less:	75,000	
		Creditors – amounts falling due within one year		
	50,000	Trade creditors 90,000		
	–	Overdraft 10,000	100,000	
(5,000)		Net current assets		(25,000)
575,000		Total assets less current liabilities		885,000
120,000		Less: Creditors – amounts falling due in more than a year		150,000
455,000				735,000
£		Capital and reserves		£
250,000		Share capital		300,000
205,000		Profit and loss account		435,000
455,000				735,000

Illustration 4.11 C Ltd: cash flow statement for year to 31 March

Sources		£		£
Profit and loss account				30,000
Depreciation				40,000
From operations				70,000
Loans				35,000
				105,000
Applications				
Fixed assets (details below)		95,000		
Working capital	£			
Stocks	10,000			
Debtors	10,000			
	20,000			
Less: Creditors	18,000	2,000		97,000
Changes to cash position				8,000
Analysis				£
Cash position: at beginning of year				20,000
at end of year				28,000
Cash position improved by				8,000

Fixed assets	£
Land and buildings	30,000
Plant and machinery	20,000
Depreciation	40,000
Investments	5,000
	95,000

Illustration 4.12 D Ltd: cash flow statement for year to 30 September

Sources			
Profit and loss account			230,000
Depreciation			80,000
From operations			310,000
Share capital			50,000
Loan capital			30,000
			390,000
Applications		£	
Fixed assets (details below)		410,000	
Working capital	£		
Stocks	35,000		
Less: Creditors	40,000	(5,000)	405,000
Changes to cash position			(15,000)
Analysis			£
Cash position: at beginning of year			5,000
at end (overdraft)			(10,000)
Position worsened by			15,000
Fixed assets			
			£
Land and buildings			250,000
Fixtures and fittings			60,000
Add back depreciation			80,000
Investments			20,000
			410,000

Again, as in so many financial situations there is nothing wrong or right about either situation but it is a fact that needs to be known so that the right questions can be asked. For example, in Illustration 4.11 cash/bank balances are shown to have increased by £8,000. How are these funds, not applied within the business at the present time, planned to be used or invested? Again, in Illustration 4.12 where cash/bank balances are shown to have been reduced by £15,000, are the funds required to finance or source investment being found out of normal bank overdraft facilities or are these balances becoming dangerously overstretched?

Indeed the importance of this view of a business's progress, by means of an analysis of the sources and uses of investment and highlighting changes in cash balances, within the cash flow statement, has gained increasing attention within recent years. This has led to the requirement that limited companies include the statement in their annual accounts, as indeed must many non-profit-making organisations such as grant-maintained schools and NHS trusts.

When the statement is prepared the information is, of course, historical, showing changes that have occurred during the year under review. Management, however, recognising the importance attached to these statements, would be foolish not to anticipate their contents. It is for this purpose that forecasts or budgeted cash flow statements are prepared for control and progress purposes throughout the year. This enables the best possible advantage to be taken of cash surpluses and the minimum damage to be caused by deficits as they occur.

Summary of cash controls

We have therefore two basic controls of cash flow: first, the day-by-day, month-by-month assessment of cash availability by means of the cash flow forecast, and, second, the overall assessment of cash movement by means of the cash flow statement.

CONSOLIDATION

We have now examined the last of the three fundamental financial information statements. In chapter 2 we reviewed the measurement of return on business investment, by means of the profit and loss account, which in our sporting analogy we termed the scoreline of business. In chapter 3 we looked at the risk of a business making a profit. We learnt how we do this by looking at the investments a business has made and how these have been financed – our money-making players, to continue our sporting analogy – in the balance sheet. Now, finally, we have looked at cash – the raw material of investment – its control and its flow, which because of its importance can only be described, within the context of the business game, as the ball itself.

We have now a basic understanding of business finance but this needs to be consolidated and reinforced. For this purpose turn to Illustration 4.13, which is a case study based on all we have covered up to this point. First, attempt the question stage by stage, without reference to the solution, and then check your work with the model answer as it is set out in Illustrations 4.14 to 4.16. Remember at each stage of the question to trace through the logic and recognise – when and if errors occur in your work – any errors you make will be *illogical*.

Once you have worked through the case study ask yourself the supplementary questions that follow it and which test your knowledge of business finance up to this point.

Illustration 4.13 Financial case study

It is planned to form A Ltd on 1 July with a share capital of £40,000, of which it intends to invest £25,000 in fixed assets – plant and machinery, etc. – and leave the remainder as cash. Its plans for the first six months are as below and you are asked to translate these into:

1. A monthly cash flow forecast
2. A forecast profit and loss account for the six months
3. A forecast balance sheet as at 31 December

Sales for six months	£600,000
Materials in sales	£240,000
Labour in sales	£180,000
Other expenses including depreciation £2,000	£140,000
Materials purchased for the period	£260,000

Cash receipts and payments for six months:

	Sales Receipts £	Materials payments £	Overheads and wages
July	40,000	60,000	
August	50,000	60,000	Paid
September	50,000	20,000	evenly
October	70,000	20,000	each
November	120,000	20,000	month
December	150,000	20,000	
	£480,000	£200,000	

Special note: Every figure is a forecast.

Illustration 4.14 A Ltd: cash flow forecast

	Jul. £	Aug. £	Sept. £	Oct. £	Nov. £	Dec. £
Receipts						
Sales	40,000	50,000	50,000	70,000	120,000	150,000
Share capital	40,000					
Sub total A	80,000	50,000	50,000	70,000	120,000	150,000
Payments						
Materials	60,000	60,000	20,000	20,000	20,000	20,000
Wages	30,000	30,000	30,000	30,000	30,000	30,000
Overheads	23,000	23,000	23,000	23,000	23,000	23,000
Fixed assets	25,000	–	–	–	–	–
Subtotal B	138,000	113,000	73,000	73,000	73,000	73,000
Balance (A – B)	(58,000)	(63,000)	(23,000)	(3,000)	47,000	77,000
Balance b/fwd	–	(58,000)	(121,000)	(144,000)	(147,000)	(100,000)
Balance c/fwd	(58,000)	(121,000)	(144,000)	(147,000)	(100,000)	(23,000)

Illustration 4.15 A Ltd: forecast profit and loss account for the six months ended 31 December

		£
Sales		600,000
	£	
Less: Materials	240,000	
Labour	180,000	
Overheads	140,000	56,000
Trading profit		40,000

Illustration 4.16 A Ltd: forecast balance sheet as at 31 December

	£	£	£
Fixed assets		25,000	
Less: Depreciation		2,000	23,000
Current assets			
Stock	20,000		
Debtors	120,000	140,000	
Less: Current liabilities			
Creditors – materials	60,000		
Bank overdraft	23,000	83,000	57,000
			80,000
Financed by:			
Share capital		40,000	
Profit and loss account		40,000	£80,000

The cash flow forecast – the supplementary questions

Once you have completed your answers and compared them with those provided in Illustrations 4.14 to 4.16, ask yourself, in the context of the cash flow forecast, this question. If you were a bank manager and A Ltd came to you for a loan to help it over this six-month period, would you say yes or no? Base your answer on what you see in the cash flow forecast only.

Think this through – your answer should be no. First, because there is insufficient security, which seems to be confined to the fixed assets purchased in July for £25,000 and second, because of the commitment of the owners. The shareholders are putting only £40,000 into the business while you, as a banker, are being asked to lend, without any say in the day-to-day running of the business, nearly four times that by October.

These then are the two facts you look for before you lend money: security and commitment. You want sufficient security to cover the amount lent and enough commitment from the owners to indicate the risk they are taking. A textbook rule for the bankers is never lend anyone more than 50 per cent of what they could lose themselves – which in our example would be no more than £20,000 (50 per cent of the share capital of £40,000), a long way short of what is needed! However don't give up now, textbook rules are often there to be broken.

So if A Ltd cannot borrow the money it needs, let's pose the next supplementary question. If it were your own business, would you welcome friends who might be willing to put in £150,000 as extra share capital? Again you should say no, and again there are two reasons: first, of course, because your friends would then control the business, and if you were investing your ideas and energy in the enterprise, you might very well not wish this to happen.

However, there is a second and much more important reason for saying no and that lies in the nature of the sources of capital. If you recall from chapter 1, share capital is permanent, and looking along the bottom line of the cash flow forecast A Ltd certainly does not need £150,000 permanently, only in September and October. Before and after that it has very different needs. In fact by the time it gets to the end of December it requires only £23,000. So if you had accepted your friends' money as share capital, you would not only have lost control of your business, but by the time you reached the end of the six months you would have £127,000 sitting in your bank account which you would no longer require.

Having dealt with these supplementary questions it can be seen that it will certainly not be easy to obtain a loan, and additional share capital, even if it were forthcoming, is not the answer. So what should we do – give up? Well, before we do that let us see if it is going to be worth the effort. In other words, the cash flow forecast shows us that there will be a real need for cash help and that to get it will not be easy – impossible, you might think. Well, before we get too depressed let us see if it is going to be worth the effort, and we do this by looking at the scoreline – the profit and loss account. After all, if this shows that the business would make large profits, it might be worthwhile putting some effort into getting hold of the money from somewhere. However, if it shows a loss, why bother?

The profit and loss account

So let's pose the first supplementary question about the profit and loss account shown in Illustration 4.15: what do you think of the profit shown of £40,000? Is it good, bad or indifferent? I hope you will answer very good indeed! This should be because you have compared this profit, not with the sales figure of £600,000, but with the capital employed of £40,000. A return on capital employed of 100 per cent in six months: not bad, you might say.

In fact it is so good that if you were a sensible manager or investor you would look to see if such profits are possible. You would be suspicious and this means you would look for comparisons. You would find out whether other companies operating in the same type of business area are making a similar profit. Would you then want to compare profit with the sales? Well, not quite – in fact you would want to have the profit and loss account reanalysed as we discussed in chapter 2.

You can see this in Illustration 4.17, where the expenses have been divided between those which are variable and those which are fixed, the direct costs and overheads as they are termed in the example. It is the difference between the direct costs and the sales figures – the gross profit – which is crucial in any comparison of profits. This illustration shows a gross profit of £300,000, which represents a ratio of 50 per cent of sales. It would be this percentage that we could then compare with similar businesses to see if their gross profits as a percentage of sales work out at approximately the same figure. If this is so, we could then say that although, having started A Ltd, we would certainly have a considerable cash-flow problem (it would be strapped for cash in the first six months), it would at the same time be making a very large profit. In fact whatever effort is required to secure finance would be well worth it if these profits could be earned.

Illustration 4.17 A Ltd: revised forecast profit and loss account for the six months ended 31 December

	£	£
Sales		600,000
Less: Direct materials	240,000	
Direct labour*	60,000	300,000
Gross profit		300,000
Less: Overheads		260,000
Trading profit		40,000

* It is assumed that the labour cost of £180,000 shown in Illustration 4.15 is divided between direct labour £60,000 and overhead labour £120,000.

The cash flow statement

Cash flow forecast and the profit and loss account together tell us something which can be illustrated in the cash flow statement set out in Illustration 4.18. This shows that the sources of funds during the six months would amount to £82,000: share capital £40,000, profits £40,000, plus depreciation £2,000. However, we have seen from the cash flow forecast that we are short of cash. We have a loan requirement at the end of December of £23,000. This therefore means that we must have invested £105,000. It also shows that the negative cash position as at 31 December is caused not by losses – after all, substantial profits are made for the six months – but by investments.

Illustration 4.18 A Ltd: forecasted cash flow statement

	£	£
Sources		
Share capital	40,000	
Profit	40,000	
Depreciation	2,000	82,000
Applications		
Investment		105,000
Negative cash flow		23,000

The balance sheet

To determine in which areas such investment will take place we need to examine the forecast balance sheet shown in Illustration 4.16. Now you have done this we will pose the final supplementary question. We already know that if A Ltd is started it will have an investment problem: it will be investing more funds that it is creating. So, looking at the balance sheet, where precisely will this be happening, in which particular investment area or areas?

And the answer is obviously in the credit it is giving its customers – its debtors or accounts receivable – which by 31 December will amount to £120,000. This might then lead us to consider whether this money could be brought in more quickly or whether we could find backers who might lend A Ltd money on the security of its unpaid invoices.

Summary and conclusion

We have just been explaining how from a simple business plan we have been able to use our knowledge gained so far, linked with our common sense, to arrive at some logical conclusions – or at least better questions. After all, we are looking at a totally logical subject which stems entirely from the market place. That is why we began by understanding the way money works in every business by means of our balls' model, and then followed this by studying the three primary questions we need to ask about the investment of money in any business:

(1) the return as given by the profit and loss account;
(2) the risk as given by the balance sheet; and finally
(3) the ready as given by the cash flow forecast.

So is this all? Have we finished? Well, not quite. After all, does a match-fit team ending a game with a winning scoreline and the ball at its feet have no need to question its past or future performance? And the same applies to a business. There are still more questions, questions we shall discover when we go on to study management accounting in Chapter 5, which deals with the supplementary questions that stem from these three primary statements.

5

THE DEVELOPMENT OF MANAGEMENT ACCOUNTING

THE EVOLUTION OF FINANCIAL INFORMATION

So far we have dealt with the three primary information statements produced to measure and explain business investment – the profit and loss account, the balance sheet and the cash flow forecast. However, these primary measurements leave many questions still to be answered; questions as to whether profits can be more, investments less or cash there.

The search for answers has created what might be described as an evolution of information, which all too often is wholly ascribed to managers and for this reason termed management accounting. The name implies that any additional information following the presentation of the profit and loss account, balance sheet and cash flow forecast or statement is to meet the exclusive interests of managers. This is not so. Information has only one catalyst – interested parties – be they managers, investors, employees or indeed the general public. It is true, however, that their executive powers put managers in a privileged position to demand such data – availability to other interested parties tends to depend more upon 'management discretion' than on established rights.

We will, however, ignore whatever exclusivity the term management accounting may imply. We will instead consider the development of what might be termed the supporting or supplementary material from the point of view of the 'interested party', and in the first place examine what I call its evolution.

We see this approach set out in Illustration 5.1, in which the stages of understanding are described under five area headings. Reading from the left – area 1 – the first step is 'Understanding money in any business', and certainly anyone who wishes to understand business finance must begin at this point.

Sources and investment of money in business

One must understand where money comes from and where it goes to, and in Illustration 5.2 you will see the financial model with which we have become familiar. In this model we describe the fact that in any business money comes in from the owners and from whatever is borrowed. For a limited company this will be its share and loan capital – shown as circle 1. We then point out that once the money is in a business it goes into three main areas: fixed assets, which are things we have no intention of selling, outside investments (these days included as one of the fixed assets), and working capital.

Illustration 5.1 The evolution of financial information

Area 1	Area 2	Area 3	Area 4	Area 5
The first step	Primary financial information	Derivative financial techniques	Comparative techniques	
Understanding	1. The return: given in the profit and loss	1. Analysis of profit and loss: – Costing – Full		
money	account	– Marginal	Budgetary control	Interpretation of data
in	2. The risk: given the balance sheet	1. Project in appraisal 2. Working capital analysis		
any			Standard costing	
business	3. The ready: given in the cash flow forecast	1. Cash flow statement		

Working capital

Working capital is money which is invested in labour, materials or merchandise and overheads, which in their turn are converted into finished goods, saleable merchandise or services. These then are sold either directly for cash, or to people or businesses who hesitate before they pay – who we refer to as debtors or accounts receivable.

It will also be remembered that in the same way a business itself takes time before it pays for the materials or merchandise, labour and overheads it uses. In these circumstances we refer to those who are waiting for their money as the creditors or accounts payable.

Illustration 5.2 The financial model

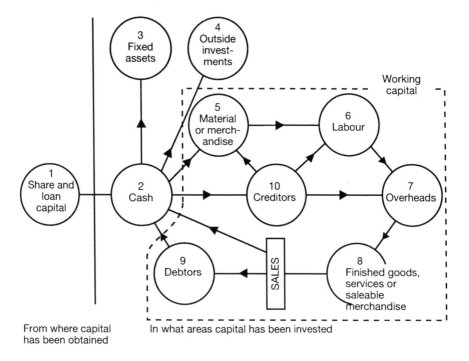

From where capital   In what areas capital has been invested
has been obtained

Primary questions

If we then return to Illustration 5.1 you will see that the second area from the left
is headed 'Primary financial information'. The primary financial information
stems, as we have seen from our previous studies, from the three primary questions raised by anyone concerned with business investment.

The profit and loss account and balance sheet

First, there are the two questions every investor asks whenever money is invested anywhere: what is the return, and what is the risk? It is in response to these
questions in business that the profit and loss account, which deals with the first
question, and the balance sheet – which creates the basis from which we can
assess the risk, the chances of making a profit – are supplied. Examples of both
these financial statements are set out as Illustrations 5.3 and 5.4.

However, in a business situation we find that answering these two primary
questions is not enough because central to the understanding of business finance
is the fact that when money is put into a business it moves or flows. It is continually changing position and growing or shrinking, depending upon how and
when the money is spent or received. This is the unique feature of a business

investment: the fact that money is moving and therefore the amount held at any point in time is continually changing. This creates the need for the third primary financial statement, the one concerned with forecasting how much cash as money the business will have at any particular time – what might be described as discovering whether the business will have 'the ready' to arrive.

The cash flow forecast

We therefore have this further need – to discover what will be our cash position over the period ahead while we are running a business. This is not something you want to know historically. You need to discover this in advance so that you can look ahead and be prepared for any eventuality. Illustration 5.5 sets out the statement that deals with this: the cash flow forecast.

Illustration 5.3 A Ltd: profit and loss account for the year ended 30 September (layout in accordance with Companies Act 1985, format 1)

	£000	£000
		£000
Turnover		170,000
Less: Cost of sales*		100,000
Gross profit		70,000
	£000	
Less: Distribution costs (these include sales expenses)	12,000	
Administration costs	18,000	30,000
Trading or operating profit:		40,000
Add: Non-trading income		
Investment income	5,000	
Profit on sale of machinery	500	5,500
		45,500
Less: Non-trading expenses:		
Interest on loans	7,000	
Loss on sale of equipment	1,000	8,000
Profit on ordinary activities before taxation		37,500
Less: Taxation		12,500
Profit on ordinary activities after taxation		25,000
Less: Proposed dividend		5,000
Retained profit		20,000

THE DERIVATIVE TECHNIQUES

Having understood these three primary statements let us continue with our evolution. In other words if we were supplied with this primary financial information, would it in itself be enough or would we ask for more? In response to this question we shall take each of the three primary financial statements which we have just described and ask ourselves in each case the question: if we got this information is it enough in itself or do we want to know more? The purpose of this is to illustrate the natural – the logical – evolution of financial information to meet the needs of the interested parties – managers, investors, and indeed the world at large, it might be argued. So let us begin with the profit and loss account.

Illustration 5.4 A Ltd: balance sheet as at 31 January (layout in accordance with Companies Act 1985, Format 1)

		£000	£000
Fixed assets:			
Tangibles (at revaluation value)		900,000	
Investments		60,000	960,000
	£000		
Current assets:			
Stock: Raw material	5,000		
Work in progress	8,000		
Finished goods	17,000		
Debtors	40,000		
Cash	10,000	80,000	
Less: Creditors – amounts falling due			
within one year		60,000	
Net current assets			20,000
Total assets less current liabilities			980,000
Less: Creditors – amounts falling due in			
more than a year			250,000
			730,000
Capital and reserves:			
Called-up share capital			270,000
Revaluation reserve			150,000
Profit and loss account			310,000
			730,000

Techniques derived from the profit and loss account

If you turn to Illustration 5.3 you will see a typical example of this statement: consider the trading or operating profit of £40,000,000. Of course, as we have already seen, whether this profit is good or bad depends on its relationship to the capital invested. Remember the key measurement of profit to capital employed we considered in chapter 4?

As well as this overall assessment of profitability, however, you have a specific question to ask about the profit figure.

The need for analysis – costing

To illustrate this point, suppose that this profit and loss account is that of your own business and that the business sells many different products or types of merchandise or proves many different services. Given this situation, the question to answer is: would it be enough to know that you have made this profit or would you want to know more about it? In this situation I have no doubt that what you would want to know is where the profit is being made? Where is it coming from – from which product or type of merchandise or service – and how much?

In other words, a central concern of anyone looking at a profit and loss account is to find out where the profit or loss (in our example, £40,000,000 profit) is being made. To do this it will clearly be necessary to analyse the sales income and the trading or operating costs of materials or merchandise, labour and overheads so as to determine which applies to which particular product, type of merchandise or service. It is this analysis which is referred to as costing.

Costing, then, is the financial technique which has been developed to meet the very natural desire of anyone looking at a profit and loss account to find out from where the trading or operating profit or loss has been made.

Illustration 5.5 A Ltd: cash flow forecast

	Month					
	1		2		3	
Receipts:	Budget	Actual	Budget	Actual	Budget	Actual
	£	£	£	£	£	£
Sale of goods – debtors	50,000		60,000		40,000	
Sale of fixed assets	5,000		–		–	
Dividends/interest received	1,000		500		2,000	
Subtotal A	56,000		60,500		42,000	
Payments:						
Material – creditors	30,000		40,000		41,000	
Wages/salaries	10,000		12,000		12,000	
Overheads	5,000		6,500		7,000	
Fixed assets purchases	4,000		10,000		12,000	
Subtotal B	49,000		68,500		72,000	
Balance (A – B)	7,000		(8,000)		(30,000)	
Balance b/fwd	2,000		9,000		1,000	
Balance c/fwd	9,000		1,000		(29,000)	

Full and marginal costing

We will be looking at the details of this technique in later chapters but at this point we need to consider a particular feature of trading or operating expenses which we introduced in chapter 2 when discussing the analysis of expenses. This is that if you relate the analysed expenses to the units of merchandise we are selling or the services we are rendering you will see that such expenses move in two ways. First, there will be those which can be attributed directly to such units and services and second, those which are incurred irrespective of the activity of the business. For example, there will be the materials, merchandise and labour which can be traced directly to the particular products, merchandise or services sold. However, many other expenses – often termed the overheads – such as rent, insurances and salaries cannot be so directly attributed. It is this division of expenses that has to be understood when considering the two types of analysis termed full and marginal costing. Full costing is the system which attempts to analyse all the trading or operating expenses of the business, while marginal costing confines its analysis to the direct expenses: those trading or operating expenses which move in sympathy or, as they say, vary – with what is produced and sold.

Simple examples of both a full and marginal cost analysis are set out in Illustrations 5.6 and 5.7 and we shall be dealing with each method of costing in the next two chapters.

Techniques derived from the balance sheet

Having considered the techniques which arise from the desire to learn more about the profit or loss presented in the profit and loss account we shall now consider what stems or evolves from the balance sheet. The statement which is concerned with the risk or chances of a business making a profit. Once again I want you to ask yourself the question: if you received this statement would it be enough for the purpose of examining risk?

Of course, to deal with this question you have to recognise the nature of the balance sheet. It is what we termed an agenda – a summary – item by item of from where the business has obtained its capital and how this same capital has been invested.

The areas in which the business is investing its money which calls for the greatest concern and management involvement. This is because their day-to-day activities involve the continual investment and reinvestment of the funds in the business.

Illustration 5.6 Full cost analysis

	Unit cost (pence)
Direct material	5
Direct labour	4
Direct expenses	3
Prime cost	12
Indirect works expense	3
Works costs	15
Indirect administrative expenses	4
Production cost	19
Selling and distribution expenses	5
Total cost	24
Profit	4
Sale price	28

Illustration 5.7 Marginal cost analysis

	Unit cost (pence)
Direct material	5
Direct labour	4
Other variable expenses	8
Marginal cost	17
Contribution or margin	11
Sale price	28

Investment areas

It will be remembered that when considering how money was invested in a business we saw that money, very broadly, is either being put into things we have no intention of selling – the fixed assets, including outside investments – or it is being put into the money-go-round – the working capital. The money being spent on materials, or merchandise, labour and overheads which are then converted into the finished goods, saleable merchandise or services to be sold.

Because money is going into these two diametrically different areas we have very different questions regarding each. To emphasise and revise this division of investment in business tackle the question set out in Illustration 5.8, and when you have completed this check your answer against Illustration 5.9.

Fixed assets

We will begin our examination of the techniques developed from the balance sheet by taking the fixed asset area. Here, the point to recognise is that, by the time you read a balance sheet and sort out what fixed assets the business owns, it is too late! Because fixed assets are not purchased for resale once they are acquired, the business is in a way 'stuck with them'. It is for this reason that the primary need of those concerned with their purchase – managers and investors – is to look before they leap!

Project appraisal techniques

In other words, they need to have enough financial data before the investment is made to help them consider its benefits to the business once it is owned. To meet this obvious requirement, over the past years 'project appraisal techniques' have been developed.

These techniques consider the facts that are known about the particular investment before it is made, and from these the desirability or otherwise of the investment is judged. We will be considering these techniques in chapter 8 when we examine their application to this business investment area.

Illustration 5.8 Model of a manufacturing business

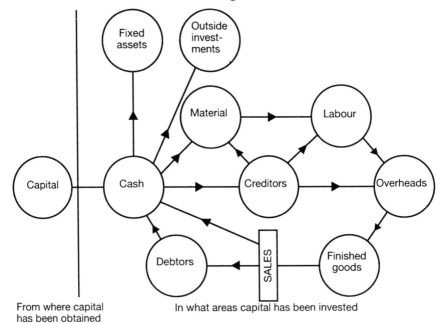

From where capital   In what areas capital has been invested
has been obtained

Place the following items in the appropriate circles of the model of a manufacturing business

1	Raw material purchased	12	Components
2	Marketing expenses	13	Land and building
3	Delivery vehicles	14	Share capital
4	Office salaries	15	Consultants' fees
5	Loans to business	16	Research and development costs
6	Bank overdraft	17	Salesmen's salaries
7	Amounts due to material suppliers	18	Investment in another business
8	Plant and machinery	19	Wages of employees
9	Rent	20	Auditors' fees
10	Labour employed to extend store	21	Amounts due from customers
11	Office equipment	22	Finished goods in warehouse

Working capital – minimising the investment

In the second area of the balance sheet – the working capital – we have the continuous requirement which we described in the first chapter: minimising the investment. There we saw that every business wishes to minimise its working capital so that it can both maximise the return on the capital employed and minimise the working capital required to support its sales. Remember how we described the working capital investment as the financial luggage a business carries on its journey to a sale?

To achieve this we also saw that a business needs to control time: to shorten the time it takes for its money to move from materials, merchandise, labour and overheads back into cash, and at the same time to maximise the time the business takes to pay for such materials, merchandise, labour and overheads. The analysis and control of the time money is invested in working capital are considered in detail in chapter 9.

Illustration 5.9 Answer to Illustration 5.8

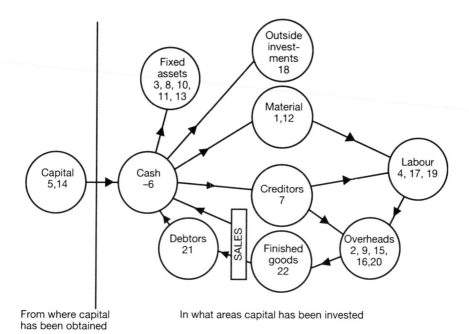

From where capital
has been obtained

In what areas capital has been invested

Notes:
1. Item 10 is an example of an expense which becomes capital because what it is
    concerned with is extending the store.
2. Item 16 is an 'intangible' item and is therefore written off as a revenue expense – see
    chapter 3.
3. Item 15 is treated as an overhead but it could be a fixed asset or capital expenditure in
    certain circumstances, for example architects' fees in respect of the construction of a
    new factory.

Techniques derived from the cash flow forecast

Let us now consider the third primary financial statement, the cash flow forecast.
In this statement we are trying to discover exactly what money will be available
throughout the period ahead while we are running the business.

It should be particularly noted that in this cash area we are dealing with the
one certain financial commodity: money itself. After all, we talk about profits
and losses and we examine balance sheets but we handle money. It is perhaps
because of our familiarity with cash that over the years managers and investors
have used money as a very central means of control.

Cash as a medium of explanation

What has happened is that managers and investors have recognised that if they translate all their plans into cash terms they will obtain a most convenient medium through which to review and control their entire business operations. This has led to the summary of information (evolved from the cash flow forecast) termed the cash flow statement, which is aimed at looking at a business in strictly cash terms. Its central purpose is to examine a business's progress in terms of:

- from where the sources of cash for investment have arisen during a period of time;
- on what has cash been invested or spent during the same time; and
- the impact these changes have had upon the cash held by the business over the period under review

The cash flow statement

It might be said that these cash flow statements summarise the business's progress, either over the past or into the future, in such a way as to highlight whether or not the business is living within or beyond its means. This was referred to in chapter 4 in which we illustrated and discussed the cash flow statement and we will mention it again in chapter 12 when we consider the interpretation of financial information. It must, however, be noted that the cash flow statement, unlike the cash flow forecast, originates nothing. It re-presents the information set out in the profit and loss account, balance sheet and cash flow forecast and as such might be described as a derivative statement from all three. Its sources of cash include profits presented in the profit and loss account, its investments additions to fixed assets set out in the balance sheet, and its cash balances are those detailed in the cash flow forecast.

The derivative techniques – summary

We have now considered the main derivative techniques which arise or evolve from the three primary financial statements, all of which are summarised in Illustration 5.1 under area 3.

(1) First, in the case of the profit and loss account, we have the need for analysis which leads to the techniques termed costing – both full and marginal.
(2) Second, in the case of the balance sheet, we have the need to look at and control investments as we make them. As regards fixed assets, including outside investments, the techniques of project appraisal have been developed to help us look before we leap! In the case of working capital, we have the continual need to control and analyse time so as to minimise the amount invested in this area.
(3) Finally, in the case of the cash flow forecast, we have the need to use cash in making clear the overall effect of a business's past actions and future plans

on its cash position: in other words, to highlight whether or not the business is 'living within or beyond its means' which we present in the cash flow statement.

THE NEED FOR COMPARISONS

Having looked at what we have termed the derivative techniques it is now necessary to turn to the next area of concern to managers and investors alike: the continual need for comparison. In every financial situation, whether you are considering your salary, your car or your house, the natural desire is to compare.

Budgetary control

Certainly when you are presented with financial information about a business there is not only a desire but a logical compulsion to compare so as to review its progress and where possible take corrective or continuing action. It is because we have this need to compare and review that in business we have produced techniques to assist us The first or primary comparative technique is the one termed budgetary control, which is the overall technique of financial comparison within business.

It is concerned primarily with translating the policies and plans pertaining to the business into their financial consequences. These take the final form of the projected profit and loss accounts, balance sheets and cash flow forecasts which will arise from such plans and comparing these with the actual figures as they become known. As well as budgeted profit and loss accounts, balance sheets and cash flow forecasts, however, budgets can be arranged throughout the business to suit particular needs. For example, budgets can be arranged around managers and around functions as well as produced within the context of the business as a whole. Indeed in many businesses the budgeted profit and loss account, balance sheet and cash flow forecast are the totals of all the functional budgets from throughout the organisation.

Budgetary control therefore meets the natural desire to compare and contrast actual against budgeted performance in financial terms and once such comparison has been made to take whatever corrective action is necessary or possible. It must be understood that budgetary control is fundamentally concerned with the conversion of plans and policies into financial measurements, but its use falls under two main heads: first in proving the financial credibility of the policies of the business as a whole, and second to compare the performance of management throughout the organisation against agreed targets or budgets of performance. Both these objectives will be dealt with in chapter 10 on budgetary control.

Standard costing

Having considered the overall comparison technique of budgetary control we must recognise that the desire for comparison in one particular area of business finance – namely costing – calls for a very analytical approach. In this area managers do not wish just to compare, they wish to take effective action as soon as possible; to correct things that have gone wrong or continue things that have gone right.

In order to obtain information to meet this requirement a technique of comparison has been developed termed standard costing. Standard costing is not a different form of costing (as it may sound from its name) but a method of comparison; a method which isolates and defines the reasons that have caused the differences, or variances as they are called. It entails much detailed analysis and control and will be dealt with further in chapter 11.

INTERPRETATION

If now you turn to Illustration 5.1 you will see that we have arrived at the final area of financial understanding, the area entitled interpretation. The interpretation of financial data is the sum of all the financial understandings we have obtained up to this point. Interpretation is therefore based on the accumulated knowledge we get from all the other financial techniques and statements we have introduced up to this stage.

We will look at interpretation in chapter 12 and will be considering the application of ratios and other analytical techniques. We will also see that in the interpretation of financial information both our financial and non-financial knowledge and experience must be harnessed. After all, it must never be forgotten that all financial information is expressing a practical business situation and therefore whatever is being reported must represent this. For this reason, too, anyone examining financial data must at the same time bear in mind the practical event which is being reported. For example, if engineers consider that the cost information regarding a product is at variance with the engineering practicalities they must be prepared to challenge the financial data.

It must never be forgotten that this interplay of practical knowledge with financial understanding is vital in the interpretation of financial data. It must also be brought very much to mind that the accounting information that we have discussed in this and previous chapters provides managers with better questions, not answers. We hope these questions will certainly lead to better answers but this does not imply that financial information in itself provides them. Answers must always depend upon the judgement of managers, investors and all those concerned with the data presented.

Illustration 5.10 Functional contribution to preparation of financial data

List the contribution beneath each heading:

1. *Buying*

2. *Production planning department*

3. *Credit control*

4. *Drawing office*

5. *Sales representatives*

6. *Production foreman*

7. *Administration*

Illustration 5.11 Examples of functional contribution to preparation of financial data

1. *Buying*
   Prices for cost and estimate purposes
   Stock valuation
   Departmental, functional budgets as applicable

2. *Production planning department*
   Times for cost and estimate purpose
   Departmental, functional budgets as applicable

3. *Credit control*
   Provision for bad and doubtful debts
   Debtor and creditor times for working capital
   Departmental, functional budgets as applicable

4. *Drawing office*
   Data for estimates of new products
   Data for capital project appraisal
   Departmental, functional budgets as applicable

5. *Sales representatives*
   Sales analysis data
   Credit control intelligence
   Departmental, functional budgets as applicable

6. *Production foreman*
   Control data on material in manufacture
   Time control and analysis of labour
   Work in progress and finished goods valuation
   Departmental, functional budgets as applicable

7. *Administration*
   Control data for administrative costs
   Departmental, functional budgets as applicable

CONCLUSION

Finally, turn to Illustration 5.10 and list the contribution of each function to the preparation of financial data. When you have done this compare your answers with those suggested in Illustration 5.11. Once this test has been completed we can proceed with our study of the derivative and comparative techniques. These techniques are often combined under the generic, although I believe misleading, heading, of management accounting, and the first of them deals with full costing.

6

FULL COSTING

As we have seen, in business there are three primary financial questions leading to the three primary statements: what is the return? (leading to the profit and loss account); what is the risk? (leading to the balance sheet); and do we have the 'ready', the available money to arrive? (leading to the cash flow forecast).

Even when these statements are available, however, it becomes clear that they are not enough in themselves. In the last chapter we saw the evolution of financial information. For example, if we know the profit or loss a business has made this will obviously pinpoint the return on the investment; but if that business is selling many different goods or types of merchandise or rendering many different services this answer would certainly be insufficient. Those concerned would want to know where it was making its profit or loss; whether it is making more profit on one item it sells or service it renders than another so that from this analysis, continuing our game analogy, the business might improve its scoreline in future. It is in response to this obvious question 'where am I making my profit or loss?' that the techniques known as costing have been developed.

COST AND PROFIT ANALYSIS

The purpose of costing is to pinpoint where the profit or loss is being made so that you can manage, organise and run your business more profitably. And indeed this desire for analysis has been with us for a very long time. (I would suggest Adam and Eve, selling apples, would have wanted to know which type of apple was giving them the greatest profit!) Costing is not a modern invention – it is one that has been part of the fabric of business life since the beginning of time.

It is from the analytical data made available through costing that we are able to translate our policies into their impact on profitability. It also enables us to produce estimates or forecasts of the cost and profitability of new activities. These are the purposes for whicht costing has been developed. It is also because of these that costing holds within itself enormous benefits – and equally enormous dangers, discussed later, when we consider the question of credibility: whether or not the information it provides can be believed.

Mechanics of analysis

Having described its purpose let us now look at the means by which cost is calculated. However, first we must understand that there are two systems of costing, based on the desire or otherwise to analyse fully the trading expenses. Both systems are therefore concerned with analysis but their difference lies in the degree of such analysis. In the first method – termed full costing – an attempt is made to analyse all the expenses contained in the trading or operating section of the profit and loss account. In the second, or partial, system – known as marginal costing – the analysis is confined to those expenses that move in sympathy or, as they say, vary with what the business produces and sells – its activity. We deal with marginal costing in a later chapter – for the present we will concentrate on full costing.

Benefits and dangers

The benefit of costing is, as already explained, in determining where the profit and loss is being made. It therefore assists us in planning a business enterprise on the most profitable lines and reviewing past performance so that improvements may be made or past achievements continued in the future.

However, as well as advantage there is danger. The danger lies in whether or not we are able to believe the information costing presents. It is, after all, a dynamic technique. It influences both judgements regarding the past and decisions regarding the future. Central to any examination of costing must therefore be the question: can we believe it? Is it credible? If the answer is 'no' we could be using highly dangerous information. If our costing data makes us believe that one particular product, type of merchandise or service is better than another but the information on which it is based is incorrect, that is not just a shame or a nuisance. It could be ruinous. In fact some cynics have said 'that more businesses have gone bust because they have had costing information than because they haven't'. This is obviously far too cynical a view to accept but there is an element of truth in it.

It must also be remembered that cost analysis is not only concerned with the past, it may affect the view of the future. For instance, when a new estimate is called for, it is often found necessary to use facts already available from costs of similar products or services. This means therefore that poor cost analysis will provide a wrong view not only of the present and past but also of future profitability.

FULL COST ANALYSIS

To help us understand full costing and recognise those areas in which credibility needs to be particularly questioned we shall run through the build-up of the full cost statement set out as Illustration 6.1.

Illustration 6.1 Full cost statement

	Unit cost pence
Direct material	5
Direct labour	4
Direct expenses	3
Prime cost	12
Indirect expenses	6
Total cost	18
Profit	7
Sale price	25

The unit of cost

In the first place, in any costing system one has to choose a suitable unit of cost to which costs can be analysed, and this in turn will be determined by the business itself. For instance, in the building or construction industry we might use the building contract as the unit, in a solicitor's practice the particular piece of litigation (the divorce, the writ, the claim for damages, etc.), whereas for a retail operation we might refer to the particular department. On the other hand, in a mass production engineering company we might use the cost of a unit within the production line. To do this the total cost of what is produced for the period, say the week, is first determined and then divided by the units produced in that period to arrive at a unit cost. Under this method it might be said that the individual unit cost is an average more than an actual cost incurred in creating the particular unit.

All this means that we choose the unit of cost which suits the business. In a manufacturing business this will normally follow the production methods whereas in a service industry or retail operation it will follow the service that is rendered or the division of merchandise presented. To test your understanding of units of cost, tackle the question set out in Illustration 6.2 and compare your answer with the solution in Illustration 6.3.

Illustration 6.2 Deciding on suitable unit costs

Consider the following business in relationship to the unit of cost most suitable to each.
1. Department store
2. Brick works
3. Chemical manufacturer
4. Insurance agency
5. Motor repairer
6. Hospital
7. Mass production car manufacturer

Illustration 6.3   Suggested answer to Illustration 6.2

1. Cost per department
2. Cost per quantity of bricks
3. Cost per process of manufacture
4. Cost per type of insurance
5. Cost per job
6. Cost per hospital bed
7. Cost per car coming off the production line based on 'average' cost per unit

Nature of expenses

Having selected the unit of cost let us now continue our understanding of a full cost by examining the nature of the expenses themselves. Once this is done it becomes clear that, broadly, they fall into two categories: those expenses which are directly attributable to the chosen unit and those which are not – in other words, expenses which are there whether or not we produce the particular unit to which we are attempting to analyse the expenses.

DIRECT EXPENSES

These are the expenses that directly relate to the unit and we record them as the unit is being produced, the services rendered or the merchandise presented. These are set out in Illustration 6.1 as direct material 5p, direct labour 4p and direct expenses 3p. Direct material and labour are the material and labour that can be traced directly to the unit we are costing and would be calculated from information received from those concerned with the use of material or the control of labour.

We may also find that there are other direct expenses, such as a royalty we have to pay to a designer on the manufacture of a particular unit, or the travelling expenses of a solicitor's clerk in obtaining necessary information regarding a search prior to the completion of a property conveyance. As we have said, we call these expenses direct and their total, as you will see from Illustration 6.1, is termed the prime cost.

Credibility

We will now return to our central question – the credibility of the information presented. Whenever anyone looks at a cost this must be the first consideration and it must be a recurring theme in understanding and using cost data. On arriving at the prime cost it should be no surprise to learn that the credibility of the data will depend largely on how accurately the direct costs have been analysed, priced and recorded – measurements which will depend very much on the grassroots recording within the business. In slang terms, more damage can be done by careless recordings by 'the bomb-happy storeman/foreman syndrome than any triple distilled cost accountant who you could meet in a day's walk'.

Accuracy of material and labour recordings

What is meant by that colourful expression is that the credibility of the data down to the prime cost depends very much upon its accurate recording as and when it takes place. The direct material cost in a manufacturing process will be made up from all the information recorded within the manufacturing processes, and a wrong entry of material issued, returned or transferred will mean that the direct material cost shown will also be wrong.

Equally, with labour, accuracy will depend upon the basic recording of the labour which goes into the manufacture of the goods or the rendering of the services. It is therefore essential that time recordings are accurate. If the recordings by those concerned with the manufacture of the unit or the rendering of the service are inaccurate, inevitably the direct labour cost information will also be wrong.

Accuracy of prices and rates

At the same time we must recognise that costing is historical (hysterical at times, you might say!). This means that the price of the material and the pay rate of labour going into the calculation of the direct material and labour cost is also historical. If, therefore, the prices of materials or the labour rates of pay are going up, what is set out in the cost may well be an unrepeatable bargain – an understatement of cost.

Material pricing

This problem of changing price is particularly important when considering direct material costs during a period of frequent price changes. This is set out in Illustration 6.4, where a material has been purchased at different prices throughout the month of March. The question arises: at what price should the material be included in those costs in which it occurs? And basically there are four positions that can be taken.

Illustration 6.4 Material prices

Purchases for March				Issues for March					
Date	Quantity kilos	Price per kilo	Total	Date	Quantity	Price per unit			
						FIFO		LIFO	
		p	£			Qty Kilos	Price p	Qty Kilos	Price p
3	1,000	50	500	4	500	500	50	500	50
10	1,500	52	780	12	1,600	500	50	100	50
						1,100	52	1,500	52
14	2,000	54	1,080	15	2,200	400	52	200	50
						1,800	54	2,000	54
20	1,600	55	880	21	1,400	200	54	1,400	55
						1,200	55		
	6,100	211	£3,240						

Basis of calculating:
Simple average price method = 211 divided by 4 = 52.75p
Weighted average price method = 3,240 divided by 6,100 = 53.1p

FIFO and LIFO

First, the materials can be priced out in logical sequence. This is shown in Illustration 6.4 under the heading FIFO (First In First Out). Second, the materials can be priced so as to reflect the most recent prices – again shown in Illustration 6.4 under the heading LIFO (Last In First Out).

LIFO is favoured during periods of rising prices as the cost will then reflect the increasing material costs. However, FIFO is more logical and therefore is often found easier to apply as it is more understandable to clerical staff, an advantage lost when computers take over.

Average price and weighted average price

There are also the third and fourth methods shown in Illustration 6.4 which reflect the average price and the weighted average price methods. Under the average price method the total of the individual prices are divided by the number of price changes to arrive at what is termed a simple average price. In Illustration 6.4, 52.75p per kilo would be the price of issue after 20 March assuming no previous issues made during the month.

However, this simple average method wholly ignores the quantities purchased at the different price changes, which is the problem the weighted average method addresses. In our example this would lead to an issue price after 20 March of 53.1p per kilo on the assumption that no previous issues have been made. This clearly is not the case but the arithmetical calculation involved to illustrate each issue price would, I feel, be beyond the scope of this book, the interest of its readers and the arithmetic skills of the author!

Rising prices and rising rates of pay

We will be dealing with the problem of rising costs in a broader context when we discuss current cost accounting in chapter 12. However, at the present time you need to be aware that the historical prices of materials and rates of pay for labour may well need to be revised if costs are to be looked at realistically.

The use of cost data

However, what is realistic depends upon the use for which the cost information is being produced. For instance, if we are using it to look ahead so as to estimate what it will cost us next time we make the product or render the service, we must be careful to take this fact into consideration. We must therefore be particularly careful in determining whether or not the cost relates to a current, historical or future cost, and select the data with care depending on how we intend to use it. For example, if the cost data is to be used to determine the future cost of producing the product or rendering the service, care must be taken to apply those rates of pay and material prices which it is considered will then apply.

INDIRECT EXPENSES

We have so far looked at direct expenses, which in the main are made up of materials and labour, but if we look at all the expenses deducted from sales before arriving at the trading or operating profit in a profit and loss account we see that there are still many other expenses apart from these. There are indeed also a large number which do not relate directly to any particular unit of cost, for instance the insurance of the buildings, the salaries of the supervisors, the wages of people who clean the offices and sweep up the factory and move the materials, the rent of the retail shop, managers' salaries and directors' fees, and so on. All these expenses are necessary in order to arrive at our trading or operating profit but they do not relate to any one particular unit of manufacture, merchandise or service. These expenses are often collectively referred to as the overheads in the profit and loss account and as indirect expenditure in costing.

Indirect expense/overhead absorption

However, despite the fact they do not relate directly to any particular unit of cost, to arrive at a full cost it is necessary to include all trading expenses – and this must mean not only the direct but also these indirect expenses. To do this it is necessary therefore to work out some way in which we can add into each unit of cost a due proportion of these indirect expenses.

You will see in Illustration 6.1 that the indirect expenses are brought in at 6p, so the question arises: how do we arrive at this figure? Well, quite simply by a series of forecasts or guesses! And in case you think this is too glib for such an exact measurement as cost data let us take an example of what we mean. In the first place, before we do any costing whatsoever, those concerned will prepare estimates for the period ahead in order to arrive at two overall forecast figures, which will form the basis for calculating the way indirect expenses will be included in a full cost.

To illustrate this let us take a practical example. Suppose we are going to be costing for a particular year, then towards the end of the previous year the cost office will seek answers to two questions, answers needed to establish the two forecasts required to calculate the basis for charging – or, as they say, absorbing – the indirect expenses.

The indirect expense for the period

The first of these will be how much we think the indirect expenses will be during the period – in most cases the year – ahead in which we will be doing our future costing. Of course many of the indirect expenses will be known with total accuracy – for example, the rent, insurances and some wages and salaries for the particular period ahead – but there are bound to be certain expenses where a measure of forecasting, dare we say guessing, will be needed. The salaries in certain circumstances may not be exactly known, and again indirect materials used in cleaning machines and telephone charges cannot be determined with total accuracy. Thus in many cases forecasts will have to be made.

This then will be the first step – to arrive at a total assessment of the likely indirect expenses during the period in which the costing will take place. This is shown in Illustration 6.5 as forecast (or guess) number 1 – the indirect expenses we think will be incurred during the period ahead for which we are producing the cost information. In this instance we are forecasting a figure of £5,000,000.

Illustration 6.5 Indirect expenditure recovery calculation

1. Forecast of indirect expenditure over year ahead	say £5,000,000
2. Forecast of activity of the business during the year ahead	
Prime cost forecast	say £10,000,000
Absorption rate £5,000,000 of £10,000,000 = 50 per cent.	

The activity for the period

Having arrived at this figure it will then be necessary to work out our forecast (or guess) number 2: what we think the activity of the business will be during the same period. Activity can be measured in many ways but in the first instance it is often found useful to measure it in terms of the sales a business expects to make during the period ahead. However, once this estimate is made, we will be able to translate it into production, service rendering or retailing capacity depending upon the industry with which we are concerned (for instance, what goods are to be produced, services rendered or counter space made available during the year ahead to meet the sales forecast), and express this in value or in quantity such as production or machine or labour hours, square footage, etc.

However, whatever measurement of activity is used it will be based on a forecast of what we believe will take place during the period ahead for which we are going to be doing our costing. Let us say in this particular instance that we have arrived at our sales budget for the year ahead and that we translate this back into the prime cost of production needed to meet these sales. In other words, we ask ourselves: if we know the planned sales for the period ahead, what will that mean in terms of the prime cost of the production needed to meet that sales demand? And say we arrive at a prime cost figure of £10,000,000 – again as set out in Illustration 6.5.

Basis for absorption

Having arrived at this figure we will see that we have now our basis for absorbing or recovering our indirect expenses. We have arrived at two figures: first, the indirect costs for the period ahead, which we have worked out to be £5,000,000, and, second, the activity for this same period translated into its prime cost value, which we have worked out to be £10,000,000.

This means that if we take the forecast indirect expenses of £5,000,000 as a percentage of the forecast prime costs of £10,000,000 we arrive at a figure of 50 per cent – a percentage which shows that for every £1 of prime cost, the business will incur 50p of indirect expenditure. Returning to Illustration 6.1 we see that having arrived at the prime cost of 12p we add 50 per cent to it (the indirect expense of 6p), which gives us a total cost of 18p.

Credibility of absorption rate

Having seen the mechanics of indirect cost recovery, let us get back to the central consideration – its credibility. And here we find that whether or not we can believe the amount brought in as indirect expenses will depend upon the accuracy or inaccuracy of a couple of forecasts or guesses – and we all know how unreliable these can be!

The indirect expense items

For instance, suppose that during the year ahead there are general wage and salary increases and the indirect expenditure rises from £5,000,000 to £6,000,000. If that were so, 50 per cent of the prime cost (assuming it remains constant at £10,000,000) would be insufficient. It would fail to recover the

£1,000,000 of extra indirect costs. And this would not be seen by looking at an individual cost, but only when the original estimate of £5,000,000 is compared with the actual indirect cost figure of £6,000,000, when this is known.

The activity achieved

However, even more important to understand is the problem of activity. For example, if due to a recession in the trade, the activity of the business did not reach £10,000,000 prime cost but only £8,000,000, we would be faced with the fact that 50 per cent of £8,000,000 would recover only £4,000,000. However, what we would also find, in all probability, is that whatever the activity may be, the vast majority of indirect expenses will not move directly – or, in sympathy – with this reduced activity. They will remain at £5,000,000. For example, it is highly unlikely that management or supervisory staff will volunteer to take a salary decrease should this recession occur (I know *you* would, but you would be an exception!). Equally, and even more certain, landlords will not reduce their rent during the same period. In other words, indirect expenditure is not necessarily bound by the activity within the business. It is therefore vital for everyone using cost data to make sure that indirect cost recovery rates, based as they are upon forecasts, are continuously checked against the facts as they are known.

FULL COST STRUCTURE – RECAPITULATION

We have now arrived at Illustration 6.1's total (full) cost of 18p, made up of the sum of the direct and indirect expenses of the particular unit.

We have seen that the accuracy of direct expenses is determined to a very large extent by the recording of material quantities and labour times within the business. We must therefore continually be watchful that such recordings are being made accurately so that the information we get is credible down to the prime cost. It must always be remembered that if we have bad labour or material control the likelihood is that we will have equally bad costing and perhaps even more dangerous, bad estimating.

We must also be aware that the values placed on the direct costs of material and labour and direct expenses will be based upon historical values unless otherwise arranged. This will therefore require most careful attention if we are using these costs also as a basis for future estimates or for trying to determine the cost of a similar product when material prices and labour rates of pay are changing.

Beyond the prime cost point the amount introduced to recover indirect expenses depends upon guesses or forecasts. For this reason we need to be ever watchful that we are reconciling these forecasts with the facts as and when they are known. We must also realise that at the end, having arrived at the total cost, it will be this figure that will be compared against whatever we use for comparison. In the case of costing products, merchandise or services we will be comparing their costs against their sales prices or against their estimated costs, and whenever we make this comparison the difference will create an emotional response from management – for or against the particular product, merchandise or service depending upon the way the comparison goes. It is for this reason that the credibility of the information produced will be central to the value of full costing to the user.

MULTI-ABSORPTION RATES

It must also be recognised that in Illustration 6.1 we have used a very simple example in which there is just one indirect rate of recovery for the entire business. In practice it is normally found that individual indirect expense recovery rates will be calculated for the different divisions of overheads, for example production indirect expenses, administrative indirect expenses and selling and distribution indirect expenses. Each of these indirect expense divisions will have a different rate of recovery, and an example of this is given in Illustration 6.6.

We also need to understand that in many of these divisions we may wish to calculate more than one indirect recovery rate. This may be important when it is considered that a particular unit of cost uses a larger proportion of indirect expenses than another, for example, a product going through four production processes compared with one going through only two. In such a case it might be considered useful to arrive at a separate indirect expense absorption rate for each process. This means therefore that in place of a single indirect recovery rate as is set out in Illustration 6.1, in practice you could have many more.

Illustration 6.6 Full cost statement with division of indirect expenses

	Unit cost (pence)
Direct material	10
Direct labour	8
Direct expenses	6
Prime cost	24
Factory indirect expenses	6
Works cost	30
Administration indirect expenses	4
Cost of production	34
Selling and distribution indirect expenses	11
Total cost	45
Profit	8
Sale price	53

COST CENTRES

When such a proliferation of analysis takes place the subdivisions into which the overheads are separated are often referred to as cost centres. A recovery rate per cost centre is then calculated and charged to the unit of cost in whatever way is felt appropriate. The reason for doing this is to arrive at a more equitable division of indirect expenses and, it is believed, a more accurate assessment of the full cost of the particular units.

However, the principles set out in Illustration 6.1 will still apply. Just because we have many more indirect recovery rates we still apply the same principles in arriving at each one. It must, though, be noted that if cost centres are established three and not just two judgements will be necessary. We must still arrive at, first, what we believe the indirect expenses will be and, second, what the activity will be when they are being incurred. But to these two we have to add a third judgement: on what basis should we divide the total forecast indirect expenses between the different cost centres? This point is specifically dealt with in the consolidation illustrations which we introduce later.

VALUE OF TIME RECOVERY BASIS

It should also be understood that in using a measurement of activity it is often preferable to translate it into time rather than value. This is because most indirect expenses relate more to time than to value, for example salaries for the month, insurance for the year and rent for the quarter. It is therefore found in practice that rates of recovery are often based on machine, labour or production hours. The reason for this is that if we use value, the amount we add on to recover indirect expenses will be increased if we have expensive direct costs, which may have no bearing on the proportion of indirect expenditure applicable to the particular cost unit. For instance, if we are producing brass rings and platinum rings, and we are adding our indirect expenses based on a percentage of the prime cost value, the platinum rings would bear a much higher proportion of indirect expenditure than the brass rings. This might not be fair, however, because it might not take any longer to manufacture or sell platinum than brass rings. An example of this is shown in Illustration 6.7.

Illustration 6.7 Effects on final cost of using direct costs time basis to calculate recovery rate

	Platinum ring	Brass ring
	p	p
Direct material	400	40
Direct labour	50	50
Direct expenses	10	10
Prime cost	460	100
Production time per ring	30 mins	20 mins
Indirect expenditure added on as 50% of prime cost	230	50
Total cost	690	150
Indirect expenditure added on a time basis at, say,		
5p per production minute	150	100
Total cost	610	200

SOME FINAL WORDS OF CAUTION ABOUT FULL COSTING

We shall now summarise our studies of full costing. Full costing is a combination of the actual cost going into the unit, made up of the direct materials, labour and expenses which make up its prime cost, and a rate or rates of recovery added so as to include the indirect expenditure in the total unit cost. These rates of recovery are based upon forecasts/budgets or assumptions of what the indirect expenses will be and the activity which it is believed will take place in the business over the period ahead. Full costing is a combination of fact and fiction and extreme caution is necessary before it is believed and acted upon; to ensure, first, that direct costs are correctly recorded and priced and, second, that the assumptions on which indirect rates of recovery are calculated are continuously checked.

Direct/indirect division

We have stressed throughout that the value of any costing system depends on its credibility. It should also be borne in mind that the division of expenses, in the first instance, between direct and indirect is one which, by its very nature, can never be 100 per cent accurate. When we talk about expenses as being direct or indirect the division is itself one which is determined by people's judgements. There will inevitably be items which may not exactly fit into either category but for which a decision will have to be made as to where they should be placed.

It could be argued, for instance, that every bit of labour from the chairman down (or up) to the lift-boy could be made direct given enough detailed recording by those concerned. But in practice this is not done and a division is made between direct and indirect labour based upon a judgement of the practicality of its recording. However, it should be noted that this division is not a uniform one – what one company might term direct expenditure another in the same industry might term indirect and vice versa – judgements might differ and impracticalities may become possibilities.

Maximising direct costs

Nevertheless, it must always be borne in mind that the objective of full costing should be to maximise the direct costs. This is for the simple reason that the higher the proportion of direct costs the more we are looking at costs which are determined when the data is being produced. It must be noted that when an indirect expense is absorbed into a cost we are dealing with expenses which inevitably will have to be reconciled against facts as and when these become known – and this will always be after the event. It has been said that once you spread an indirect expense you spread discontent. There is always another judgement as to how such expenses should be absorbed! A manager will already have examined the cost before a reconciliation can be made of the indirect costs recovered against those actually incurred. This means therefore that any sensible manager must always view a full cost with a considerable measure of caution below the prime cost point.

CONSOLIDATION AND CONCLUSION

It is now time to test our understanding against the more complex exercise set out in Illustration 6.8. Here you will see a set of facts relating to the costs of three products, A, B and C, divided between:

(1) the direct cost data provided from the control records for the three products as they are produced;
(2) the forecast or budgeted indirect expenses established for the year during which the direct cost data (1) is provided;
(3) the total forecasts or budgets for the same year for the direct materials, labour, expenses and sales of the three products; and finally,
(4) the bases which are to be used for the recovery of factory, administrative and selling and distribution indirect expenses.

From all these facts you are asked to produce the full cost analysis of these three products, presented in the way set out in Illustration 6.6.

Illustration 6.8 Full cost exercise

X Ltd produces three main products, A, B and C. An analysis of the cost data for these products presents the following information:

		Product	
1. Direct cost data	A	B	C
(a) Direct material:			
Type D (15p per kilo)	12 kilos	6 kilos	14 kilos
Type E (12p per kilo)	11 kilos	11 kilos	11 kilos
Type F (5p per kilo)	13 kilos	12 kilos	6 kilos
(b) Direct labour:			
Dept G (60p per hour)	1 hr	½ hr	3 hrs
Dept H (80p per hour)	4 hrs	4 hrs	2 hrs
Dept I (70p per hour)	3 hrs	–	1 hr
(c) Direct expenses per unit	10p	5p	15p

2. Budgeted indirect expenses for year:

	Factory expenses	Administrative expenses	Selling and distribution expenses
	£	£	£
Salaries	15,000	131,000	48,000
Rent	3,700	1,800	1,400
Insurance	2,000		
Depreciation: plant and machinery	16,000		
Indirect wages	22,100		
Telephone		700	
Stationery		1,100	

		£
Commission (0.5% of sales price)		A 3,000
		B 5,000
		C 4,500
		12,500
Advertising		411,000
	58,800	134,600	472,900

3. Total budget for year:
   (a) Direct material, say, £650,000: materials required   D 1,890,000 kilos
   E 2,173,000 kilos
   F 2,048,000 kilos
   (b) Direct labour, say, £850,000: available for product   A   300,000 hours
   B   450,000 hours
   C   360,000 hours

(c) Direct expenses, say, £20,000
(d) Budgeted sales: A £600,000   B £1,000,000   C £900,000
(e) Selling price: A £16.   B £10   C £15

4.   Indirect factory expenses are to be apportioned on the following bases and recovered based on direct labour hours:

	A	B	C
Rent and rates	on the bases of floor area		
Factory salaries	40%	30%	30%
Factory insurance	20%	60%	20%
Depreciation plant and machinery	25%	50%	25%
Factory indirect wages	40%	20%	40%

Floor area of factory used for product:

A = 200,000 sq feet
B = 300,000 sq feet
C = 100,000 sq feet

5.   Administrative indirect expenses will be recovered based on the budgeted work's cost.

Selling and distribution expenses will be recovered based on the budgeted cost of production.

You are asked to calculate:
(1)   prime cost for each product;
(2)   works cost for each product;
(3)   cost of production for each product;
(4)   total cost for each product;
(5)   profit/loss for each product.

Once you have completed your answer you should check this with the one given in Illustration 6.9 and trace through any errors that may occur. The ways in which the indirect costs, with particular reference to the factory indirect expenses, are recovered are set out for your information in Illustration 6.10. You should study this with particular reference to cost centres and how they are used in the recovery of the factory overheads. You will notice that each product A, B and C is a cost centre in itself. This is for simplification purposes in this example as in practice you may find cost centres selected in many other forms. For example, a particular production process may be a cost centre or a support section such as a drawing officer or tool design may fulfil the purpose.

Having chosen the cost centre, however, the first step is to analyse each individual expense under each cost centre head. In our example you will see from Illustration 6.10 that this involves the apportionment of each indirect factory expense in the way recommended in Illustration 6.8, paragraph 4. Only after completing this apportionment and arriving at an analysis of the total indirect factory expenses under each cost centre head are the rates per direct labour hour calculated.

It is also of interest to note that in the case of factory indirect expenses amounting to £58,800 a considerable effort is made to arrive at the rates of recovery involving cost centres and activity translated into time, i.e. labour hours. However, in the case of both administrative indirect expenses amounting to £134,600 and sales and distribution indirect expenses amounting to £469,400 no such use of cost centres or activity translation is used in arriving at the appropriate recovery rates. In their case the total expense figure is left unanalysed and a percentage based on the total value of units produced is used as a recovery base.

Illustration 6.9 Suggested answer to Illustration 6.8

	Products		
	A	B	C
	p	p	p
Direct material	377	282	372
Direct labour	590	350	410
Direct expenses	10	5	15
(1) Prime cost	977	637	797
Factory expenses (see Illustration 6.10)	54	210	31
(2) Works cost	1,031	657	828
Administrative expenses (9%)	93	59	75
(3 Cost of production	1,124	716	903
Selling and distribution expenses (27%)	303	193	244
Commission (0.5% of sales price)	8	5	7
(4) Total cost	1,435	914	1,154
(5) Profit/loss	165	86	346
Sales price	1,600	1,000	1,500

Perhaps, if you managed this business, you might raise the question of the cost effectiveness of the costing system itself bearing some relationship to the value of the data presented. Costing, after all, has one primary concern – the analysis of expenditure. For this reason, it might be thought that the time and effort expended in producing cost data should be in proportion to the amounts analysed.

Having completed this consolidation assignment and left you with the need to relate cost to benefit we continue our study of the analysis of profit and loss in the next chapter, which deals with marginal costing.

Illustration 6.10 Calculation of administrative expenses and selling and distribution expenses on cost rate

Total budgeted costs for year:	£	
Direct material	650,000	
Direct labour	850,000	
Direct expenses	20,000	
Factory expenses	58,800	
Works cost 1,578,800		
Administrative expenses	134,600 = say 9% of works cost	
Cost of production	1,713,400	
Selling and distribution expenses *less*:		
Commission treated as a direct expense and		
charged to each product per unit of sales	460,400 = say 27% of cost of	
	2,173,800 production	

Products	Total £	%	A £	%	B £	%	C £
Factory expenses							
Salaries	15,000	40	6,000	30	4,500	30	4,500
Rent (floor area)	3,700		1,233		1,850		617
Insurance	2,000	20	400	60	1,200	20	400
Depreciation plant and machinery	16,000	25	4,000	50	8,000	25	4,000
Indirect wages	22,100	40	8,840	20	4,420	40	8,840
	58,800		20,473		19,970		18,357
Labour hours (direct) 1,110,000			300,000		450,000		360,000
Rate per direct labour hour 5.3p			6.8p		4.4p		5.1p
Direct labour hours taken per product			8 hrs		4.5 hrs		6 hrs
Factory expenses absorbed per product on direct labour hour basis (to nearest p)			54p		20p		31p

7

MARGINAL COSTING

Having dealt with full costing we now turn our attention to the alternative system of expense analysis known as marginal costing. To understand this we must get back to our bar stools – in other words, examine expenses from a direct and personal point of view.

THE BREAKEVEN CHART

For example, if you were starting a business how would you think of the expense and income side of it? The first thing you might do is recognise the relationship between cost and income with regard to what you intend to produce and sell. To explain this, turn to Illustration 7.1, which sets out in a visual form the way everyone running a business must think about the relationship between trading expense and income. (You may recall this diagram, which we first introduced in chapter 2 as Illustration 2.8.)

Illustration 7.1 breakeven chart

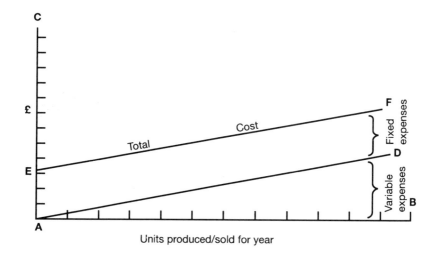

Variable expenses

Illustration 7.1 shows a horizontal axis (AB) which measures the volume of output/sales during a year in units and a vertical axis (AC) which is scaled into £s dealing with monetary value. If we look at our expense to income relationship over a year we will find that expenses will respond to sales and output very broadly in two ways. The first is shown by the line AD, which describes the fact that some expenses move in direct sympathy with what we produce and sell – for instance, the materials and direct labour that go into the product, the commission payable to sales staff, the royalty paid to the designer every time the product is produced. All these are examples of what are termed variable expenses: those which exist only as a result of the business's activity. If the business produces and sells nothing they are not incurred; if the business produces and sells its products, merchandise or services they will be incurred in direct proportion to the activity achieved.

Fixed expenses

However, it must also be noted that we have many other expenses which are there whatever we do – the rent, the salaries of our administrators, insurance premiums, and so on. These are all examples of the other type of expense, which we refer to as fixed expenses or costs. If we produce nothing we are still committed to these and as we go on producing and selling they in fact remain constant for the immediate period ahead – the year in our illustration. These fixed expenses are shown on the vertical axis (AC) in Illustration 7.1 as the distance AE.

Total costs

It is also for this reason that the line EF can be drawn in the chart representing the total cost at whatever level of activity the business achieves. This line EF runs parallel with the variable expense line AD, the distance between them representing fixed expenses AE.

What we have described so far is the fact that expenses fall into two broad categories: the one which moves in direct sympathy with what we produce and sell, known as variable expenses, and the other, which remains constant irrespective of what we produce and sell over a given period of time – termed the fixed expenses. From the illustration it can be seen that if nothing is sold during the year the total cost will be the fixed expenses and the total costs of whatever is sold beyond this zero point will be read as the variable expenses relating to the particular sales achieved plus the fixed expenses for the year.

Sales income

Let us now continue by taking our view of the breakeven chart a little further. Consider Illustration 7.2, where we add the cumulative sales income to the chart in Illustration 7.1. In other words, we consider what we will make from selling our goods, merchandise and services over the same period as our expenses are being incurred – the accumulated income as and when it arrives based upon our sales for the year. To illustrate this we have put in the line AG representing such sales values, depending upon the volume of sales achieved over the year.

Illustration 7.2 Breakeven chart with sales income

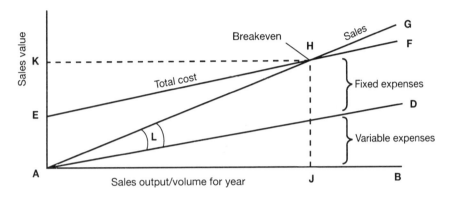

The breakeven point

As we can see from the chart set out in Illustration 7.2, this sales line breaks through the total cost line EF at the point H. This represents the point which is described in terms of the value or the volume of sales which must be achieved for the business to 'break even' depending on whether you draw the dotted line down to the horizontal or across to the vertical axes at points J and K.

Contribution

The breakeven point, as it is called, is the point at which the total income from our sales exceeds the variable expenses of these by the amount of the total fixed costs for the period. To illustrate this situation let us take a very simple example of a business with one product which is sold for £100 and for which the unit variable cost is £70. The excess, or difference between sales value and variable cost, is therefore £30. If the total fixed costs for the year amounted to £3,000,000 the breakeven point could be measured in a unit volume of 100,000, i.e. £3,000,000 divided by £30, or sales value of £10,000,000, i.e. 100,000 units x £100.

Alternative diagram

For information an alternative form of breakeven chart is set out in Illustration 7.3. You will see from this that the fixed and variable expense lines are drawn in reverse order from that shown in Illustration 7.2 and that no angle of contribution is established. It might also be criticised on the grounds that although it provides a graphical translation of the breakeven point it has the disadvantage of suggesting that sales first break through the fixed expenses before recovering the variable expenses.

Illustration 7.3 Alternative breakeven chart

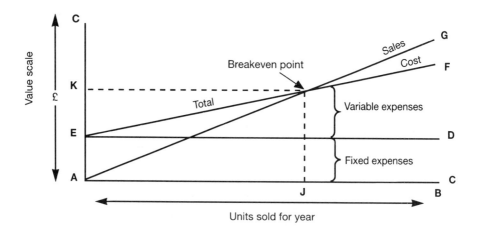

For this reason the breakeven chart in Illustration 7.2 is used throughout this book for reference purposes. Mind you, criticism is raised in this case as well. This is because people are confused between the total cost line EF and the fixed expenses total AE. This is caused by the seeming contradiction between fixed expenses, which should remain the same although the total cost line EF increases with activity. To avoid such confusion it must be remembered that the fixed costs are reflected by the distance between the two parallel lines – the variable expense line AD and the total cost line EG. In this view of breakeven the fixed expenses are shown as a constant distance between two parallel lines.

Contribution/margin/profit

Having described the breakeven chart, as it is known, let us stand back for a minute and consider the concept which is behind this view of expenditure in relation to sales. This is that on the sale of a unit, whether it is a unit of manufacture, merchandise or service, we do not generate profit or loss at all. We generate the difference between the sale price and the variable cost of the particular unit. It is this difference that may be termed the margin or, more usually, the contribution.

Under the concepts of marginal costing what must be recognised is that neither the margin nor the contribution is a profit. What is demonstrated is that a profit is not established for any business until the breakeven point has been reached. In other words, not until all the fixed costs for the period have been fully recovered can a business consider that it has made a profit. This is because up to the point of breakeven, it is committed to its fixed expenses for the period and these will have to be met whatever volume or value of sales is achieved. In fact the critical point to examine is the angle of contribution, labelled L in Illustration 7.2.

A narrow angle indicates a competitive market place in which contributions are small and profit is likely to be delayed until well through the period of time in which it is being measured. We need therefore to control and, where possible, reduce fixed expenses and this must be a constant theme of financial control.

On the other hand, a wide angle indicates a less competitive or even speculative market place in which a profit is made early in the measured period. However, just as profits are earned early so are losses if sales volumes are not achieved. The ease of profit making during 'good times' may create the temptation to loosen the control on fixed expenses and this must be resisted in every possible way.

MARGINAL COSTING

Based upon the concept set out in Illustration 7.2 the system known as marginal costing has been developed. This is a system of expense analysis which over the short term – say twelve months – recognises that expenses move in the way we have just described. Because of this it becomes evident that in examining the cost of a unit the only costs that can truly be related to it are those which are variable, because those which are fixed exist whether or not a particular product is produced, merchandise presented or service rendered.

Under marginal costing, therefore, a unit of cost does not give a business profit: it provides – so long as sales value exceeds variable cost – a contribution. Profit happens only when the total contributions gained from all that is sold equals the total of the fixed expenses for the particular period.

Consider Illustration 7.4. Tackle the question, expressing the breakeven in units and sales value in each case. When you have done this check your answers with Illustration 7.5 (down to the broken line).

P/V ratio

Breakeven can therefore be expressed in units or sales value and if sales can be related to time then breakeven can be located to a particular month of the year. For example, if in the case of business A it was planned to sell 400,000 units a month the business should break even in mid-August, assuming that sales were achieved evenly throughout the calendar year. Contribution can also be related to the sales price as a percentage and this percentage in turn can be translated into pence per £1. For example, a contribution of 30 per cent of the sales price for a particular product means that for every £1 of sales of the product a contribution of 30p will arise. To practise this way of looking at contributions to sales values study the three examples in Illustration 7.4 and the calculations below the broken line in Illustration 7.5.

Illustration 7.4 Expense/income relationship

Consider the expense/income relationship for the following three businesses and calculate the breakeven point in each case:

Business	A	B	C
Sale price of products	20p	35p	40p
Variable expense of products	15p	28p	22p
Fixed costs	£150,000	£280,000	£360,000

Illustration 7.5 Calculations of breakeven points in Illustration 7.4

		A	B	C
Contribution of business		5p	7p	18p
Breakeven = $\dfrac{\text{Fixed expenses}}{\text{Contribution}}$ =		$\dfrac{£150,00}{5p}$	$\dfrac{£280,00}{7p}$	$\dfrac{£360,000}{18p}$
Units	=	3,000,000	4,000,000	2,000,000
Sales value	=	£600,000	£1,400,000	£800,000
Contribution/sales price	=	$\dfrac{5}{20}$	$\dfrac{7}{35}$	$\dfrac{18}{40}$
As a %	=	25%	20%	45%
Pence per £	=	25p	20p	45p

Marginal costing is often referred to as the analysis of cost/profit/volume and the ratio of contribution to sales price which we have just discussed is sometimes termed the profit/volume or P/V ratio. As we have seen, this ratio can be expressed as the percentage the contribution bears to the sales value, either of one unit sold or the total sales of the organisation. This is demonstrated in Illustration 7.6 and some of the uses of the ratio are set out in Illustrations 7.7 and 7.8.

An example of the use of the P/V ratio is when additional fixed expenses are under discussion and management wishes to know what additional sales must be generated to justify them. For instance, if the P/V ratio is 20 per cent, additional annual fixed expenses of £10,000 will increase the breakeven point measured in sales value by £50,000 (£10,000 divided by 20 per cent). This means that the business will have to increase its sales by £50,000 to recover the increased fixed costs of £10,000.

Illustration 7.6 P/V ratio

	Unit data	Total unit data
Contribution	30p	£600,000
Sales price/turnover	45p	£1,000,000
P/V ratio	66%	60%

Illustration 7.7 Using the P/V ratio: breakeven

The breakeven point can be determined by dividing the fixed expenses by the P/V ratio:

		£	%
	Sale price	110	100
	Variable costs	77	70
	Contribution	33	30
	P/V ratio	= 30%	
If	Fixed expenses	= £750,000	
Then	Breakeven point	= £2,500,000	(£750,000 divided by 30%)

Illustration 7.8 Using the P/V ratio: profit

When the breakeven point is known, profits and losses are easily determined through the P/V ratio:

		£
	Budgeted sales	4,000,000
	Sales value at breakeven point	2,500,000
	Sales value beyond breakeven point	1,500,000
If	P/V ratio = 30%	
Then	Estimated profit = £450,000 (30% x £1,500,000)	

Summary

Marginal costing is a system of analysis which concentrates on the variable expenses and by doing so highlights the difference between them and the relevant sales values. This difference is called the contribution or margin and is a measurement that can be calculated for units or for the total sales achieved over a period of time.

Marginal costing, then, is concerned with an examination of the contribution. However, it must be emphasised that marginal cost does not in any way ignore fixed costs – it simply does not analyse them. To understand this point as regards marginal costing, turn to Illustration 7.9, which contains a full cost analysis and, alongside it, the equivalent marginal cost analysis. In the full cost all expenses – direct, variable and fixed cost items – are brought into the analysis. However, in the case of the marginal cost the analysis is confined entirely to the direct or variable expenses.

Illustration 7.9 Full and marginal cost layout

	Product A	
	Full cost (pence)	Marginal cost (pence)
Direct material	10	10
Direct labour	8	8
Direct expenses	2	2
Prime cost	20	20
Works expenses: Fixed	6	-
Variable	4	4
Works cost	30	-
Administration expenses: Fixed	10	-
Variable	2	2
Cost of production	42	-
Selling and distribution expenses: Fixed	14	-
Variable	11	11
Cost of sales	67	-
Marginal cost	-	37
Net profit	8	-
Contribution	-	38
Sale price	75	75

Direct, variable and fixed costs or expenses

The terms variable and direct cost, or indirect and fixed expenses, can pose a problem of definition. This is because in practice, apart from materials and directly variable costs such as commissions and royalties, most other expenses are, in part, both variable and fixed. For example, labour used to render a service while the service is actually being rendered is variable and direct to the service, but if no work is available and the labour is still employed such labour cost becomes a fixed expense and is indirect in respect of any particular service.

For this reason the terms direct and variable cost become interchangeable in marginal costing. Another case of duplicate jargon! (And do remember the words 'cost' and 'expense' are also interchangeable.)

THE USE OF MARGINAL COSTING

Having taken this first view of marginal costing it is necessary to stand back and look more closely at its meaning and significance to those using the information it provides. The first thing to understand about marginal costing is that it is used very much in the pricing and forecasting field of management. Of course it is also used in the historical view of what a unit has cost and how a business has performed. When marginal costing information is available, however, managers will inevitably use it in looking forward and translating their plans into profit assessments and in examining and determining their future pricing policies.

What I am emphasising here is that marginal costing is a highly dynamic technique. It is not used purely in the somewhat static role of full costing. You could say that one of the central points to understand about marginal costing is that it is actively used. It is not confined to the filing cabinet but will take an active part in management decisions, especially in policy-making areas such as pricing and marketing.

LIMITATIONS OF MARGINAL COSTING

For this reason management using marginal costing data must be aware of its limitations, which can be described with regard, first, to time and, second, to output or sales.

Time

To illustrate the limitation of time consider the breakeven point set out in Illustration 7.2. This point is based on the facts which are available when the lines AD, AE and AG are drawn and any changes in these facts will affect the breakeven point H.

Management must therefore make sure that the facts they are using are brought up to date. Nothing is more dangerous than management discussing the breakeven point or the contributions of each unit as if they were incontrovertible facts established for all time. For example, it must be understood that the breakeven point will alter whenever there is a change in any of the costs forecast – whether they are variable or fixed – or when changes are made to the sale prices used. These must be brought into account as soon as they occur.

In other words, the data on which the breakeven point and marginal costing data has been established must be continually revised and reviewed.

Output or sales

Having considered the limitation of time we must now consider the second limitation – the limitation of activity, whether measured in output or sales. This is caused because marginal costing is always based upon an assumption of a given minimum and maximum output/sales within the business situation. To illustrate this let us turn to Illustration 7.10, where we see a breakeven chart in which two vertical lines run from M to N (to the left of the breakeven point) and O to P (to its right).

These two lines represent what might be described as the parameters upon which the breakeven information has been produced. The minimum limit means that the variable cost and fixed cost lines drawn in the illustration are based upon the assumption that we shall never sell less than a minimum quantity of the product. In Illustration 7.10 this is described by the line MN. If we do not reach this minimum output or sales value (points N and R) the costs will react in a way not described in the diagram. The variable costs will not necessarily disappear to nothing as the illustration suggests – they will in many cases become fixed. For example, much of the direct skilled labour will still be employed for a time, even if there is insufficient production for them to be fully employed, and their wages would therefore become a fixed cost. Equally, many fixed expenses such as administrative wages and salaries might in fact be cut if the minimum output or sales is not reached.

Illustration 7.10 Breakeven chart – output limitations

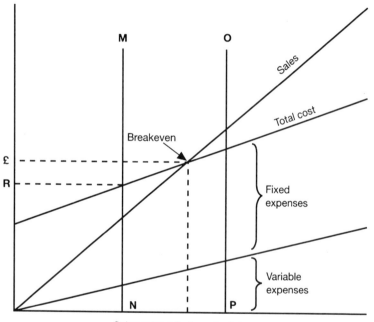

Sales output /volume (units)

And this is equally true at the other end of the scale. If you get beyond a certain volume of output/sales (marked by the line OP in Illustration 7.10), then once again the variable and fixed costs will not respond in the way set out in the chart. For example, it is very likely that many of the variable costs will increase per unit produced. The business may become more wasteful or careless with its materials or merchandise or it will have to pay overtime to its labour to perform the necessary extra work. It may also be found that if it exceeds a certain normal output or sales volume the fixed cost might increase. It might have to employ more supervision or it may have to rent more space in order to obtain the extra capacity to store the goods or present the merchandise that it is now wishing to sell.

Coupled with this problem of increasing costs when a business exceeds a certain normal output/sales level, if it wishes to sell more of its goods, merchandise or services, it might well have to reduce its sale prices. The combination of these factors might well mean that, although you increase your sales and output, you do not achieve the profit level you would normally expect. In fact you might even make a loss, in what might be termed a trading pincer movement. This is shown in Illustration 7.11 by the continuation of the total cost and sales lines, which show how changes in fixed and variable costs and sale prices affect the total profitability of the business. Indeed, increased activity eventually achieves a loss.

Illustration 7.11 Breakeven chart – cost changes

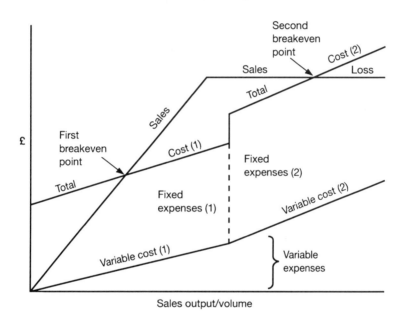

Sales output/volume

Historical use of marginal costing

Bearing in mind, therefore, the limitations of marginal costing let us go on to see how the information it reveals can be used in making business decisions.

As already mentioned, in addition to using marginal costing in analysing historical costs it has a very wide application in decisions concerned with marketing and pricing. To illustrate these applications let us first consider the trading and pricing problems of business over the past years; what we find is that, whenever we do, there is an application for marginal costing.

MARGINAL COSTING AND PRICING POLICY

Market domination

To illustrate this let us go back a hundred years or so and consider the situation that arose when many of the larger enterprises began to establish dominance in their particular market. An example of this is shown in Illustration 7.12, which sets out the costs of two units. We will assume that these represent the costs of units produced by two different manufacturing companies in the same industry and that product A is produced by a large multi-product manufacturer, product B by a smaller, single-product manufacturer. Based on the two full cost analyses, product A costs 10p and is sold for 12p with a profit of 2p, whereas product B which costs 8p is sold for 10p and thus has the same profit of 2p.

Illustration 7.12 Unit costs

	Large company Product A (pence)		Small company Product B (pence)
Direct costs	4		4
Variable cost		6	
Indirect costs	6		4
Fixed cost		4	
Total cost	10	10	8
Profit	2		2
Sale price	12		10

What we see here is that a small company producing the single unit is selling that unit at a lower price than its larger competitor in the same market place. It is also clear that, in this situation, if the larger manufacturer wished to dominate the market place in the sale of this particular unit, it would have to eliminate or at least curtail the activities of its opposition. So how best could this be done?

Obviously, one of the more effective ways would be to reduce its own sales price, but before this could be done the larger company would need to know what minimum sale price it could adopt. It is in establishing that 'minimum sale price' that marginal costing – which analyses costs into those which are variable as opposed to those that are fixed – comes into its own. We can see from Illustration 7.12 that if the large manufacturer does this it reveals the variable cost of the unit as 6p and the fixed cost as 4p. And having established these facts it is not too difficult to work out that if the large manufacturer sells more than one type of unit, it could, for a limited period, decide to recover its fixed costs from these other units. It could then decide to sell product A at something which will recover its variable costs and perhaps be satisfied with making only a very small contribution above that.

For instance, the larger manufacturer might decide to sell A at 7p, which would leave the small manufacturer in a very difficult position because it has no other products over which it can spread its fixed costs. In this situation the minimum price it could sell product B for, without making a loss, would be 8p.

It was based upon this view of pricing and the treatment of fixed costs that many monopolies were established at the turn of the century: capturing markets from smaller, 'annoying' competitors by reducing sale prices for limited periods of time. The method might be described as 'blitzing out' the competition.

Pricing during a recession

If we go on from this point of time to a period of recession and slump, once again we see the need to establish minimum sale prices to meet the market-place problem that arises: it no longer wants your goods, merchandise or services unless the price is set very attractively. In this situation it might be said that any sale price which recovers some of the fixed costs is better than one that sells nothing at all! After all, the fixed costs will continue whatever happens.

We can trace this view by studying the breakeven chart in Illustration 7.2. Here you will see that whether a sale is made or not the fixed costs will still continue, and therefore any sale price which recovers the variable costs and provides some contribution towards the fixed costs will reduce the eventual loss. It will certainly be better financially than not selling anything at all. It was indeed this application of marginal costing to pricing within a recessionary period which provided and indeed still provides a lifeline to survival during such economic times. Mind you, you cannot continue selling at what is a loss for ever but for a limited period it may have an application as a means of survival.

The 'other label' approach

The third application of marginal costing to pricing policies can be seen in the use of 'other label' techniques to meet competitive market situations – techniques adopted when the desire to reduce prices has to be reconciled with justifying such action. In such a situation what we find is that many businesses attract additional sales by reducing their sale prices while at the same time disguising their products, merchandise or services by means of 'another label'. An example of this is a supermarket selling 'own label' colas which are actually produced by the manufacturer of a well-known brand. Or a solicitor may offer to undertake legal work for a client at a special price because he or she is a friend. Such action obtains two objectives: more sales achieved through reduced sale prices, at the same time not offending past or present customers or clients who have previously purchased the same goods, merchandise or services at higher prices. The lower price which attracts extra business is 'justified'.

Here again, to establish such lower sale prices the marginal cost is used to produce a reference point for the revised price. For an example of this situation turn to Illustration 7.13 and examine the breakeven chart set out there. In this chart you will notice that production capacity is marked by the vertical line ST and the sales demand based on normal sale prices by the vertical line YZ. We therefore have the area ZT which represents free, indeed unused, production capacity. It is to fill this free capacity that many companies adopt the 'other label' sales policy, marketing their excess capacity under another brand label, coupled with a price reduction, in order to attract the necessary additional sales volume. At this stage it is important to emphasise the fact that such 'other label' techniques are not confined to retail sales operations – baked beans and washing powder. They are equally evident in such sales techniques as bulk discount, the 'old boy or girl' network – because you are a friend we can give you a special price – and subscription reductions.

Illustration 7.13 Breakeven chart showing sales and production limits

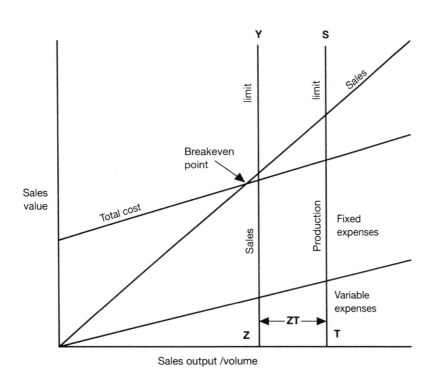

Brand label switch problems

It must, however, be understood that if a business uses such selling methods two problems exist.

(1) The first is to establish what is free capacity. It is too easy to decide what is free capacity only to find that once you have committed yourself to filling it with work at a lower sale price you are forced, having now reached full

capacity, to refuse higher priced work once demand flows back to the business. In other words, you can over react to a short-term situation.

(2) The second problem, however, is even more important to understand: if you adopt the policy of selling your free capacity at lower than normal sale prices you must make sure that the business maintains a strict control of its sales mix. You must confine your lower prices to items which will fill the free capacity and not allow these to eat into your otherwise high-profit making capacity. Central to this second problem is an understanding of the arithmetic of profit.

THE ARITHMETIC OF PROFIT

Consider Illustration 7.14. You will see that there are three products, A, B and C, with sale prices of 10p, 15p and 8p respectively. In column 2 we have the variable cost of each product, namely 5p, 10p and 7p, which thus gives a contribution for A of 5p, B of 5p and C of 1p. If we then relate the contribution to the sales value for each product we arrive at the following relationships (given in column 4): in the case of A, 5p contribution divided by 10p sale price gives us a relationship of 0.5; for B the relationship (5p divided by 15p) is 0.33; and, finally, for C a penny divided by 8p gives 0.125.

These relationships tell us that, in the case of A, 50 per cent of whatever sales value we achieve will be contribution – in other words, if we sell a pound's worth of A 50p will be variable cost and 50p contribution. For every pound of B we sell 33p will be contribution and 67p variable cost, and in the case of C 12.5p will be contribution and 87.5p variable cost.

The sales mix

If we then turn to the final columns we will see, first, the budgeted sales mix. This is the mix of sales between the three products we are planning to sell for the period ahead. Assuming that the budgeted sales mix of A, B and C is 80, 10 and 10 per cent respectively, as shown in the illustration, we can establish the relationship of contributions to sales values within this mix by very simple multiplication and addition.

Illustration 7.14 The arithmetic of profit

Products	Sales price	Variable cost	Contribution	Contribution to sales price	Budgeted sales Mix %	c/sp
	(pence)	(pence)	(pence)	(pence)	%	(pence)
A	10	5	5	0.50	80	0.40
B	15	10	5	0.33	10	0.03
C	8	7	1	0.125	10	0.01
						0.44

Fixed costs   = £880,000 divided by 44p
Sales to breakeven   = £2 million

Sales mix and breakeven calculation

For instance, if we multiply the 0.5 that we have established for product A by 80 per cent we arrive at the figure of 0.40 x £1, for product B (0.33 by 10 per cent) 0.03 x £1 and, finally, for product C (0.125 by 10 per cent) we arrive at 0.10 x £1.

Having established these individual amounts we can then add them up to arrive at a total of 0.44 of £1. Now let us look at this overall. What we are saying is that every time we sell a pound's worth of our goods in the mix that we have just been discussing (80 per cent A, 10 per cent B, 10 per cent C), we shall arrive at a contribution of 44p.

It will therefore be seen that if the fixed costs we are trying to recover for the year from our business amount to £880,000, the sales value we must achieve (based on the same mix) to recover these fixed costs can be calculated by dividing the £880,000 by 44p. And if we do this we arrive at the sales value of £2,000,000. The breakeven point therefore is sales of £2,000,000.

Budget/actual comparison

We can now take this a step further. We can see what would happen if we found that our actual sales mix does not agree with our budgeted sales mix. For instance, if we do not achieve a mix of 80 per cent A, 10 per cent B and 10 per cent C, but our mix in fact becomes 10 per cent A, 10 per cent B and 80 per cent C, the question we have to solve is: what does that mean in terms of the profits and the sales value required to break even?

To deal with this we need to turn to Illustration 7.15. Here we see that in order to arrive at our answer we must recalculate our relationship of contribution to sales price based on this new mix. In other words, we must multiply the 0.5 for A not by 80 per cent but by 10 per cent. For B the multiplication remains the same because the sales mix is still 10 per cent, but in the case of C we must multiply 0.125 not by 10 per cent but by 80 per cent. If we do all this we come to a very different figure, made up of 0.05 for A plus 0.03 for B and 0.10 for C, giving us a total of 18p.

Illustration 7.15 Revision of sales mix

Products	Contribution to sales	Actual sales mix %	Actual contribution to sales price (pence)
A	0.50	10	0.05
B	0.33	10	0.03
C	0.125	80	0.10
			0.18

Fixed costs	= £880,000 divided by 0.18p
Sales value to breakeven	= £4.9 million

What we have now discovered is that when we sell in this new mix, instead of arriving at a contribution of 44p per £1 we sell, we now arrive at a contribution of only 18p. In other words, between the budget and the actual mix every time we sell a pound's worth of our products we are losing, or reducing our profits by, 26p – the difference between our budget and our actual contribution figures.

We can also see that to break even we would now have to achieve sales, based on this actual mix, of £4.9 million – calculated by dividing £880,000 by 0.18. A very different figure from the budgeted sales value of £2,000,000!

All this is the arithmetic of profit, which must be clearly understood by all those who seek to establish sales policies which require pricing adjustments within a sales mix. At the present time more and more businesses are entering into a much more competitive market place and a full understanding of this 'profit arithmetic' must be established throughout such organisations: not simply by accountants but by all those concerned with pricing and selling the products, merchandise or services.

CONTRIBUTION AND LIMITING FACTORS

Having looked at contribution in relation to sales value it is useful to carry our thoughts on the use of marginal costing a step further. We have so far mentioned that marginal costing information provides us with minimum sale price levels below which we must not fall – namely the variable cost.

We have also seen that marginal costing gives us a way of examining the contribution of individual units in relation to the sales value. It is in fact central to profit comparison between products, merchandise or services sold because it defines the true differences between them. After all, costs deducted after arriving at the contribution refer to fixed expenses, which bear no direct relationship to any particular units sold. This means that it is the measurement of contribution which separates one product, item of merchandise or service from another.

Because contribution is so central to product definition from a profit point of view, in many cases it is found useful to examine it, in relation not just to sales value but to other factors. For example, within every business there may be limitations – of time, of storage space, of expertise, of capital or finance – and when this happens it is necessary to consider the need to maximise profit, not in relation to sales, but in relation to the particular limitation.

Limitation of time

To help us understand this let us turn to Illustration 7.16, which considers the problem of time limitations in relation to the three products that we have been examining in Illustrations 7.14 and 7.15. We will assume that there is a demand for our products which far exceeds our production capacity. We will also assume the following facts: that it takes three minutes of manufacturing time to make A, two minutes to make B and half a minute to make C.

Illustration 7.16 Contribution per limiting factor of time

Product	Contribution (pence)	Production time (mins)	Contribution to production time (pence per min.)
A	5	3	1.7
B	5	2	2.5
C	1	½	2.0

The problem posed is to decide which of the three products we should concentrate on during a limited period of time available for manufacture. In this situation the relationship of contribution to sales value is no longer relevant – we need to look for a measurement of contribution not against sales value but against the limited production time. We find that A gives us (5p divided by 3 minutes) approximately 1.7p per minute, B (5p divided by 2 minutes) 2.5p per minute, and C (1p divided by ½ minute) 2p.

So if we are limited by production time then from a profit-maximisation point of view, we would concentrate first on selling B, second on C and finally on A. In other words, not quite but very nearly in reverse order of preference from that which we established when we looked at contribution to sales value in Illustration 7.14.

Price selection

However, as well as using the measurement of contribution when looking at established sale prices of products, merchandise or services it may also be found useful when selecting ideal future price levels.

To examine this situation let us consider Illustration 7.17. In this we have a product which we decide to market and we have to agree upon its sales price. We will assume that the marketing department advises us that, depending upon the size of the market we wish to obtain, the sale price could range from 20p to 40p. We will also assume that we select the sale prices set out in the illustration and that the variable or direct cost of this particular unit is estimated at 15p. If this is so then the contribution – depending on the sale price decided upon – would range from 5p to 25p per unit. Suppose, too, that we decide that this particular unit must give us a minimum contribution of, say, £200,000 to make it worthwhile producing and selling it at all.

Illustration 7.17 Contribution and price selection

	Suggested sale prices (pence)				
Product	20	25	30	35	40
Variable cost	15	15	15	15	15
Contribution	5	10	15	20	25

Minimum contribution required from product – £200,000

The 'contribution' breakeven chart

To solve the problem of which price should be chosen we can produce what we might term a visual agenda (as set out in Illustration 7.18). This shows a breakeven chart which is different from the ones we have so far examined because it is concerned solely with presenting the cumulative contributions in relation to the volume of sales achieved. As you will see from the chart we have two vertical lines, AB and CD, scaled so as to set out the value of profit above and loss below the two points X and Y. These two points X and Y are joined by a horizontal line, which is scaled in units sold, the complete chart taking a form similar to a rugby goalpost. Within this chart the cumulative contributions, attributable to the different sale prices, can be drawn and compared with the sales volumes predicted.

Reading and plotting the chart

The chart begins by marking £200,000 at point E on the loss or negative portion of vertical axis AB. This indicates the minimum contribution which this unit is targeted to recover whatever sale price is selected. Having established this at point E the contributions from the different sale prices are then drawn to indicate the cumulative contribution they each make depending upon the volume of sales achieved. These are set out in Illustration 7.19. For example, EF is the line relating to the sale price of 20p, EG to 25p, EH to 30p, and so on. In addition, these lines indicate at points K, L, M, N and O the volume of sales at each price required to break even, that is, to recover the £200,000 contribution target.

Illlustration 7.18 'Contribution' breakeven chart – stage I

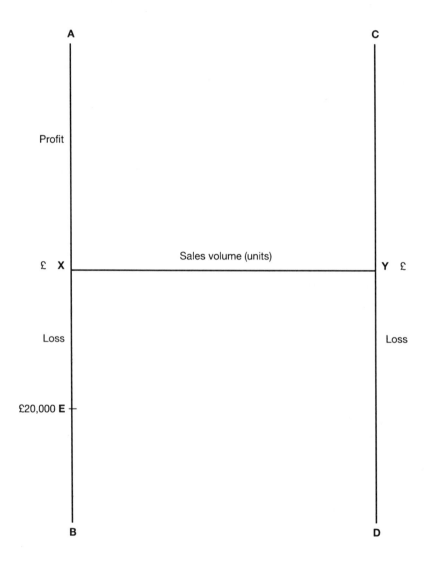

Illustration 7.19 'Contribution' breakeven chart – stage II

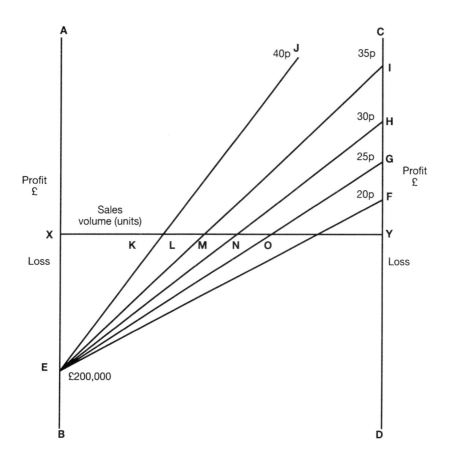

Having done this it is then possible to examine these lines in relation to the market forecasts, which are set out in Illustration 7.20. To decide these, you could ask the marketing side of the business what volume of sales are anticipated at these different sale prices and mark these, as in Illustration 7.20, at points R, S, T, U and V.

From this we can then determine what we feel is the most suitable sale price by deciding which particular unit price gives us the maximum profit in relation to our production capacity. In this particular case 30p, 25p, 35p and 20p would be the order of profitability, and 40p would be dismissed as it does not even reach breakeven. It fails to cover the minimum contribution.

Illustration 7.20 'Contribution' breakeven chart – stage III

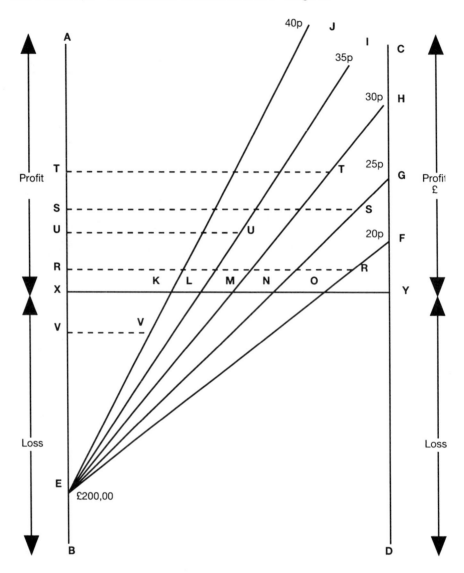

It must be recognised, however, that the maximisation of immediate profit may not always be in the best long-term interests of the business. For instance, other considerations might favour a price which may not give us such a high profit but which might establish us in a market place which fits into our particular range of products. Or we might wish to establish a lower sale price so as to attract more business, which in turn will keep the skills of the workforce more fully employed to meet future anticipated demand.

SUMMARY

We have now examined marginal costing and the way in which it can be used and adapted to meet different management problems.

Definition of marginal costing

Marginal costing is a method of analysing expenses so as to highlight the fact that they either move in sympathy with what we produce and sell or are of a fixed nature: fixed in that they are not directly influenced by sales or production volume but more by time – rent for the quarter, salaries for the month, insurance for the year. It must be recognised that this division is not absolute and in fact many expenses fall into neither category – in other words, they are neither fixed nor variable but a little of each. An example of this sort of expense would be depreciation on plant and machinery. This, it can be argued, varies in accordance with the use of the particular item but also contains a fixed part – the obsolescence – which is going on whether it is used or not.

We could also argue that such things as wages can often be partly variable and partly fixed. They are variable in the case of production labour so long as production continues, but once production is held up or is no longer continued, such expenses can and often do become fixed. The skilled operator waiting for work becomes a fixed cost and it is for this reason that we must be particularly careful not to treat the division of fixed and variable expenses in too rigid a manner. The division needs to be continually reviewed in accordance with situations as they develop.

The second point to emphasise is that in the division of fixed and variable expenses the fact that marginal costing is concerned with the analysis of variable expenses does not imply that the fixed costs are being ignored. It is true they are not being analysed, but this certainly should not mean that they are being ignored. Throughout any system of marginal costing, contributions must be compared with fixed costs and emphasis must always be placed upon making sure that such fixed costs are as planned and are being recovered by the contributions obtained from the products, merchandise or services being sold.

Having arrived at this overall view of contribution and marginal costing it is necessary to consider how this way of looking at the expense to income relationship can be used to deal with management problems. However, once again certain points must first be emphasised.

Limitation of data

To begin with there are the limitations which are inherent in this view of costing. What is meant by this is that, whenever we consider fixed and variable costs and the sales and breakeven points, it must be remembered that all these measurements of expense and income are based on assumptions. In other words, once we have established the breakeven point any event which alters expenses or sale prices – or indeed the sales mix – will change the breakeven point. For this reason the revision of marginal cost information must be a constant requirement by management.

Implicit assumptions

Second, when we look at the measurement of breakeven and variable and fixed costs and sale prices we must appreciate that they are all based on an assumption of minimum and maximum output sales levels. Once a business falls below or rises above these levels the relationship between the expenses and sales may also change.

Management use of marginal costing

Having recognised very clearly the limitations and assumptions of the information we use in establishing a marginal cost it is necessary to consider the use that can be made of such data.

Sale price guidelines

The first use is in establishing sale price guidelines. For instance, to meet different marketing situations – to take advantage of them – we may feel that an adjustment of the sale price could be advantageous. If this need arises, then knowing the variable cost of the different units we are selling could be of considerable help. It would allow us to recognise that this is the value below which a sale price would not recover the variable expense of the unit and above which we would at least make a contribution towards our fixed costs.

Establishing such a minimum sale price can be particularly useful in highly competitive market places and could have a very real application when we wish to steer our marketing policies in different directions.

Concentration on the controllable within recognised limitations

A further point is that because marginal costing concentrates our view upon the contribution of each unit we sell, it enables us to examine our products, merchandise and services in the light of those costs which are controllable. It also enables management to study the contributions discovered in relation to particular limiting factors such as time, space or capital invested.

Sales price selection

Finally, by the use of marginal cost analysis it is possible to review the effects of different sale prices for the same product, merchandise or service by means of the revised breakeven chart set out in Illustration 7.20. This may prove a valuable way of bringing together the many considerations which have to be taken into account in establishing a sale price within the context of the business's overall strategy. Indeed, the chart illustrated might be described as a visual agenda.

Illustration 7.21 Marginal costing exercise

B Ltd sells five product lines. The five products are manufactured on a bank of 60 power presses, any of which may be used on each of the five products. It is estimated that each press can produce 40 hours' work per week. The data relating to the products is as follows:

Product	Total cost £	Variable cost £	Selling price per unit £	No of press hrs	Estimated demand per month
A	26	20	30	3	1,400
B	35	28	40	6	1,900
C	72	52	85	7	300
D	20	15	30	5	1,800
E	18	14	30	4	600

Fixed costs amount to £23,400 per month.

What combination of products would produce the maximum profit assuming the business is limited by press hours?

Illustration 7.22 Suggested answer to Illustration 7.21

Product	Selling price per unit £	Variable cost £	Contribution per unit £	Hours required	Contribution per hour £	Best product
A	30	20	10	3	3.3	3
B	40	28	12	6	2.0	5
C	85	52	33	7	4.7	1
D	30	15	15	5	3.0	4
E	30	14	16	4	4.0	2

To maximise the profits based on 9,600 available per month, produce:

Product	Demand	Produce	Hours		Total hours	Contribution £
C	300	300	7	=	2,100	9,900
E	600	600	4	=	2,400	9,600
A	1,400	1,400	3	=	4,200	14,000
D	1,800	180	5	=	900	2,700
					9,600	36,200
					Less fixed costs	23,400
					Net profit	12,800

Consolidation

To consolidate your studies of marginal costing, attempt the question set out in Illustration 7.21. When you have completed it check your answer with Illustration 7.22 and revise those sections in this chapter which explain the points of difficulty you experienced, before proceeding.

CONCLUSION

This then completes our study of both full and marginal costing. The question which perhaps remain is why there should be two methods of analysing expense. The answer lies in the the market place around us. Full costing is very much the method used when sale prices can be determined by those selling the product, the service or the merchandise. It is therefore concerned with a method of analysis by which the direct cost of each unit is established and to which a suitable absorption rate of overheads and profits is added so as to arrive at the sale price.

Marginal costing is, however, designed to meet a rather different market place, one dominated by the buyer or the competitor. Its concern, as we have seen, is in the pricing, marketing and profit-measurement fields within a competitive world.

8

PROJECT APPRAISAL

INTRODUCTION

In chapter 5 we began to examine the evolution of financial information from the profit and loss account, the balance sheet and the cash flow forecast. We discussed how information has been developed or evolved to meet the needs of the thinking manager. For instance, in the case of the profit or loss we have the analytical techniques of full and marginal costing, discussed in the last chapter.

To remind you of this pattern, look again at Illustration 5.1 and you will see that, in the same way, evolution arises from the balance sheet. The balance sheet sets out from where a business has obtained its money, its capital, and where this same money is invested right now. Managers are much concerned with the areas in which the capital is invested. They may be unable to influence directly all the sources of capital but they certainly need to be aware of how it is invested. After all, where it is invested is a direct result of their actions and the way managers do this will greatly influence the chances, or risks, of profits or losses being made. To refresh your memory of the way money is invested in business, look at the form of the business model set out in Illustration 8.1.

Here we see the two areas of investment: fixed assets including outside investment, and working capital. So let us begin by looking at the first of these – the fixed assets, the things we buy with no intention of selling – and ask ourselves: would it be sufficient simply to read about what we own as fixed assets on the balance sheet? The answer, I hope, is a definite 'no'. By that time it would be too late! We would already own them. In other words, if we had bought the 'wrong ones' it would be too late to correct the matter – we would be 'stuck' with them!

So let us look at the techniques available to help managers plan and control this vital investment area.

Illustration 8.1 Investment of money in business – the business model

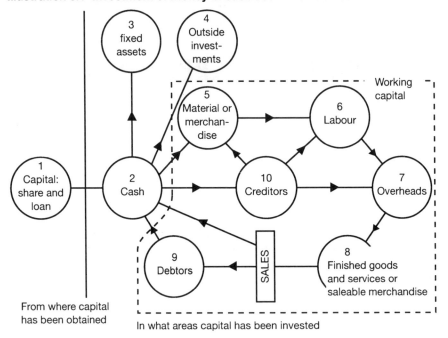

PROJECT APPRAISAL

In the first place we must appreciate that although we can very broadly describe investment in business as going into things we have no intention of selling – the fixed assets – or into things we do intend to sell – the working capital – there are exceptions. There are in many businesses a certain number of investments which are neither one thing nor the other. We might term them the 'hybrid' investments. For example, consider an advertising campaign or an investment in long-term research and development or (dare we mention) training! They are aimed at making our products, etc. more saleable, improving the products, etc. we sell and increasing the skills of those who make and sell them. However, it may be some time before such investment is reflected in any improvement in sales. It is the need management has to address the problem of assessing the value of such expenditure that has been the catalyst for the technique termed 'project appraisal'; a need stemming from the nature of investments in fixed assets and other long-term projects – to assess their relative financial value to the business over the period during which they provide benefits. Project appraisal techniques have been developed in response to this need.

We use the term project to encompass not only investments in fixed assets but all investments, where the money locked up does not come back into the business immediately or within the normal annual trading cycle.

In order to study the techniques that we use, put yourself in the position of an investing manager. Then consider the situation that arises where you are concerned with investing in a fixed asset or project such as we have been discussing; one from which the benefit will not be immediate.

Fact gathering

In examining this consider what financial information you would need on which you could base your judgements. However, to enable you do do this let us consider a practical situation. Imagine that we are considering an investment in plant and machinery which our production manager wishes to make. He or she approaches us and provides us with all the technical details regarding the proposed investment.

However, when this is completed, we would also require certain financial facts about the proposition and it is these you should think through for yourself.

The cost

So, what is the first fact you would want to know? Of course the answer is, quite simply, the cost. You obviously need to know exactly how much money will be required to purchase the particular item of plant and machinery. Let us say in this case a figure of £40,000.

This may appear a simple, round sum of money but it is never that easy! In fact this is often the most difficult figure to assess. After all, it is not just the face cost of the machine, or whatever, you need to consider. There is also the supporting investment in such things as the stocks which may need to be increased to support the manufacture of the extra products which will be produced by the new machine; and the extra investment in the debtors or receivables – the customers who will buy the extra products once the new machine is operational – but who will not pay for them immediately. And we must never forget the training of the people who will operate the new machine.

All these and other costs will need to be taken into account in arriving at the cost of the machine. So you can see that this very first figure – the cost – will not be as easy to access as it might first appear. Indeed it is often these other, 'hidden' costs which can present the greatest difficulty and distort the final assessment of the project: failing to recognise the parking requirements when assessing the cost of a supermarket extension; the additional office equipment and furniture when extending an estate agent's branches.

The benefits

Now let us proceed and ask ourselves: if we know the cost, what else do we want to know? One immediate response would be that we want to know the effect of this purchase on our profits. In other words, what will be the result to us as far as the investment is concerned – what benefits will it afford the business in financial terms? And, remembering our earlier studies, the measurement of profit immediately comes to mind.

However, we have a rather odd situation when we try to trace profit to a particular project. To explain this we might begin in the way shown in Illustration 8.2. We might ask ourselves what the additional sales will be if we buy this machine and write those down. Of course we would have to deduct the costs – the materials, labour and all the other expenses like rent, insurance, maintenance, power, and the depreciation and so on – which would accompany these sales. We would therefore arrive at a calculation of the profit or loss. At this point, however, pause and think this through a little more – and to help you in this look at Illustration 8.3. This is a visual illustration of the problem that confronts managers when they are considering an investment of this nature.

Illustration 8.2 Project appraisal

Profit and loss account relating to plant and machinery investment is as set out below:

		£	£
Sales			31,000
Less:	Materials	15,000	
	Labour	5,000	
	Rent	400	
	Depreciation	7,000	
	Power	1,000	
	Maintenance	600	29,000
Net profit			2,000

Illustration 8.3 Graphic display of decision problem

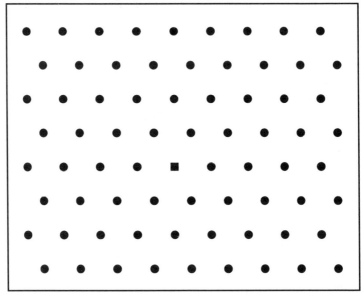

● = All other project proposals
■ = Plant and machinery (cost £40,000) proposal

What this illustrates is that managers, in this situation, have in front of them many projects that they have to consider, not – as in this case – the particular proposition costing £40,000 (marked ■ in Illustration 8.3). They also have all the spots in the rectangle, representing other project decisions that have to be made in the management of the business. From this, what becomes clear is that the measurement which we must bring to bear upon one particular project must be one which precisely relates to it. The measurement used must be unique to the project under consideration.

In other words, we have to find some measurement which will specifically pick out the project in front of us from all the others under consideration. No measurement which assumes a particular way of spreading or absorbing the overheads to a particular project can be said to be wholly accurate. After all, in Illustration 8.2 how did we calculate the amount of rent, power or maintenance charged against the sales? Remember our studies of full costing and the assumptions (guesses?) that go into calculating overhead recovery rates. When facing up to this problem managers find that they cannot use the measurement of profit and loss in appraising the benefits derived from a particular project. They have to find some other measure.

CASH FLOW

To understand the measurement chosen, let us return to the financial model in Illustration 8.1 and ask ourselves which is the most sensitive area – in financial terms – when one considers anything you do in a business. In other words, which circle in our financial model will be affected whatever we do – whether we buy or sell, whether we invest in this item or not, whether we get money by bringing capital in, whether we pay bills, and so on? What we will find, thinking this through, is that the most sensitive area of all is cash itself – the pulse of the business.

Measurement of cash flow

Financially, whatever we do will eventually affect cash. It is because of this that when we measure the financial implications of a particular project we use cash as the medium of measurement, and this is done in a totally pragmatic way. We simply ask ourselves, when a project or fixed asset investment is being considered, exactly how it will affect the cash circulating in the business throughout its life.

For instance, in the particular situation we are considering, if we invest £40,000 in the project in year 0 – when we purchase the item – cash will be reduced by £40,000. There will, as they say, be a negative cash flow in Year 0 of £40,000. The cash circle (2) in our model will shrink by that amount. We then consider the effect on cash during the project's life. To do this we must first decide, in the light of the particular project, its life span – in this case, say, four years. So our next question is: what will be the effect on the cash flow year by year over those four years if we do purchase the item?

Cash flow and profit

To illustrate the difference between cash flow and profit let us return to Illustration 8.2 and consider the difference in the figures set out when we calculate the profit in year 1 and those shown in Illustration 8.4, which sets out what is termed the gross cash flow. We see first that, if we make sales, it will certainly affect cash. So this amount will continue to be used in the assessment of the gross cash flow as it was for profit in year 1. We can also see that the materials going into the extra units that will be produced from the new machine will also affect cash – so this will remain the same as will the additional labour.

Illustration 8.4 Cash-flow assessment of project in year 1: calculation of gross cash flow

		£	£
Sales			31,000
Less:	Materials	15,000	
	Labour	5,000	
	Power	1,000	
	Special repairs	200	21,200
Gross cash flow			9,800

However, when we come to the other expenses like rent, power and maintenance, etc., we have to be careful. For each we must ask ourselves whether it is additional expense or one that would be there whether or not we bought the machine. For example, if we find that the rent is not additional but simply apportioned to the project it will not come into the calculation of the gross cash flow. Or again, if we find that we will be using the existing maintenance staff to look after the new machine, the only difference being a certain amount on special repairs, then only these should be brought into the gross cash flow calculation.

We must also remember that depreciation is, as we saw when we discussed the profit and loss account and the cash flow forecast in chapters 2 and 4, a profit and loss account expense which does not affect cash. Its purpose, you will remember, is to reduce the profit you could otherwise take out of the business (dividends in the case of limited companies). However, when we examine the effect upon cash in each year from this investment we have to ignore depreciation. This is because depreciation reduces profit not cash.

So, if we turn again to Illustration 8.4 we see the reassessment of the figures that we had shown in Illustration 8.2 as an assessment of profit into an assessment of the increase or reduction in cash: the measurement known as the gross cash flow.

The gross cash flow

The gross cash flow is a most important measurement for us to understand and it is one we have not used before. It is, however, the only one we can use in making project decisions because of its unique ability to differentiate between one project and another by measuring its effect upon the business in cash terms – the pulse of the business. It is therefore vital that we should understand the difference between the measurement of profit and loss and that of the gross cash flow.

In order to test this understanding turn to the question in Illustration 8.5, which reinforces what we have learned so far. When you have completed your answer compare it with that in Illustration 8.6 before proceeding further at this stage.

Illustration 8.5 Project appraisal exercise

Set out the following figures in the calculation of the gross cash flows for each of the three years:

Years	1	2	3
	£	£	£
Additional sales	20,000	25,000	15,000
Material in sales	10,000	12,000	6,000
Labour in sales	5,000	7,000	2,000
Other extra expenses in sales	2,000	3,000	500
Reapportioned expenses already incurred	1,500	1,500	400
Depreciation	5,000	5,000	5,000
Additional power	300	300	100
Maintenance costs			
– reapportioned	150	150	150
– additional	50	50	50

Illustration 8.6 Suggested answer to Illustration 8.5

	1		2		3	
	£	£	£	£	£	£
Sales		20,000		25,000		15,000
Less: Materials	10,000		12,000		6,000	
Labour	5,000		7,000		2,000	
Extra expenses	2,000		3,000		500	
Power	300		300		100	
Maintenance	50	17,350	50	22,350	50	8,650
Gross cash flow		2,650		2,650		6,350

Profit plus depreciation and cash flow

However, to understand cash flow fully it is necessary to look just a little further at this measurement and to recognise that if we are creating an increase to the gross cash flow this will indeed have an effect on the profit or loss of the business as a whole. We will in fact realise that the growth of cash in total represents the additional net profit before taxation and any depreciation that the business has charged before striking such profit.

In other words, if in year 1 the business we are discussing does invest £40,000 in this fixed asset, its profits will be increased by £2,800 – which is £9,800 growth in the gross cash flow shown in Illustration 8.4, less the depreciation of £7,000 (from Illustration 8.2). It also means there will be tax to pay on these additional profits – and as we all know tax certainly affects cash when it is paid!

The net cash flow

Taxation can be a very important factor in the assessment of a project because a project such as an investment in machinery will involve paying more corporation tax on the additional profits it helps to create as well as attracting capital allowances. These are allowances, awarded by statute, which have the effect of reducing taxation for those businesses which invest in certain favoured capital expenditure items. The items which attract such allowances and the amount of these have been a significant part of fiscal policy in the past although in recent years the benefits have been reduced in succeeding budgets.

It is because taxation has to be taken into consideration before a final cash flow figure can be calculated that the amount before tax is referred to as the gross cash flow (GCF) and after tax as the net cash flow (NCF).

Detailed treatment of taxation is beyond the scope of this book so the figures used under the title net cash flow assume that taxation adjustments have already been made. These include both the corporation tax payable on the additional profits and the capital allowance benefits where applicable. They would also take account of any government grants that may be available at the time the investment is made. A simple illustration of taxation and government grant adjustments is included in Illustration 8.7, which should be studied. This shows the gross cash flows for the four-year life of the project introduced in Illustrations 8.2 and 8.4, and sets out the effect of the assumed taxation and government grant adjustments applicable.

It is emphasised that these adjustments are illustrating principles and are based on assumed taxation rates, capital allowances and government grants. In most situations managers would be expected to calculate the gross cash flow figures only and the financial function would supply the taxation adjustments. However, all those responsible for the investment proposal – both those submitting the data and those deciding upon its merit – should understand the principles upon which the figures are calculated.

As regards our project, let us now continue by considering Illustration 8.7 further. Here we see that the figures after the taxation, etc. adjustments have been placed under the head net cash flow, or NCF. As we have seen, the net cash flow is the amount by which the cash is affected year by year within the business because of the particular investment. Our illustration shows the following figures:

In year 1 –	we have a positive net cash flow of	£25,000
In year 2 –		£15,000
In year 3 –		£10,000

In the fourth and final year, which includes an estimate of the scrap value at the end of the machine's life (£600), we have a positive net cash flow of £3,000.

Now let us look at how this information can be used in appraising a particular project and again we shall return to our questioning situation.

Illustration 8.7 Project appraisal (continued)

Cost of plant and machinery	£40,000
Year	Net cash flow (NCF)
	£
1	25,000
2	15,000
3	10,000
4	3,000
Total	53,000

Note on net cash flow calculation

Years:	1	2	3	4
	£	£	£	£
Gross cash flows	9,800	22,500	15,400	500
Less: Corporation tax @, say,	4,900	11,250	7,700	250
50%	4,900	11,250	7,700	250

Add back:
Capital allowances @, say, 25%
of plant and machinery cost
(£40,000) on reducing balance

	1	2	3	4
(see calculation below)	5,000	3,750	2,817	2,110
Government grant	15,000	–	–	–
Scrap value	–	–	–	600
	£24,900		£10,517	£2,960
Net cash flow	(say £25,000)	£15,000	(say £10,000)	(say £3,000)

Capital allowance calculation:

Year	Original cost	Capital allowance	Tax saving @ 50%
	£	£	£
1	40,000	10,000	5,000
	10,000		
2	30,000	7,500	3,750
	7,500		
3	22,500	5,625	2,817
	5,625		
4	16,875	4,219	2,110

THE PAYBACK PERIOD

First, think about how you might look at the financial data that we have in front of us in Illustration 8.7 and ask yourself: if you were in the position of making the 'yes' or 'no' decision, which would it be? And before you rush into an answer, consider also the fact that as an investor you would need to steel yourself with a certain amount of pessimism before accepting or rejecting any particular investment idea. This is because it has been found from the beginning of time that those putting forward propositions want financiers to say 'yes'! In other words there is the constant danger of 'inbuilt optimism' in the figures presented.

It is for this reason that investors have always tried to arm themselves with a degree of pessimism, so as to make their judgements as dispassionately as possible. It is to create, perhaps, just such a 'flattening' approach that investors have sought a quick measurement in looking at projects. What they have looked for is how quickly they will get their money back based on the figures presented.

If you consider this approach you will see that the response of an investor is precisely the same as that of any person heading for a situation in which the commitment, once made will be final. It is not important what the situation is. Anyone who is to make such a decision needs to 'look before they leap'. And certainly a most useful measurement would be to consider the escape route. In other words how quickly can you back out if all goes wrong?

In the case of business investment, therefore, the first measurement that is often used in looking at the data that we have just produced in Illustration 8.7 is to see how long it would take to get our money back. You are paying out £40,000 on this particular project: in year 1 you get back £25,000, in year 2 a further £15,000, and so on. Thus, by the end of year 2, based on the figures in front of us, we will have recouped our original £40,000 investment. This measurement is termed the 'payback', and it is the one used most often when an investment is appraised.

The payback period may be considered in isolation or in comparison with other projects. In other words, a set payback period might be agreed for different project types or projects might be selected based on which of them give the quickest return of cash. A criticism of this measurement is that it is a fairly blunt tool to guide project – largely capital – investment within business. However, it has the advantage of immediate and simple application and perhaps accuracy. This is because it gives emphasis to cash forecasts earlier than later, which is often more checkable and therefore more reliable as a basis for decision-making. As mentioned previously, in practice many organisations set payback periods for different categories of projects and these then become the first filter through which projects must pass. For example, if three years were the payback period required in Illustration 8.7 the project under consideration would meet this criterion.

RETURN ON CAPITAL INVESTED

Unless someone had suggested the approach, however, many people looking at the figures we have just gathered together might not immediately think of using the payback method. I think many would try to calculate the return on the investment made. After all, this is what business investment is all about – maximising the return on the capital employed

Average return

Illustration 8.8 shows that there are three stages in calculating the return on the capital invested or employed in our example project. First, we have added all the net cash flows, which in this case came to a total of £55,000. Next, we have deducted from this figure the original cost of the investment (£40,000), leaving an excess or total return of £13,000 over its four-year life and struck an annual average return of £3,250 (£13,00 divided by 4). Finally, this figure is related to the average capital invested: another figure that needs to be calculated.

Illustration 8.8 Average return on average capital invested

Year	NCF		£
0	£	Cost of plant and machinery	40,000
1	25,000		
2	15,000		
3	10,000		
4	3,000		
	53,000		
Less: Cost	40,000		
Difference	13,000		

Average return = 13,000 divided by 4   =   3,250
Average capital employed = 40,000 divided by 2   =   20,000

Average return on average capital employed $= \dfrac{3,250}{20,000} =$ 16.75%

Average capital invested

We are, in our example, investing £40,000 but the amount locked up does not stay the same throughout the period. By the end of the fourth year the original money invested has returned into the business. So you might say the average amount of money invested at any time over the four years would be £20,000 – half the original cost. This is explained by means of the diagram in Illustration 8.9, where you see the mid-point of the money outstanding over the four years to be £20,000. This represents the fact that for the first two years more than

£20,000 and for the second two years less than £20,000 is being invested. (This is of course based on the assumption that an equal amount of money is paid back into the business each year which in this case is not strictly true.)

Illustration 8.9 Average capital invested

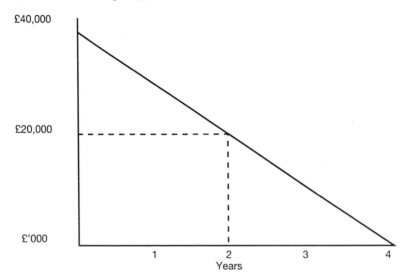

Average return on average capital invested

If we then relate the average annual return of £3,750 to the average capital invested of £20,000 we are able to calculate our average return on average capital employed. This gives us a rate of approximately 16.25 per cent and we can then compare this with the rate of return we might be looking for in our business. If we were obliged to borrow the money for this project we could compare this 16.25 per cent with the interest charged by the lender (at the present time very attractive but lenders are very fickle, remember).

THE PROBLEM OF TIME AND MONEY

All this may sound very logical, but think about it for a moment. What we have just proved by these calculations is a financial absurdity! To illustrate this absurdity let us consider the question of whether you would rather I gave you £100 now or £100 in a year's time – even assuming there is no monetary inflation and you trusted me.

Without any hesitation, no doubt everyone would prefer to have the money right now – for the very simple reason that if you have money now you can use it. You can re-invest it – and it will be worth £100 plus whatever rate of interest you can earn over the year, as opposed to the alternative of exactly £100 at the end of the year.

Now if this is true of the £100 it is equally true of the figures we have been looking at in Illustration 8.8. For instance, I would much prefer £1 of the £25,000 offered to me in year 1 than £1 of the £3,000 in year 4. After all, the sooner we get the money back into circulation the sooner we can re-invest it and therefore the sooner we can obtain a further return on the money. It is because this is true that what we have just illustrated, in calculating the average return on the average capital invested, does not make financial sense. Remember all we did was add up all the years' net cash flows into a single total, irrespective of when they arose, before dividing them by four.

DISCOUNT FACTORS

It is for this reason that in the area of project investment people have looked to discount factors to address this problem of time and money.

To help understand discount factors, turn to Illustration 8.10 and study the examples given. You will see that we have the factors for nought to five years and for different rates of interest between 8 and 16 per cent. To illustrate their use let us take the discount factors for 10 per cent and that for year 1 is 0.909. The meaning of this factor is that if you invest 0.909 of £1 now, in year 0 as we say, in one year's time at 10 per cent interest it will grow to £1. In year 2 you will find the factor for 10 per cent stands at 0.826, and again this means that if you invest 0.826 of £1 now (in year 0), in two years' time at 10 per cent compound interest it will grow to £1, and so we could go on.

Illustration 8.10   Discount factors

Year	8%	10%	12%	14%	15%	16%
0	1.000	1.000	1.000	1.000	1.000	1.000
1	0.926	0.909	0.893	0.877	0.870	0.862
2	0.857	0.826	0.797	0.769	0.757	0.743
3	0.794	0.751	0.712	0.675	0.658	0.641
4	0.735	0.683	0.636	0.592	0.572	0.552
5	0.681	0.621	0.568	0.519	0.497	0.476

It is useful to become familiar with these discount factor tables, so to reinforce your knowledge look at Illustration 8.11. This sets out a question for you to tackle to aid familiarity. Once you have completed this, check your answers with Illustration 8.12 before proceeding.

Using discount factors

Having explained the meaning of discount factors we shall now see how they can be applied in the appraisal of investments. To illustrate this, in the context of the example we have been examining throughout this chapter, we shall say in the first instance that we require a return of 16 per cent on our investment. That 16 per cent is our criterion and thus we use the appropriate discount factors for 16 per cent in Illustration 8.10. These are:

Year 1   0.862
Year 2   0.743
Year 3   0.641
Year 4   0.552

Illustration 8.11 Discount factor exercise

Set out the discount factors for the following:
1.   12 per cent in year 4
2.   15 per cent in year 3
3.   16 per cent in year 5
4.   8 per cent in year 1
5.   14 per cent in year 2
6.   10 per cent in year 4

Illustration 8.12 Solution to Illustration 8.11

1.   0.636
2.   0.658
3.   0.476
4.   0.926
5.   0.769
6.   0.683

If you turn to Illustration 8.13, you will see that these factors have been placed against the net cash flow figures for each of the four years.

Illustration 8.13 Discount factors for NCFs in project appraisal

Year	Net cash flow £	Discount factors 16%
0	(40,000)	1.000
1	25,000	0.862
2	15,000	0.743
3	10,000	0.641
4	3,000	0.552

Having arrived at these factors we can then proceed to the next stage, which is to multiply the amounts we have calculated as the net cash flows for each of the four years by the appropriate discount factor. This is shown in Illustration 8.14 and by it we arrive at the amount we need to invest now, in year 0, to give us the net cash flows for each of the four years.

Illustration 8.14 Calculation of present values

Year	NCF £		Discount factors 16%		Present value £
0	(40,000)	x	1.000	=	(40,000)
1	25,000	x	0.862	=	21,550
2	15,000	x	0.743	=	11,145
3	10,000	x	0.641	=	6,410
4	5,000	x	0.552	=	1,656

THE PRESENT VALUES

What we have done by multiplying the net cash flows by these factors is to discover how much we need to invest now, in year 0, at 16 per cent to arrive at the net cash flows forecast for each year. For example, in order to arrive at £25,000 at the end of year 1, assuming a rate of interest of 16 per cent, we would have to invest £21,550 in year 0.

Again, to arrive at £15,000 at the end of year 2 – assuming a rate of 16 per cent compound interest – we would have to invest £11,145. And to arrive at £10,000 at the end of year 3, we would have to invest £6,410 now. Finally, to arrive at £3,000 in four years' time, we would need to invest £1,656 now. We call the individual result of this multiplication the 'present value' as it represents the present value of investment in year 0 required to give us the forecast net cash flow for each year based on the interest rate chosen.

Having arrived at these individual values we can finally add them all up, and we will see from Illustration 8.15 that we come to a total of £40,761. This is the total amount that we would have to invest now, in year 0, at 16 per cent compound interest, to give us the amounts that we have calculated as the net cash flows for each of the years 1 to 4 in our illustration.

Illustration 8.15 Discounted cash flow calculation

Year	NCF £		16% DF		Present value £	£
0	(40,000)	x	1.000	=		(40,000)
1	25,000	x	0.862	=	21,550	
2	15,000	x	0.743	=	11,145	
3	10,000	x	0.641	=	6,410	
4	3,000	x	0.552	=	1,656	40,761
			Positive net present value			761

DISCOUNTED CASH FLOW APPRAISAL TECHNIQUE

However, we are being asked to invest only £40,000 now so in financial terms we have a bargain. We are getting more than 16 per cent as a return on the £40,000 investment because at 16 per cent we would have to invest more – in fact £40,761. Thus, if a 16 per cent return is our criterion we would agree to the investment because we are getting a higher return.

This technique is referred to as the discounted cash flow method. What is being done by this approach is that the net cash flows for each of the years in question are being multiplied by the discount factors for the particular rate of return required. By doing this we arrive at the amount that we would have to invest to give us these net cash flows.

In this particular example it amounts to £40,761, which we are then comparing with the proposed investment amount: in this case £40,000. From this comparison we are able to see whether or not the investment is giving us the appropriate return. From this it can also be seen that by using discount factors for percentages in excess of 16 per cent we could find out precisely what return we are getting on £40,000. In other words we could find the discount factors for the appropriate percentage which would convert £25,000, £15,000, £10,000 and £3,000 into a total present value of precisely £40,000.

Internal rate of return

You will see from Illustration 8.16 that the appropriate percentage is approximately 19. This percentage is termed the internal rate of return (IRR). However, if we were simply seeking a return of 16 per cent Illustration 8.15 demonstrates that we are obtaining at least this. We have what is termed a positive net present value, or NPV as it is known – the positive values equal £40,761 against the negative value of £40,000.

Illustration 8.16 Calculation of internal rate of return

Year	NCF		18%		Present value	
	£		DF		£	£
0	(40,000)	x	1.000	=		(40,000)
1	25,000	x	0.847	=	21,175	
2	15,000	x	0.718	=	10,770	
3	10,000	x	0.609	=	6,090	
4	3,000	x	0.516	=	1,548	39,583
		Negative net present value				(427)

The internal rate of return (IRR) is therefore approximately 18%.

Consolidation

Now in order to reinforce your knowledge so far turn to Illustration 8.17, which sets out three different investment proposals together with the appropriate discount factors for 15 per cent. Make the necessary calculations to assess whether or not you would agree to the investment based on these financial facts using the discounted cash flow method. Once you have completed this task compare your answers with Illustration 8.18 before continuing.

Illustration 8.17 Investment proposal decision

From the following financial facts regarding three different proposals calculate whether or not they meet the discounted cash flow criterion.

		1 £	2 £	3 £
Investment cost		30,000	28,000	45,000
Net cash flows				
Year	1	15,000	12,000	20,000
	2	10,000	8,000	30,000
	3	10,000	6,000	10,000
	4	5,000	6,000	5,000
	5	–	4,000	–

The rate of return required = 15%

Discount factors for 15%: Year 1 0.870
2 0.757
3 0.658
4 0.572
5 0.497

Illustration 8.18 Answer to Illustration 8.17

Proposal				1 £		2 £		3 £
Investment cost:				30,000		28,000		45,000
Year	DF 15%		NCF £		NCF £		NCF £	
1	0.870	x 15,000	= 13,050	12,000 = 10,440	20,000 = 17,400
2	0.757	x 10,000	= 7,570	8,000 = 6,056	30,000 = 22,710
3	0.658	x 10,000	= 6,580	6,000 = 3,948	10,000 = 6,580
4	0.572	x 5,000	= 2,860	6,000 = 3,432	5,000 = 2,860
5	0.497	x –	= –	4,000 = 1,988	–
			30,060	25,864	49,550
NPV			+60	–2,136	+4,550

MANAGEMENT CONSIDERATION

Having examined the arithmetic of project appraisal techniques we shall now look at them from a decision-making point of view. The first necessity is for us to return to one of the principles discussed in chapter 1: accountants do not provide answers, they provide better questions. This point must be strongly kept in mind when using project appraisal techniques. What must be understood is that, whatever the arithmetical answer arrived at from the information presented, it is wholly dependent on the accuracy or inaccuracy of the net cash flow calculations. And we must remember that these are built up from a series of forecasts or guesses! Never forget that in nearly every project there are certain facts which cannot be financially evaluated with complete certainty.

Risk analysis

To illustrate the difficulty of achieving accuracy in assessing the net cash flows, consider the point that in evaluating any project there must be an optimistic and a pessimistic view. For this reason it is very important in making an assessment based upon financial data to look at the likelihood, i.e. the chances or the risk, of the figures actually materialising.

Factors may arise which are completely outside the control of managers such as monetary inflation or changes in the world economy, or the invention of newer and better methods of operation or technology, and so on. All these will change the forecast cash flows.

It is possible to use arithmetical means to assist in the field of risk analysis but their use is best left to specialist texts on the subject. Suffice it to say that risk analysis is an area of concern and its consideration must be ever present in the minds of those responsible for decision-making.

Non-financially measurable considerations

It must always be remembered that there are certain features in any project which will be difficult – in some cases impossible – to assess financially with any degree of accuracy but which are central to any judgement. For instance, how do you assess the ability of the person in charge of a project to overcome a future crisis? Anyone concerned with decision-making must recognise that, however well planned a project may be, it will inevitably hit a crisis. This holds true whether the project is the simple purchase of a piece of plant and machinery or one of the more complex investment areas such as research and development or marketing.

Projects inevitably bring with them crises and when they occur the calibre and qualities (or even luck!) of the person in charge of the project will become central to its success or failure. It is for this reason that management must guard against an over-glib, mechanistic assessment of projects: for instance once having met the criteria set for a project under a discounted cash flow or a payback calculation then all is well! What is vital is that managers using project appraisal techniques should realise that their decisions must be assessed from many standpoints.

In other words, although the financial data may support or reject the decision, many other considerations are required outside the financial measurements set out in this chapter. This is not to say that such techniques as discounted cash flow and payback are not important, but they must not be considered omnipotent. They are corroborating not determining evidence.

Rate of return

Finally, we must consider the rate of return that is used. How do we choose the 16 per cent or whatever? In the first instance we must look very closely at what we expect to receive on the funds we are employing in the particular project, and it is therefore necessary for management to consider the source of the funds which are being invested. For instance, if the money being used to finance a project is being borrowed the rate of return must be one that covers the interest on the borrowed capital. In other words, if you are borrowing money at 10 per cent the rate of return must be in excess of this.

However, after allowing for a measure of safety – say in this instance 16 per cent – it must be recognised that anything in excess of 16 per cent is a rate of infinity so far as the shareholders of the company are concerned. They are getting that extra percentage on no investment on their own part at all. On the other hand, if the funds are being provided by the shareholders of the company themselves, the rate of return which will satisfy them must be the managers' decision, based on what they feel will satisfy the shareholders.

It must also never be forgotten that the managers, although responsible to investors, have a very large measure of freedom in meeting this responsibility. There is no reason that management should not ask for different returns from different projects, some above and some below the overall shareholders' target. After all, so long as the total return on the capital employed satisfies investors then the manner in which this is made up among the different projects or investments is of no concern to them. You might term this both the freedom and the responsibility of management.

SUMMARY OF PROJECT APPRAISAL

The net cash flow

To summarise project appraisal we first gather together the financial facts regarding the particular project, and the measurement we use to do this is the net cash flow.

The first thing required is the investment cost. It must be understood in this calculation that all additional investment must be brought into consideration, for example working capital in the form of stocks and debtors which may have to be increased on the installation of a new piece of plant and machinery, etc. This must be taken into account in calculating the cost of the new machine (or whatever) because it is necessary to find out the effect upon the total net cash flow year by year.

This entails careful assessment of the cash effect of the project with regard to both its inflows and outflows. To this end we must make sure we ignore expenses already being incurred, and add back depreciation and any other expense, deducted before arriving at profit, which does not affect cash. Finally, we must ensure that the effects of taxation are included in the calculation.

When we have brought these financial facts together it is then necessary to use our particular yardstick in the appraisal of the investment.

The appraisal methods – the yardsticks

There are three yardsticks that can be used. The first, based on the healthy cynicism of investors, is the payback method – looking to see how quickly we get our money back for further use. The second is the very simple average return on average capital invested method, which has the great disadvantage of ignoring when the money is flowing into the business. And finally we have the discounted cash flow (DCF) method, which takes into account the timing of the annual net cash flows (NCFs) as well as compound – as distinct from simple – interest (an arithmetical point of some importance when considering interest over a period of time).

Further considerations

However, whichever technique we use we must recognise the fact that project appraisal techniques do not give us answers. They provide us with better questions and therefore a better approach to the investment decision.

The basis of data

If I look at an investment and see from a project appraisal assessment that the answer is yes or no, this is not the end from a management decision point of view. It must be recognised that the data on which the financial facts are considered is based on forecasts and these may be wrong because of over-optimism, or over-pessimism, or because certain facts are not fully known at the time of making the decision.

Management must also understand that in project decision-making certain highly relevant facts cannot be quantified financially – the ability or otherwise of project leaders to overcome crises, the sensitivity to error of the data on which project appraisal assessments are based. However, such considerations must be borne firmly in mind by managers.

Monitoring data

It is also vital that once projects have been agreed the data contained in the appraisal is monitored as the years go by to see how clearly it matches the facts as they emerge. Such post-project audits, as they are sometimes termed, can serve as useful reminders of where errors can occur and can be used to improve future project proposals. In other words, used as a means of improving future appraisals rather than the basis of a witch hunt!

BUYING OR LEASING

Before we end this chapter I want to turn to the problem of buying or leasing. The problem involves two separate questions: assessing the benefit of the investment to the business however it is made, and deciding whether, if it is worthwhile, the investment should be bought or hired. In doing this you must avoid the temptation to mix the two questions. For instance, you must separate the assessment of whether or not you should obtain a new machine from whether or not you should buy or lease it. These are two quite separate management decisions.

Illustration 8.19 Data for lease or buy decision

Rate of interest required	12%
Cost of computers if bought	£60,000
Rental if hired	£15,000 per annum
Period of rental agreement	5 years
Annual maintenance cost if bought	£650
Scrap value at end of 5 years	£10,000
at end of 6 years	£5,000
Free maintenance if hired	£500 per annum
Savings per year if computers introduced	£20,000
Period computers will be used if bought	6 years
Corporation tax	take as 50% (for simplicity's sake only!)

Calculate whether to buy or hire/lease

Illustration 8.20 Project appraisal – calculation of net cash flow

Stage I: If bought

Year:		1	2	3	4	5	6
		£	£	£	£	£	£
Capital allowances savings on corporation tax @ 50% say		7,500	6,250	4,050	3,000	2,300	1,500
Scrap value							5,000
Annual savings	£20,000						
Less: Maintenance	650						
	19,350						
Less: Tax @ 50%	9,675	9,675	9,675	9,675	9,675	9,675	9,675
		17,175	15,925	13,725	12,675	11,975	16,175

Stage II: If bought and not hired

Year:		1	2	3	4	5
Capital allowances		£	£	£	£	£
(as above)		7,500	6,250	4,050	3,000	2,300
Annual rental payable	£15,000					
Tax @ 50%	7,500					
	7,500					
Less: Free maintenance	500	7,000	7,000	7,000	7,000	7,000
Scrap value						10,000
		14,500	13,250	11,050	10,000	19,300

Whether to obtain the item

If you turn to Illustrations 8.19, 8.20 and 8.21 you will see how these two considerations are kept separate. In the first instance, described as Stage I in Illustrations 8.20 and 8.21 you will see that we assume that we will buy and we
consider the facts based on a buying situation. We take as an example an investment in computers costing £60,000 from which we then show the appropriate
net cash flows year by year, in this case the saving of clerical costs by their use.
Having calculated the net cash flows we come to the decision that the answer is
yes. We should obtain the new computer. Go through Illustration 8.19 and Stage
I of Illustrations 8.20 and 8.21 carefully as they set out all the principles we have
discussed in this chapter so far.

Illustration 8.21 Project appraisal – lease or buy calculation

Stage I: If bought

Year						£
0	Cost of computers					60,000

	NCF £		Discount factor 12%		Present value £	
1	17,175	x	0.893	=	15,337	
2	15,925	x	0.797	=	12,692	
3	13,728	x	0.712	=	9,772	
4	12,675	x	0.636	=	8,061	
5	11,975	x	0.568	=	6,802	
6	16,175	x	0.507	=	8,201	60,865
Positive net present value						865

Stage II: If bought and not leased

Year						£
0	Cost of computers					60,000

	NCF £		Discount factor 12%		Present value £	
1	14,500	x	0.893	=	12,949	
2	13,250	x	0.797	=	10,560	
3	11,050	x	0.712	=	7,868	
4	10,000	x	0.636	=	6,360	
5	19,300	x	0.568	=	10,962	48,699
			Negative net present value			11,301

Conclusion based on data provided is to lease the computers.

Whether to buy or lease the item

It is now necessary, having decided that we will proceed with the investment, to go to the next stage and decide whether we should buy or lease the computers. You will see from Stage II in Illustrations 8.20 and 8.21 that we have a whole series of new facts in front of us on which to make this second decision. In considering the leasing or the buying question the important fact to bear in mind is that we must ignore anything which is common to both situations. We need to say to ourselves if we buy what is the difference between that or hiring/leasing?

The first difference obviously is that if we buy we will incur the cost of £60,000 which we will not incur if we hire. We then go on year by year asking ourselves what the difference is between buying and leasing. You will see that we totally ignore the benefit we will obtain from the new office computers, because this is common to both situations. In fact the only matters that we bring in are first, the fact that if we buy we will save the annual rental, and, second, we will lose the benefit of the annual maintenance which the rental firm provides us free of charge. In addition, we will lose the tax benefit of being able to charge the rental against our profits for tax purposes, but we will obtain the tax benefit of the capital allowances if we buy.

You will see all these calculations set out in Stage II of Illustrations 8.20 and 8.21 so that year by year we are able to put in a net cash flow figure showing the difference between buying and leasing. You will also see the period of comparison is linked with the rental agreement of five years, bringing into the final year our assessment of the scrap value of the computer as a benefit which arises to the buyer and not the hirer.

Examine these illustrations very carefully and then test your understanding by tackling the question set out in Illustration 8.22. Compare your answers with Illustrations 8.23 and 8.24 and note particularly areas of difficulty that require revision.

Illustration 8.22 Data for lease or buy decision

Cost of machine if bought	£120,000
Rental if hired	£40,000 per annum
Annual maintenance cost if bought	£5,000
Maintenance provided free by rental firm worth per annum	£1,000
Scrap value at end of 6-year life	£10,000
Scrap value at end of 5-year life	£12,000
Savings per year if machine introduced	£50,000
Rate of interest required	12% per annum

Illustration 8.23 Project appraisal – calculation of net cash flow

Stage I: If bought

Year:		1	2	3	4	5	6
		£	£	£	£	£	£
Capital allowances Savings on corporation tax @ 50% say		20,000	10,000	7,500	5,625	4,110	3,100
Scrap value							10,000

Savings per year	£50,000						
Less: Maintenance	5,000						
	45,000						
Less: Tax @ 50%	22,500	22,500	22,500	22,500	22,500	22,500	22,500
		42,500	32,500	30,000	28,125	26,610	35,600

Stage II: If bought and not leased

Year:	1	2	3	4	5
Capital allowances (as above)	£	£	£	£	£
	20,000	10,000	7,500	5,625	4,110

Savings: Annual rent	£40,000					
Tax @ 50%	20,000					
	20,000					
Less: Value of free						
maintenance	1,000	19,000	19,000	19,000	19,000	19,000
Scrap value						12,000
		39,000	29,000	26,500	24,625	35,110

Illustration 8.24 Project appraisal – lease or buy calculation

Stage I: If bought

Year				£
0	Cost of machine			120,000

	NCF	Discount factor	Present value	
	£	12%	£	
1	42,500	x 0.893 =	37,953	
2	32,500	x 0.797 =	25,903	
3	30,000	x 0.712 =	21,360	
4	28,125	x 0.636 =	17,888	
5	26,610	x 0.568 =	15,115	
6	35,600	x 0.507 =	18,049	
			136,268	
Positive net present value			16,268	

Stage II: If bought and not leased

Year				£
0	Cost of machine			120,000

	NCF	Discount factor	Present value	
	£	12%	£	
1	39,000	x 0.893 =	34,827	
2	29,000	x 0.797 =	23,113	
3	26,500	x 0.712 =	18,868	
4	24,625	x 0.636 =	15,662	
5	35,110	x 0.568 =	19,942	112,412
	Negative net present value			7,588

Conclusion based on data provided is to lease machine.

CONCLUSION

Having completed our studies of project appraisal we can now proceed to the next area of investment, that concerned with working capital – the financial luggage a business carries on its way to a sale.

9

THE CONTROL OF WORKING CAPITAL

INTRODUCTION

In the previous chapter we discussed the methods which have been developed to examine the fixed asset investment set out in the balance sheet. Project appraisal techniques concern themselves with investments which tie up money. They are designed to assist decision-makers in such situations before the commitment of funds. Now let us turn our attention to the second and perhaps the more difficult, but equally important, area of investment to control – the working capital.

The working capital of a business, shown in Illustration 9.1, is concerned with the investment of money in materials or merchandise, labour and overheads, pending its return back to the business when the finished goods, saleable merchandise or services are sold and paid for. As an investment it is made up therefore of the money tied up in materials or merchandise, labour and overheads less the amount that may be owed at any time to those from whom we have purchased them.

Working capital is indeed a net area of investment. If we return to Illustration 9.1 we can see that it is made up of the total invested in circles 4, 5, 6, 7 and 8, less what is owed in circle 9.

WORKING CAPITAL IN MANUFACTURING INDUSTRY

For a manufacturing business we can examine working capital as set out in Illustration 9.2. Here we show the investment in labour, materials and overheads as raw material, work in progress and finished goods stocks. To this we add the debtors or receivables – the amounts due to us from our customers to whom we have sold our goods but who have not yet paid for them – less the credit taken from our creditors (or payables) for the materials, labour and overheads which have gone into such stocks and debtors but who have not themselves yet been paid.

In chapter 1, when we discussed working capital, we pointed out that, from the point of view of managing or investing in a business, it should be everyone's ambition to minimise the amount of money tied up in this area for two major reasons. The first is that everyone's investment goal is to maximise the return on the capital employed, and if we can make the same profit with less working capital, it must be better.

Illustration 9.1 Business model showing working capital area

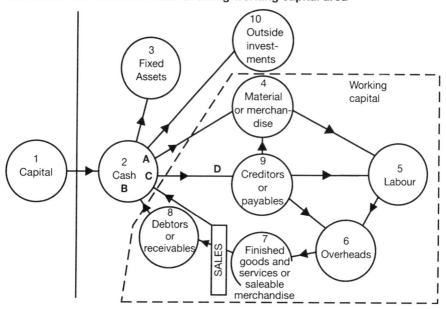

From where capital has been obtained

In what areas capital has been invested

However, there is the second reason that people wish to minimise working capital, which is far more dynamic than the basic need to maximise the return on capital employed (although it does indeed help us to improve this as well). This is that if you wish to expand a business then it is vital to make sure that you are not held back because of a lack of capital.

Every business, whatever its size, is limited in the end by the total capital that it can obtain. Within the parameters of its capital, however, a business is continually being limited by the two barriers to progress: what it can sell – the problem of the market place – and/or what it can produce, present as merchandise or render as services: the capacity of its fixed assets. However, if it needs working capital this in itself could limit its progress. To illustrate this point: if a business finds that for every £1 of sales it needs 10p of working capital to finance it, that business could find itself held back, not because it could not sell and/or could not produce, but because it did not have the necessary 10 pences.

Illustration 9.2 Alternative business model setting out working capital in manufacturing industry

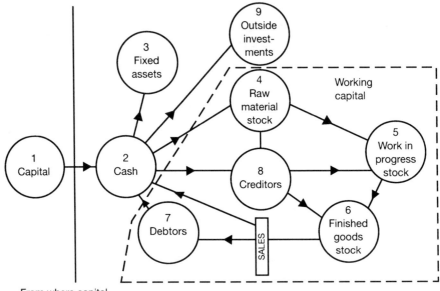

From where capital has been obtained

In what areas capital has been invested

It is not coincidental that the great business expanders make ways of minimising their working capital a first priority. For example, Henry Ford in producing the Model T decided to paint it black and sell it to agents for cash as soon as the cars were produced. All these policies enabled him to minimise his working capital and therefore minimise the limitations to his expansion plans.

CONTROL OF WORKING CAPITAL

Any examination of working capital points very clearly to the fact that if a business wishes to minimise this investment it must control time. If we turn to the model in Illustration 9.1 it will be seen that to minimise working capital the objective must be to turn the materials or merchandise, labour and overheads as quickly as possible back into cash and to maximise, within agreed limits, the credit: the time it takes before meeting the amounts due to its material suppliers, providers of labour and overheads.

This then is the overall objective – to minimise working capital. We must, however, recognise that objectives such as this are not unchangeable. Circumstances may arise when they need to be modified. For example, it might be useful in certain circumstances to hold materials over a considerable period of time where there is the fear of a commodity shortage. Or it may be useful to mass produce finished goods pending a forecast demand explosion. But these are exceptions that in a way prove rather than disprove the rule.

Working capital, as suggested earlier, might be described as the financial luggage a business carries on its journey to a sale. It can also be said that the great controllers of working capital have always been sales and marketing people. They use their marketing skills to reduce the time delays that delay a business minimising its working capital. Henry Ford with his Model T was doing just that: marketing a product in such a way as to minimise the money locked up in working capital.

To control working capital we must therefore control time. But it is also necessary to recognise that the inherent difficulty in this lies in the need to co-ordinate the different functions responsible for each area of working capital. It has to be understood that, however dominant sales and marketing policies may be in the overall control of working capital, they depend on the co-operation of the other functions.

Areas of responsibility

To understand this, turn to Illustration 9.3. Here we see once again the financial model, but we have now introduced the names of the functions which will have a say in the control of time in each area. For instance, the control of time when materials are in store will be in the hands of purchasing, and once material, labour and overheads are in production the time needed to convert them into finished goods or services will be in the hands of production or service renderers (and indeed perhaps personnel). We then see that once materials, labour and overheads are translated into finished goods or services the time during which such items are unsold becomes the direct concern of sales and marketing. Finally, once finished goods or services are sold many customers do not pay immediately – they take time as debtors or receivables – while conversely the materials, labour and overheads which go into what is produced will in most cases not be paid for immediately. The business will take time, or credit, before it pays its creditors or payables. And the control of this time given and taken becomes the concern of the finance function.

It will also be seen when we consider these areas, that in each case there will be an overlap in control. For instance, production (as well as the purchasing function) will have to be concerned about the time during which material is held in store – it wants it when it is needed for use, and in quantities which are not too much but not too little ('just in time', did I hear?). There will also be the concern of marketing in the credit taken by debtors as too much chasing to reduce the length of credit may make future sales difficult, even impossible. And purchasing will be interested in the length of credit taken before paying suppliers for materials as too long a delay may jeopardise future deliveries and so the continuity of supplies.

Illustration 9.3 Business model showing functions controlling time in working capital areas

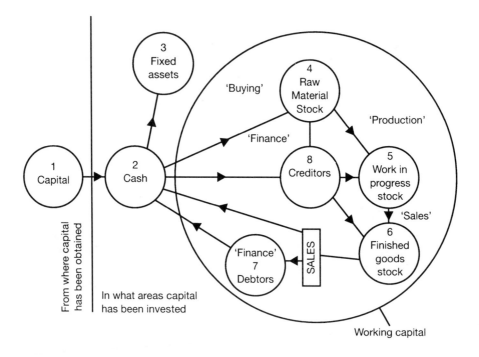

It is this interlinking and overlapping which make working capital increasingly difficult to control once businesses grow and functions are created under different managers. It is not therefore coincidental that smaller businesses can normally control their working capital much more effectively than larger concerns. This is for the simple reason that in a one-person business that person is buyer, production manager, sales manager and accountant and can therefore keep an eye on each individual area.

However, as businesses grow and different people head the different functions we find that difficulties arise as the interlinking and overlapping grow. The orchestration of management, so vital for effective working capital control, becomes increasingly difficult as businesses expand.

It is also often found that as a business grows it is difficult for people who may have a very real contribution to make in controlling working capital to see how they fit in. To illustrate this point consider the question set in Illustration 9.4 and see if you can show the responsibility of the different functions in the control of working capital. Check your answers with the suggestions made in Illustration 9.5 before you carry on.

Illustration 9.4 Control of working capital exercise

Consider how the following functions influence the control of working capital:
1.   Buying
2.   Production control
3.   Sales and marketing
4.   Quality control
5.   Accounting

Illustration 9.5 Suggested answers to Illustration 9.4

1.   *Buying*. The provision of material to enable the business to meet the production and sales requirements.
2.   *Production control*. The conversion of material, labour and overheads as quickly as possible into saleable finished goods.
3.   *Sales and marketing*. The conversion of finished goods, saleable merchandise or services into sales and cash.
4.   *Quality control*. The rectification of quality problems as soon as possible so as to reduce delay to a minimum and maximise the attractiveness of what we sell to our customers.
5.   *Accounting*. The supervision of credit control so as to minimise delay from debtors and maximise the delay allowed by creditors within the agreed credit periods.

WORKING CAPITAL CONTROL IN PRACTICE

Having examined working capital in an overall way it is now necessary to approach its control from a practical point of view. To do this we shall once again think through a situation for ourselves. Consider in the first instance the problem of a manufacturing business producing goods. We will take a set of facts, from the production to the sale of its goods, and see how they fit together from the point of view of working capital control.

To do this turn first to Illustration 9.6 and follow the figures through. You will see from the illustration that we place at the top the words 'material', 'labour' and 'overheads'. What we are then doing is to trace the time delays from the moment the costs of materials, labour and overheads are incurred by the business to their eventual conversion back into cash once the goods we have sold have been paid for.

The material time cycle

So let us begin at the beginning by taking materials. We will say in this case that on average we hold our materials for a fortnight before they go into production. What we therefore see under the materials head is half a month in the raw material store.

We can then proceed to the next stage, production cycle, meaning the time it takes to convert the material into finished goods. And again half a month is considered the average time of the production cycle in this particular business.

As we continue, the third area of delay is termed finished goods stock, which is the average time finished goods are stored before being sent out to customers, when a sale is made. Here we will say that the time is one month.

Finally, we come to the fourth area: debtors or receivables, the time taken by our customers before they pay. In this case, we shall say it is on average two months.

So if we add the materials column we come to a total of four months. However, to work out the time delay in converting materials back into cash we must deduct the time the business itself takes before it pays for such materials. Let us say that the delay is normally two months, and we arrive at a net time of two months. This is the time during which money will be locked up in respect of materials before it comes back at the point when the goods into which it goes are sold and paid for.

Illustration 9.6 Working capital control – time data

Working capital areas:	Material months	Labour months	Overheads months
Raw material store	½	½	½
Production cycle	½	½	½
Finished goods store	1	1	1
Debtors/receivables	2	2	2
Gross time	4	4	4
Less: Credit time taken	(2)	(½)	(1)
Net time	2	3½	(3)

The labour and overheads time cycle

If we now look at the columns dealing with labour and overheads we will see that down to the gross time they are identical to materials – four months. This is because in a manufacturing business materials dominate. While they are in store you will still be paying for the labour and overheads. Again, while the material is in production and while your finished goods are being stored, you will still have to pay for your labour and overheads. This situation continues while your customers are not paying.

So we reach the same subtotal of four months. However, when we look at the credit that we can take from our labour and our overhead suppliers we find that the time differs from that shown for materials. For instance, we normally cannot take more than a maximum of one month's credit from our employees, and in some cases this will be reduced to one week before we pay them. We might therefore have to accept the fact that on average, in this area, we are limited to a fortnight's credit and in the case of overheads we might be able to obtain, say, one month's credit before having to meet the bills.

We can see therefore that the bottom line for labour and overheads reads 3½ months and 3 months respectively.

Functional influence on time delays

Having examined these time cycles let us now get to grips with a real understanding of the individual time areas and the functions which influence each. To do this turn to Illustration 9.7, where the areas for delay set out in Illustration 9.6 are repeated but we have added the different functions which influence each.

Illustration 9.7 Functional influences on time delays

Working capital delay areas:	Functions which influence delay:
Raw material store	Buying
	Production
	Marketing and sales
Production cycle	Production
	Buying
	Marketing and sales
Finished goods store	Marketing and sales
	Production
	Buying
Debtors/receivables	Finance/accounting
	Sales/marketing
Creditors/payables	Finance/accounting
	Buying
	Labour negotiators
	Overhead buyers

For example, in the case of 'raw material store', if we try to minimise the time delay between the material coming in and being used, three main functions would have to be concerned with the necessary corrective action: buying, production and marketing/sales. This is because if we wish to reduce time 'in store' buyers would be most obviously concerned in arranging their purchasing policies to facilitate this. However, we also have to take account of the problems of production because production would have to furnish buyers with the necessary information on which to base their purchasing policies. In addition to this it would also be vital for marketing to play its part in providing sales plans to enable production to plan and buyers then to create the correct buying policies to minimise the time delays, making sure the material arrives 'just in time'.

Again, to reduce production time would also involve more than one function. Here we would be concerned with not only the production but also the other functions with a contribution to make. It would certainly be necessary for buyers to provide precisely the materials needed to meet day-to-day production requirements. However, sales and marketing would also be very much involved in order to ensure that the production plans are based on the real needs of the market place.

And again, as we come into the finished goods area we see the same three functions. After all, although the control of time in the finished goods store will be influenced mainly by sales and marketing there will obviously be a need for co-operation with the other functions. Production must ensure that what is produced is precisely what sales or marketing requires, and to some extent buyers may also be involved in this area. This is because the length of time goods are held in the finished goods store may well be influenced by the availability of some final component or packaging device which is the responsibility of the purchasing function.

Finally we come to the credit area – both the credit we take and the credit we give. Here the financial function will have considerable influence but again we find that we cannot ignore the other functions. The influence of sales and marketing on the credit which is taken from us by debtors or receivables can be crucial, and indeed the contribution of buyers and those negotiating labour and overhead credit terms can be equally important in ensuring the maximum credit time allowed is obtained.

Summary and consolidation

It is vital at this stage for us to understand fully the intertwining and interweaving of functions in the control of working capital. Not only do we have different functions affecting each individual area but we also have the overlaps between them. However good the credit control may be, for example, if production keep producing poor quality goods then customers may well express their disappointment by delaying payment. Or again, however good production control may be, if buyers never have the raw materials which are required, production hold-ups will ensue, creating an increase in the work in progress stock investment.

To consider this problem of time control try the exercise in Illustration 9.8. This sets out a series of jobs in a typical business and poses the question: how do the holders of each of these influence the control of working capital? In what way do they influence the time in converting materials, labour and overheads back into cash? When you have pondered this question give what you consider to be the appropriate answers and then (and only then) turn to the solution suggested in Illustration 9.9. Finally, consider your own influence over the working capital investment within your own business. How might you and your colleagues be able to reduce it?

Illustration 9.8 Personal responsibility for time delays exercise

Consider the following jobs and their responsibility in the control of working capital:
1. Storekeeper
2. Production controller
3. Retail salesperson
4. Production inspector
5. Designer

Illustration 9.9 Suggested answers to Illustration 9.8

1. *Storekeeper.* Time material in store.
2. *Production controller.* Time of converting material, labour and overheads into finished goods.
3. *Retail salesperson.* Time of converting stock on shelves into cash in the till.
4. *Production inspector.* Time of correcting any production faults.
5. *Designer.* Providing designs which minimise the time of manufacture.

SERVICE INDUSTRIES AND WORKING CAPITAL

We have so far looked in the main at working capital in the context of a manufacturing business. So let us now turn our attention to service industries. In this situation we are also concerned with converting material, labour and overheads back into cash but there may well be a different emphasis. That is, in a service industry little, if any, material may be translated back into our finished services. However, the general concept underlining the control of working capital applies equally. To enable you to become familiar with this and understand that the control of working capital is just as vital in a service business turn to Illustration 9.10, which illustrates the time cycles that apply to the service provided by a particular business – in this case, the delivery of goods to customers. From this data calculate the working capital time requirements for this particular business and when you have done that compare your answer with Illustration 9.11.

RETAILERS AND WORKING CAPITAL

In Illustration 9.12 you will see the timing facts regarding the working capital of a retailer. Here we see that merchandise is bought and held pending sale and that although credit is taken from the merchandise suppliers, employees and overhead providers where possible, no credit other than that inherent in the use of cheques, credit cards, etc., is given to customers. Again work through this example and compare your answer with that shown in Illustration 9.13.

Illustration 9.10 Working capital time cycle data in a service industry

A firm concerned with delivery of goods throughout the UK provides you with the following information regarding its working capital time cycles. Summarise these times for this business.

	Weeks
Average time between accepting delivery order and delivery	3
Average time between delivery and invoice despatch	2
Average time taken by receivables/debtors before payment	6
Credit taken: Material (fuel etc.)	4
Labour	2
Overheads	3

Illustration 9.11 Suggested answers to Illustration 9.10

Working capital areas:	Material weeks	Labour weeks	Overhead weeks
Accepting order to delivery	3	3	3
Delivery to invoice despatch	2	2	2
Debtors	6	6	6
Gross time	11	11	11
Less: Credit time taken	(4)	(2)	(3)
Net time	7	9	8

Illustration 9.12 Working capital time cycle data for a retailer

A company concerned with retailing throughout Europe provides you with the following information regarding its working capital cycle time. Summarise these times for this business.

	Weeks
Merchandise stored in warehouse	3
Average shelf-life of merchandise before sale	4
Average credit taken	2
(caused mainly by credit card use, etc.)	
Credit taken: Merchandise	8
Labour	2
Overheads	4

Illustration 9.13 Suggested answer to Illustration 9.12

Working capital areas:	Merchandise weeks	Labour weeks	Overhead weeks
Warehouse storage	3	3	3
Shelf-life	4	4	4
Debtors	2	2	2
Gross time	9	9	9
Less: Credit time taken	8	2	4
Net time	1	7	5

TIME AND MONEY

Having examined the time cycles within working capital we will now look at the relationship of time and money in this area. First turn to Illustration 9.14, which sets out a budgeted profit and loss account for a twelve-month period.

Illustration 9.14 Budgeted profit and loss account

	% of sales	Budgeted annual cost £	£
Annual sales budget			5,000,000
Costs:			
Material	40	2,000,000	
Labour	20	1,000,000	
Overheads	20	1,000,000	
Total cost			4,000,000
Profit	20		1,000,000
	100		

This budget states that the business is planning to sell goods to the value of £5,000,000 and that the material, labour and overhead cost amount to 40, 20 and 20 per cent of such sales respectively, thus leaving a profit of 20 per cent. The budgeted costs for the twelve months thusx amount to £2,000,000 for materials and £1,000,000 each for labour and overheads. Let us now apply the time cycles in Illustration 9.6 to these basic financial facts, so as to calculate the working capital requirement of this business.

Calculating the working capital requirement

If you turn to Illustration 9.15 you will see that we have done precisely this. We have applied the time cycles shown in Illustration 9.6 to the values we have just seen in Illustration 9.14.

To do this we multiply the budgeted costs of materials, labour and overheads by the appropriate months calculated in Illustration 9.6 and this gives us the working capital investment that we will require to support the planned £5,000,000 annual sales. For example, if we look at materials the annual figure of £2,000,000 is multiplied by $\frac{1}{6}$ which is $\frac{2}{12}$ of a year. Representing the net time material is invested as part of the working capital. We will also see in the case of labour we multiply the £1,000,000, the annual figure, by $3\frac{1}{2}$ over 12 months and in the case of overheads we multiply the £1,000,000 figure by $\frac{1}{4}$ which is 3 over 12 months. These figures are then totalled to give a sum of approximately

£870,000 which is the working capital investment this business must make to support its sales budget of £5,000,000.

Illustration 9.15 Budgeted profit and loss statement

Annual sales budget			£5,000,000
	% of sales	Budgeted annual costs	Working capital required (approx)
Costs:		£	£
Material	40	2,000,000 x 1/6 =	330,000
Labour	20	1,000,000 x 3.5/12 =	290,000
Overheads	20	1,000,000 x 1/4 =	250,000
Profit	20		
	100		870,000
Or working capital per £1 of sales:		$\dfrac{£870,000}{£5,000,000}$ = 17p	

In other words, what we are saying in this particular illustration is that to support £5,000,000 worth of sales we will need an investment of £870,000 as working capital. Or in simple figures, we could say that for every £1 we plan to sell, we will need to generate 17p to finance the necessary working capital to support it – calculated by dividing the £870,000 working capital by the £5,000,000 sales.

The limitation of overtrading

The measurement of working capital to sales is vital to understand because of what it is telling us. Every time we sell a pound's worth of our goods we not only need to find customers to sell to and fixed assets to produce with, but we also need to find 17p to finance the extra working capital required to support the extra sales.

If we go back to our earlier discussions about working capital you will remember that we talked about the limitation of working capital. If we do not minimise this it could limit our progress. This is precisely what this 17p means! It means that if we wish to sell an extra pound's worth of our goods, merchandise or services and we do not have whatever is needed (in this case 17p) to invest as working capital, we could be held back. Not because we cannot produce the goods, display the merchandise or render the services with the fixed assets or skills we possess, nor because we cannot find customers to sell them to – but because we do not have 17p (or its equivalent in the particular situation). It is this problem that is often loosely termed 'overtrading': the situation that occurs when a business tries to sell more than it can support with its available working capital – the penalty of over-expansion.

THE CONSEQUENCES OF SAVING WORKING CAPITAL

Having seen and examined the implications of working capital and its control or otherwise, let us take a further step and discuss the effect of saving working capital. In other words, what does it mean to us financially, when we are running a business, whether or not we reduce this investment. To illustrate this, go back to Illustration 9.6 and ask yourselves what the result would be if we could reduce the time cycle by, say, a fortnight.

We have already seen that the control of working capital implies the control of time, so let us now consider the financial implications of saving time – in this case a fortnight. Clearly if this happened the bottom line would then be reduced for materials, labour and overheads by half a month in each case: material time would be reduced to one and a half months, labour to three months and overheads to two and a half months.

It would also mean, if we take the figures we have been looking at in Illustration 9.14, that the total investment in working capital would be reduced by a fortnight's worth of the annual cost of materials, labour and overheads. You will see that this total cost comes to £4,000,000, and a fortnight's worth of this amount – taking a fortnight as 1/24th of a year – gives us an annual saving of approximately £170,000.

Now the question is: what does this mean to us financially in running a business? And to answer this let us turn to Illustration 9.16, which shows two approaches to saving working capital.

Illustration 9.16 Two approaches to the saving of working capital

First approach:	
Saving (2 weeks)	= £170,000
Return on investment expected	= 15%
Return on saving	= £25,500 (15% of £170,000)
Second approach:	
Saving	= £170,000
Working capital to sales expressed as pence per £1	= 17p
Additional sales which saving can support	= £1,000,000
Profit on sales per budget	= 20% = £200,000

Investment savings

In the first instance we look at the saving and say: 'If we can save £170,000 of working capital, we have £170,000 we can use elsewhere. And if in our business we can obtain a return of, say, 15 per cent on what we invest, the result of this saving would be that every year we could increase our profits by £25,500 – which is 15 per cent of £170,000.'

However, even if this is true, we still have to reduce this additional profit figure by the cost of a fortnight's saving. After all, you do not reduce the working capital time cycle by a fortnight without it costing you money. You might have to improve your material control and/or your production control and/or your credit control systems, and all this would increase expenditure on more staff, more procedures and more administration.

In fact, if you examined the cost of the saving in comparison with its benefits, it might well be found that there is nothing in it to justify the effort. This is certainly true in the example in Illustration 9,17, where the cost of the saving is given as £30,000 per annum. There you will see from the first part of the answer in Illustration 9.18 that the return on the saving, at £26,250, is less than the costs of achieving it.

Employee savings

However, this is only one way of looking at the working capital saving and it is certainly not the way in which a dynamic business considers it. Such a business would not look at the saving of working capital in relation to the interest on money saved – a banker's view it might be said. It would examine the situation along very different lines. It would ask itself, as is shown in the second approach in Illustration 9.16, 'What is the effect of the saving – in this case £170,000 – on sales?' In other words it would see that it now has £170,000 to support further sales.

We have already seen from Illustration 9.15 that the relationship of working capital to sales is 17p per £1 sold, and if the business can save £170,000 of working capital, it has this money available to support further sales. These would equal – if we take the relationship of 17p per £1 of sales – sufficient funds to support additional sales of £1,000,000 (£170,000 divided by 17p). It can also be seen, taking the profit to sales relationship set out in Illustration 9.14 of 20 per cent, that we have a possibility of additional profits of £200,000 (20 per cent of the additional sales of £1,000,000).

Other factors

This, of course, may not be the full picture. There may well be adjustments to this figure, as we have already discussed in the cost of saving the working capital. It must also be remembered, thinking back to when we were examining the profit and loss account in chapter 2, and marginal costing in chapter 7, that there are many expenses, especially those which relate to overheads, which will not move in direct proportion with sales. For this reason the profit we obtain when our sales exceed the budget might well be in excess of the 20 per cent which we have used in this illustration. This is because although the variable costs increase in proportion with activity, the fixed expenses or overheads will mainly be more time than 'activity' related. (If this is at all unclear revise your studies of the profit and loss account, and those on marginal costing, referred to above.)

There is also the need to ensure that the fixed asset investment is sufficient to meet the increased sales needs, whether these be increased production or retail or service-rendering capacity. However, even if such needs required an investment of, say, 50 per cent of the amount saved, in our example it would still leave £85,000 to support further sales, which in turn would provide increased profits of £100,000 (check this calculation if you doubt me): quite enough to meet the additional cost of such savings.

The benefits from saving working capital

It can be seen from this second approach to the control of working capital that to an expanding business the benefits to be obtained from minimising working capital are great indeed. It should also be noted that these benefits are not only the goal of the person who invests money in a business, but also that of anyone who considers his or her own position within a business. Employees' salaries or wages – and their entire employment conditions – are very much wrapped up in the ability of the business to expand. Similarly, the benefits investors hope to gain from working capital control depend largely upon the involvement of managers and indeed all employees throughout the business.

Turn now to Illustration 9.17 and examine the facts shown there together with the possible time savings, and calculate the two approaches to the benefits from saving working capital time that we have just discussed. When you have done this and compared your answer with Illustration 9.18, then turn to Illustration 9.19. Work through the example to test your understanding of this area of financial control and when you have completed your answer check it with Illustration 9.20.

Illustration 9.17 Calculation of saving of working capital exercise

---

Calculate the two approaches to working capital saving from the following facts:

Working capital required per £1 of sales	15p
Saving possible by improved time control	£210,000
Cost of saving working capital time	£30,000
Budgeted profit on sales	20%
Interest on investment expected	12.5%

Illustration 9.18 Suggested answer to Illustration 9.17

First approach:

Saving	=	£210,000
Return on saving (@ 12.5%)	=	£26,250
Less: Cost of saving	=	£30,000
Loss from saving		£3,750

Second approach:

Saving		£210,000
Additional sales from savings	=	£1,400,000 (£210,000 divided by 15p)
Profit from additional sales	=	£280,000 (£1,400,000 x 20%)
Less: Cost of saving	=	£30,000
Profit from saving		£250,000

Illustration 9.19 Calculation of working capital exercise

The following facts refer to a manufacturing business. You are asked to prepare an estimate of the working capital required to support its sales.

	Delay time (weeks)
Raw material store	6
Production cycle	2
Finished goods store	3
Debtors	6
Creditors: Material	6
Labour	1
Overheads	4
Sales budget for 12 months	£12,000,000

Costs	%
Material	30
Labour	25
Overheads	20

Illustration 9.20 Suggested answer to Illustration 9.19

	Materials weeks	Labour weeks	Overheads weeks
Raw material store	6	6	6
Production cycle	2	2	2
Finished goods store	3	3	3
Debtors	6	6	6
	17	17	17

Less: Creditors	(6)	(1)	(4)
Net working capital time	11	16	13
Say	2.75 months	4 months	3.25 months

Working capital calculation

Sales budget for 12 months			£12,000,000

Cost	% of sales	Annual £	£
Material	30	3,600,000 × 2.75/12	825,000
Labour	25	3,000,000 × 1/3	1,000,000
Overheads	20	2,400,000 × 3.25/12	650,000
			2,475,000

Or 21p of working capital per £1 of sales (approx)

SUMMARY AND CONCLUSION

To summarise the points introduced in this chapter we must begin at the beginning with the definition of working capital. It is the moving area – the money-go-round – in which money is being converted into and out of materials, labour and overheads over a period of time. This means that its control lies in the way we manage time.

Looking at Illustration 9.1, it is fundamental to the control of working capital to move the money as fast as we can from point A back to point B, and as slowly as we can – within agreed limits – between points C and D. We must understand that those concerned with this control include virtually every person employed in a business. Not only those in senior positions of authority but also those in seemingly unimportant jobs may have considerable influence upon this area of investment – consider the effect of storekeepers on material storage time or sales personnel in spotting the first signs of doubtful debts.

Having understood working capital as an investment, it is then necessary to see the interrelationships of functions within each area. This can be done by examining Illustration 9.3 and seeing how individual functions have an influence on and relate to one another in each of the main areas of delay. Finally we must understand how the control of working capital time relates directly to the profitability of an enterprise. It increases its ability to take advantage of marketing possibilities by reducing one of the limitations to its expansion plans – the level of working capital investment required to support its sales. This is shown in Illustrations 9.6, 9.14, 9.15 and 9.16, and these examples should be studied carefully before continuing to the next chapter, on budgetary control.

10

BUDGETARY CONTROL

INTRODUCTION

So far we have discussed the techniques, stemming from the profit and loss account and the balance sheet, developed to meet the demands of the thinking manager. For instance, from the profit and loss account the need to discover where the profit or loss is being made leads to the techniques known as costing. From the balance sheet come the questions regarding investment, which led to project appraisal techniques being developed to help managers 'look before they leap'; to meet the questions regarding investment in fixed assets and other 'locked up' areas of money such as research and development and marketing before benefits arise from it.

We also saw in the last chapter that the objective, so far as working capital is concerned, is to minimise the investment, to reduce the financial luggage – the stocks and debtors less creditors – and that this is done by the analysis and control of time: the time involved in moving the money round the working capital cycle, or money-go-round as we have called it. Finally, in chapter 4 we saw how the detailed analysis of cash set out in the cash flow forecast may be recast into a summary of overall cash movement, a summary presented in what is termed the cash flow statement, the purpose of which is to encapsulate the progress of the business in such a way as to answer perhaps the final and most pragmatic cash question of all: 'Has the business lived within or beyond its means?' And we shall be referring again to this way of looking at a business's progress when we consider interpretation in chapter 12.

However, now let us turn our attention to the recurring question that haunts every thinking manager, when financial information about what has happened is presented: 'What can I compare it against?' It is to meet this constant need for comparison that the financial technique termed budgetary control has been developed.

Budgetary control is nothing new. It has been with us in business for a very long time. Indeed one only has to go back into the history of business to find that managers have always done some form of budgeting – planning and reviewing the progress of their businesses. After all, 2,000 years ago someone was quoted as saying: 'What man ever built a house before first counting its cost?'

THE BUSINESS PLAN

Budgeting is the natural end-piece to the business plan: a plan setting out your analysis of your present position, a mission statement as to how you see the purpose of your business developing and the strategy by which such purposes and objectives might be achieved. Having expressed the plan in words, however, there is the need for evaluation – to set out the financial implications of your proposals. It is this aspect of planning with which budgetary control is concerned: The translation of your business plan over the short term (normally in detail over the twelve months ahead) into the financial measurements and progressing these against the facts as they become known.

Imagine yourself starting a business. Inevitably you would find yourself looking at your plans and your policies so that you could see whether or not it was likely to go well or even be possible. To illustrate this point refer to Illustration 10.1, which sets out the financial situation of a company so far as its future plans are concerned. It must be stressed that in this illustration we have confined our view forward to six months, which in any real-life situation would be far too short a period. However, we shall refer to the period of a budget later in this chapter.

Illustration 10.1 Budgetary control exercise

A Ltd is formed with share capital of £140,000 of which it invests £40,000 in land and buildings, £25,000 in plant and machinery and £20,000 in motor vehicles and the remainder it leaves as cash. Its plans for the first six months are as follows:

Sales for six months	£650,000
Materials in sales	£280,000
Labour in sales	£180,000
Overheads (including depreciation:	
Plant and machinery	£5,000
Motor vehicles	£5,000) £160,000
Materials purchased for the period	£300,000

Cash receipts and payments for six months:

	Sales receipts £	Payments material £	Overheads and wages £
July	30,000	70,000	
August	60,000	70,000	paid
September	40,000	10,000	evenly
October	80,000	10,000	each month
November	110,000	20,000	
December	160,000	20,000	
Total	480,000	200,000	

Note: There is no work in progress or finished goods stocks at 31 December. From the above facts construct the budgeted:

(a) cash flow forecast for July to December;
(b) profit and loss account for the six months ended 31 December;
(c) balance sheet as at 31 December.

You will see in the illustration that the business is planning to sell a certain volume of goods and that it estimates that these will cost so much. You will also see that the business plans to raise money by issuing share capital and there are certain investments that have to be made in items such as land and buildings, plant and machinery, and motor vehicles – in other words, fixed assets. You should tackle the questions set in this illustration and see how out of this business plan expressed in money values (evaluated) we produce the three major statements: the planned or, as we say, the budgeted cash flow forecast, profit and loss account and balance sheet.

As you tackle the questions and read through the suggested answers in Illustrations 10.2, 10.3 and 10.4 you might recall a similar illustration which we studied at the end of chapter 4. You will recognise that what in fact is happening is that we are proving the financial credibility of the policies of this particular company. It is all very well having great plans for the future, but they must be financially possible. Each of these three major statements is proving one or other aspect of the financial credibility of this particular business's plan.

First, if we follow this plan, what will be the return – what will be the growth or shrinkage of the money we are investing in the business? This leads us to the profit and loss account. Second, if we start this business where will our money be invested and from where will it have been funded at any point of time during the planned period? In the case of the illustration we have chosen six months from the beginning of the business. We are therefore setting out the balance sheet, the 'snapshot', of where the money will be and from where it will have been obtained as at 31 December. Finally, we need to look at whether we have the ability to arrive, the 'ready', in cash terms. We determine this by means of the budgeted cash flow forecast. In fact, in constructing the budgets for these three measurements the cash flow forecast will come first. As Illustration 10.2 shows, there is a cash need of £130,000 by September and unless this need can be financed there is no point in proceeding to the profit and loss account or the balance sheet. (If you find this point unclear revise your studies on cash flow forecasting in chapter 4.)

Illustration 10.2 A Ltd: budgeted cash flow forecast: July to December

	Jul. £	Aug. £	Sept. £	Oct. £	Nov. £	Dec. £	Total £
Receipts:							
Share capital	140,000	–	–	–	–	–	140,000
Sales	30,000	60,000	40,000	80,000	110,000	160,000	480,000
A	170,000	60,000	40,000	80,000	110,000	160,000	620,000
Payments:							
Fixed assets	85,000	–	–	–	–	–	85,000
Materials	70,000	70,000	10,000	10,000	20,000	20,000	200,000
Wages	30,000	30,000	30,000	30,000	30,000	30,000	180,000
Overheads	25,000	25,000	25,000	25,000	25,000	25,000	150,000

B	210,000	125,000	65,000	65,000	75,000	75,000	615,000
Balance (A – B)	(40,000)	(65,000)	(25,000)	15,000	35,000	85,000	
Balance b/fwd	–	(40,000)	(105,000)	(130,000)	(115,000)	(80,000)	
Balance c/fwd	(40,000)	(105,000)	(130,000)	(115,000)	(80,000)	5,000	5,000

Illustration 10.3 A Ltd: budgeted profit and loss account for the six months ended 31 December

	£	£
Sales		650,000
Less: Materials	280,000	
Labour	180,000	
Overheads	160,000	620,000
Profit		30,000

Illustration 10.4 A Ltd: budgeted balance sheet as at 31 December

	Cost £	Depreciation to date £	£
Fixed assets:			
Land and buildings	40,000	–	40,000
Plant and machinery	25,000	5,000	20,000
Motor vehicles	20,000	5,000	15,000
	85,000	10,000	75,000
Working capital:			
Current assets:			
Stock of raw materials	20,000		
Debtors	170,000		
Cash at bank	5,000	195,000	
Less: Current liabilities			
Creditors		100,000	95,000
			170,000
Financed by:			
Share capital			140,000
Retained profits			30,000
			170,000

BUDGETING FOR POLICY-MAKERS

What we have just done is to look at budgeting as it applies to the policy-makers of a business. And whether we are sitting on a bar stool planning our own small business or round a boardroom table planning the policies of a multinational corporation, we need to subject our plans, our policies, our dreams, our ideas to these same three credibility tests of finance. What will be the return? What will be the risk? And will we have the ready – the cash – to arrive? These three Rs of finance are indeed the financial thermometers of every business plan.

BUDGETARY CONTROL AND NON-POLICY-MAKERS

However, we find that this form of budgeting, which we might refer to as 'boardroom budgeting', is only part of today's budgetary control system. What we now see is that present-day business budgeting is no longer confined to the policy-makers. As businesses expand more, so more people within the enterprise become concerned with the investment, receipt and expenditure of its money as regards both its planning and progress. It is therefore necessary to extend its control to people outside the policy-makers.

It is for this reason that modern-day budgeting has taken on an additional role. We still have budgeting within the boardroom – dealing with the policy of the business – but we now see it extended to those who are not concerned necessarily with policy-making. What we find is that managers operating at all levels are taking part more and more in the budgeting process. Budgetary control is now adapted to meet their needs, not as policy-makers, but as controllers of income, expense, investment and cash flow within their own particular spheres of influence.

To demonstrate this point regarding the involvement of people with money in business consider the financial model set out again as Illustration 10.5. Place against each circle the function, e.g buying, sales, production and finance, which will influence the expense, income or investment concerned and check your answer with Illustration 10.6. From this illustration it becomes clear that – with the possible exception of outside investments – all areas of expense, income and investment are influenced to some extent by managers from every function and at all levels within the organisation.

THE BEHAVIOURAL PROBLEM

The primary role of budgeting is to prove the credibility of the business plan: whether the profit in relation to the capital employed justifies the investment and whether there will be adequate cash flow – the bus fare – to arrive. We also have its second or non-policy-proving role, which involves setting out forecasts of expense, income, investment and cash flow that can be controlled by individual managers and which are regularly progressed. This second application of budgetary control has brought with it a great increase in forecasting and a great deal more progressing than took place when budgeting was confined to the boardroom. Perhaps most important of all, however, it has brought out the problem of the behavioural response to comparison. When you subject people to personal comparison they behave in a particular way – they do not like it. And because they do not like it, they resist it.

Illustration 10.5 Influences on expenses, income or investment

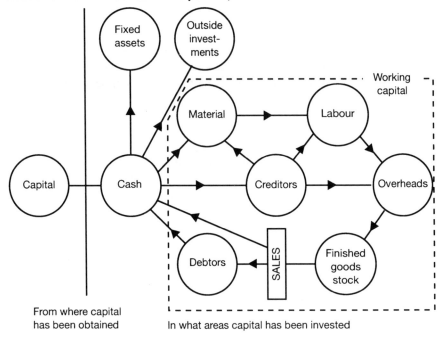

Question: Place against each circle the function which will influence expenses, income or investment

All managers concerned with projects
Most managers in the business
Distribution
Finance
Buying
Sales/marketing
Policy-makers
Personnel/production

This resistance and the consequences that flow from it become a major problem in this second role of budgetary control. Managers asked to compare their own performance against financial targets or budgets prepared around their activities may be tempted to overstate expenses and understate income and sales so that revenue budgets will easily be attained, while revenue and capital or fixed asset expenditure will be exaggerated more to increase personal prestige than for the good of the business as a whole.

We need therefore to anticipate such a response and try to avoid its consequences. To begin with, any business introducing budgetary control must understand that managers not only resist comparison but are well equipped to do this, because they have two well-tried 'defence barriers': irrelevance and impossibility.

Illustration 10.6 Suggested answer to Illustration 10.5

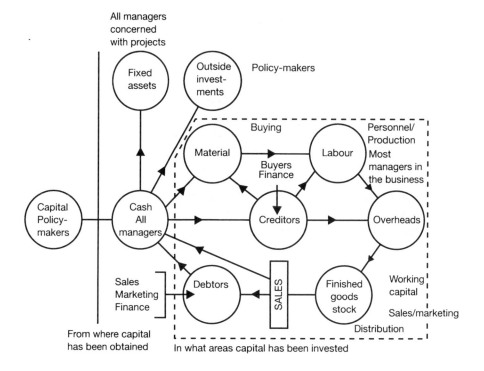

Irrelevance

Irrelevance has long been used as a defence against comparisons. Take, for example, religions, which are based upon 'example figures' in human form against whom their followers are compared. Here the excuse of those wishing to avoid such comparison has so often been: 'his hair was longer than mine', 'he lived in the desert', 'he had no job', 'he wasn't married'; not arguing his 'rightness', simply questioning his 'relevance'. In other words, this resistance barrier is nothing new and for this reason it is essential to recognise it if budgeting is to be effective. Successful budgeting presupposes that the items which managers are expected to control and progress should be relevant to them and subject to their influence.

It is therefore vital that managers take part in the preparation of their own budgets and that they are fully conversant with and appreciate their influence on each expense, income and investment for which they are made responsible. A key point of successful budgeting is to make sure that managers are fully involved at the planning stage. Managers should therefore agree their budgets before the period of control and progress begins, so as to avoid the excuse of irrelevance. For this reason every item placed within the budget of any manager must be fully agreed and understood by those concerned.

Impossibility

Having considered the problem of irrelevance the second defence – impossibility – has to be tackled. From a behavioural point of view budgeting has all the attributes of a game. Managers are being asked to achieve certain objectives to meet the agreed budget. And if you are going to get people to play positively, it is essential that the game can be won.

After all, if from the very start those asked to play know it is impossible to win, the natural human response will be either to change the rules – cheat – or, if that is impossible, ruin the game. You can see this if you watch children at play with adults when the adults are taking the game seriously. In order to make the game winnable children will do one of two things: either cheat or begin to play another game. In other words, they will convert the impossible game into one which is possible to win or at least enjoyable to lose!

These are very important points to recognise in budgeting – because the identical negative response described here will take place unless great care is taken to anticipate what might be termed the 'behavioural problems of comparison'. For this reason it is important not only that all budgets are agreed with managers but that the level of efficiency, on which the budgets are set, is possible to achieve. If not, the chances are that they will either cheat – in other words they will arrange the budgets in such a way that although people will think they are impossible or at least difficult to attain they will in fact be very easy indeed – or if this is not possible they will opt out of the system. They will play another game. They will not even try, but sulk noisily.

These then are the two cardinal rules that we must apply when we are involving people in personal comparison, rules which apply to managers in a budgeting situation as much as to any human comparative activity. The comparison must be relevant, and it must be possible to achieve.

'Below the line' items

Despite these two behavioural rules it may still be necessary to include items which, although not be the direct responsibility of particular managers, may be of interest to them. In this circumstance such items may well be included and referred to as 'below the line items', indicating that no responsibility for their control lies with the managers to whom the budget is addressed.

BUDGET PRESENTATION

A revenue budget

In the process of budgetary control it is usual practice to consider expenditure under the two headings of capital expenditure (money being spent on items not intended for resale) and revenue expenditure (items which are going into what is sold) which when sales are made will produce (we hope a greater amount of) revenue income. Based on this division, budgets once prepared are referred to as revenue and capital budgets.

A typical example of a revenue budget is set out in Illustration 10.7. You will see that the budget relates to items of expenditure, within a department, of a revenue nature: expenditure which will be deducted from sales before arriving at the profit or loss of the business in the profit and loss account.

Illustration 10.7 Revenue budget for production department to month 6

| Expense | This month | | To date | | | Remarks |
	Actual £	Budget £	Actual £	Budget £	Variance £	
Indirect wages	9,650	10,000	65,400	70,000	4,600	Overtime less
Rent	1,000	1,000	6,000	6,000	–	
Insurance	480	500	2,800	3,000	200	
Depreciation	1,900	2,000	10,600	12,000	1,400	Plant not purchased
Electricity	1,250	1,500	9,000	8,000	(1,000)	Cost increase
Plant repair, etc	900	750	8,000	6,000	(2,000)	Major breakdown

In a revenue budget the comparison which is of major interest is normally between the cumulative figures to date. This is because the actual monthly figures can sometimes be distorted by an unusual expense (or lack of one) in a particular month. The cumulative amounts, therefore, are of particular importance to those concerned with taking corrective action. It is also useful to include space for remarks and explanations, as these will bring out points which may be necessary to consider, if you are to get full value from the comparison. This is particularly important if the comparison has become distorted because of factors outside the control of the particular manager for whom the budget has been prepared.

A capital expenditure budget

It should be remembered that what is included in the capital expenditure budget will be limited to the 'domestic' definition of this investment area. As we discussed earlier, in many organisations the decision as to what is classed as capital as opposed to revenue is determined more by size than purpose. For instance, a multi-million-pound enterprise may well decide to classify as revenue expenditure items which in smaller businesses would be treated as capital. (If this matter is in any way unclear, refer back to chapter 1.)

Illustration 10.8 sets out a budget relating to capital or fixed asset expenditure. Where capital expenditure is of a continuing nature, it may be useful to examine the expense to date plus an estimate of what is necessary to complete the project, compared with the total original budget. This indeed is the budget format illustrated, which includes three comparisons: this month, the cumulative figures to date, and the figures to date plus an estimate of what has still to be done to complete the project.

It is also emphasised that capital expenditure budgets can seldom be confined to the immediate year ahead, which is the period normally selected for revenue budgets. For capital expenditure many organisations budget in considerable detail over the next five to ten years and even beyond this in outline. However, budgeting, like planning, should always be kept under strict control. It can become a diversion from facing up to the reality of today! Again we have an example of the behavioural response conflicting with the commercial objective. For this reason it is recommended that detailed budgets beyond three years, even in the case of capital expenditure, should be entertained only if proved to be necessary. In all other cases budgeting beyond this period should be confined to six monthly or quarterly estimates in outline only.

PROGRESSING BUDGETS

After looking at the setting of budgets and the way in which they can be presented we shall now consider the main rules for progressing them. First, it must be noted that budgeting is primarily a technique of communication, involving people in planning where they are going, progressing this against where they have been and noting any differences. For this reason the progressing of budgets must meet the criteria of good communications. After all, if you get people interested in setting budgets and then proceed to bore them in the way in which they are progressed you inevitably lose a great deal of the earlier advantage. For this reason care must be taken over the way in which information is progressed and in doing this we have to look at the two major rules of communication: the *form* in which information is communicated and the *frequency* or *timing* of its presentation.

Form of presentation

As regards the form of presentation it is necessary to consider very carefully the way which will best suit the different levels of managers who are to be involved in budgeting. Neat columns of figures may well serve the purpose for many managers and certainly accountants, but there may also be those who do not find the 'columns of figures' approach conducive to understanding. Indeed they may well find presentations such as graphs or other visual methods more appropriate. It may also be found that it is helpful to present information in different ways – quantities, time, etc., as well as values. This is especially true in periods of inflation or for those managers who use such non-financial measurements in their control procedures.

Illustration 10.8 Capital expenditure budget

	'A' Factory				Month 6			
	This month		Accumulated to date		Total cost			
Capital project	Actual	Budget	Actual	Budget	Actual cost plus estimate to complete	Total budget cost	Difference	Remarks
	£	£	£	£	£	£	£	
Extension to Parts Store	5,100	11,200	131,000	120,000	240,000	210,000	+30,000	Alteration to specification agreed per Directors' Minute dated 6/12/—

An example of how graphs can replace columns of figures and how quantities can be used in place of values is set out in Illustration 10.9. This shows two graphs, the first comparing the actual and budgeted value of materials used and the second comparing the actual and budgeted quantities used of the same materials. Here you see that (b) indicates an over-usage of material quantity while (a) has a more confusing picture, presumably because of fluctuating material prices.

Illustration 10.9 Comparison of materials usage: (a) by value; (b) by quantity

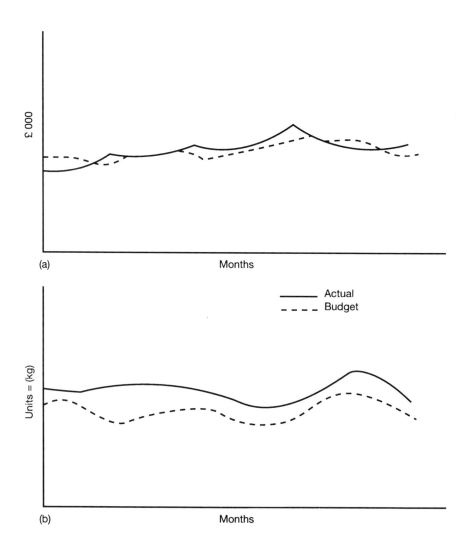

The Z chart

To illustrate a more comprehensive use of graphs turn to Illustration 10.10, which sets out data relating to sales for a twelve-month period. This includes the monthly and cumulative budgeted sales figures accompanied by the actual sales figures as they become known. The graph in Illustration 10.11 is based on these figures.

Illustration 10.10 Data and calculations for graph in Illustration 10.11

	Budget		Actual		Moving annual average	
	Monthly	Cumulative	Monthly	Cumulative	Budget	Actual
	£	£	£	£	£	£
January	5,000	5,000	5,000	5,000	60,000	60,000
February	4,900	9,900	4,800	9,800	59,400	58,800
March	5,200	15,100	5,300	15,100	60,400	60,400
April	4,800	19,900	5,400	20,500	59,700	61,500
May	5,100	25,000	4,700	25,200	60,000	60,480
June	5,010	30,010	4,800	30,000	60,020	60,000
July	4,950	34,960	4,900	34,900	59,931	59,829
August	5,100	40,060	5,200	40,100	60,090	60,150
September	5,000	45,060	5,300	45,400	60,080	60,533
October	4,800	49,860	4,700	50,100	59,832	60,120
November	5,100	54,960	5,200	55,300	59,956	60,327
December	4,900	59,860	5,600	60,900	59,860	60,900

Moving annual average calculation:
Example for June:

$$\text{Budget} = \frac{£30,010}{6} \times 12 = £60,020$$

$$\text{Actual} = \frac{£30,000}{6} \times 12 = £60,000$$

Here you will see, first, that the figures are presented to show the actual monthly sales as they become available compared with those set out in the sales budget. Second, we see the cumulative actual sales month by month compared with the cumulative budgeted sales. Finally, we show the moving annual average sales, which are based on the average monthly figures. You will see how these are calculated in the notes attached to Illustration 10.10.

The graph in Illustration 10.11 – known as a Z chart – is a way of showing the budget and actual sales figures in three ways – monthly, cumulative and the moving annual average: three comparisons on one chart. It is stressed however that this chart demonstrates the 'idea' of a Z chart and does not reflect the figures illustrated in Illustration 10.10. For those who would like to practice their ability at constructing such a chart I would suggest you should reach for your graph paper using the data presented in Illustration 10.11.

Illustration 10.11 Z chart produced from data in illustration 10.10

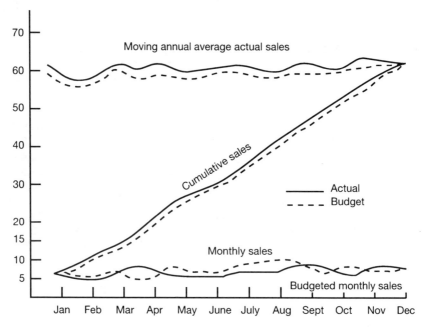

Summarising data

There are also certain other points regarding the form of presentation which should be borne in mind. The first is that if budget information is summarised on one piece of paper it can delay the information. For example, if managers receive a summary of expenditure within their departments at monthly intervals, and all the information is available by the end of the month with the exception of one item, which does not arrive, say, for 14 days, everything will be delayed until that time arrives. It therefore has to be recognised that if speedy present-ation is required summarising data can add to delay. Presentation can thus be made speedier if managers will accept partly completed data. Also connected with speed of presentation is the accuracy of the data presented. If those receiv-ing information require it to be accurate to the nearest penny there will certainly be delay, compared with the availability of similar data plus or minus a certain tolerance level of accuracy. It will be necessary to agree such levels with man-agers but once this has been done the speed of presentation will certainly be accelerated. So questions need to be addressed as to the importance of speed and the importance of the completeness and accuracy of the data presented.

Personal investigation

It is also suggested that, if possible, managers should seek out the information for themselves and so avoid altogether the clerical procedure of copying. Initialling the source material may also have additional merits: for example, managers visiting the wages office at weekly intervals to initial the wages that are under their control will save the clerical time, effort and possible error of resummarising such information on the budget statement. It may also ensure that, because of personal involvement in the data perusal process, the information is more closely studied and corrective action taken than if it were summarised on a form convenient for parking in the pending tray!

Frequency

This brings us to the second point to consider in 'budget communication': the frequency or timing of its presentation. When communicating budgets to managers timing is often vital. For example, if managers are told weeks or months after the event that something is going wrong regarding the expenditure or income over which they are responsible, the opportunity to take corrective action will be delayed, if not lost altogether.

It is therefore essential to look carefully at timing, to make sure that we are presenting budget/actual comparisons at a frequency which suits the managers concerned. It must also be noted that the right frequency for the policy-makers may not always be right for line managers or function heads. We must remember that once we take budgeting out of the boardroom, the managers most able to correct situations that have gone wrong or perpetuate those that have gone right, are very often in reverse order to their seniority. It is the individual who digs the hole too deep who will be able to make that hole the right depth next time – provided he or she is told, as soon as possible, the depth of the hole just dug! We must look at the lines of communication in progressing budgets and this line must be as short as possible.

The timing with which budgets are presented and progressed is central to the effectiveness of budgetary control. The rules of budgetary control communication are summarised in Illustration 10.12, which should form a checklist when considering the effectiveness of this technique within any business.

Illustration 10.12 Rules of budgetary control communication

Types of budget:	Purpose:
Policy-makers	To provide credibility of policy
Managers	Efficiency comparison

Two cardinal rules:	
Make sure comparison is	– Relevant to managers' sphere of influence
	– Possible to achieve

For successful communication examine:	
	– Form of communication
	– Speed or timing of communication
	– Frequency of communication

BUDGETING MYTHS

Having considered the rules of communication in budgetary control we now need to consider some of the myths which surround it as a technique.

Saves money?

The first myth claims that budgetary control saves money. This may indeed be true but it will depend very much upon the effectiveness of the system. If budgeting is not carefully introduced it can work in the opposite way. Indeed it may not save money at all, but inspire money to be spent on things which without budgetary control would never have been thought of or indeed missed. Budgetary control may well, in fact, become a technique which encourages managers to include more expenditure than is really necessary and less income than in fact they could achieve to avoid blame for failure to achieve targets. Always remember the behavioural aspect of budgeting!

One of the real problems of budgeting can be placing too much stress on the fact that unless budgets are achieved the manager will be subject to discipline. This can lead to managers over-insuring themselves by setting relatively easy budgets, and then making sure that they achieve only the budget figures agreed. It is therefore vital to avoid budgets being treated this way. Every item of expense and income must be looked at on its merits and rigidity should have no part to play in the system.

Flexible budgeting

However we organise and manage our business it is important to make sure that our budgets are flexible. In Illustration 10.13 you will see in the first column a budget based on one level of activity and therefore showing just one set of figures against which actuals would be compared. If we adopt a flexible budget approach, however, the budget figures would depend upon the level of activity that is actually attained. This 'flexible budget' approach is set out in the second column. Here it can be seen that if activity alters then the variable costs – in this case direct material, direct labour and the variable overheads – will be adjusted in line with that activity.

Illustration 10.13 Flexible budgeting

	Fixed		Flexible	
Budgeted activity	24,000 units		Actual activity	18,000
Budgeted costs on above level of activity during four-week period:			Budgeted costs on actual level of activity during four-week period:	
	£			£
Direct material	30,000			22,500
Direct labour	60,000			45,000
Variable overheads	12,000			9,000
Fixed overheads	10,000			10,000
	112,000			86,500

This flexible approach to budgeting will make it possible to adapt the budget to meet changing circumstances and so make it usable to compare with actuals irrespective of the activity achieved. To test your understanding of flexible budgets tackle the question in Illustration 10.14 and then compare your answer with Illustration 10.15. As you will find, your ability to answer will test your memory of the concepts of marginal costing which we discussed in chapter 7.

Illustration 10.14 Flexible budgeting exercise

X Ltd manufactures a product for which the activity levels in the assembly department vary widely from month to month. The following statement shows the departmental overhead budget based on average level of activity of 20,000 units production per four-week period.

	Budget average for four-week period £
Direct material	10,000
Direct labour	20,000
Variable overheads	5,000
Fixed overheads	7,500
Depreciation	2,500
	45,000
Production (units)	20,000

You are required to prepare a flexible four-week budget at levels of production of 16,000, 22,000 and 24,000 units.

Illustration 10.15 Answer to Illustration 10.14

Units of production	16,000	22,000	24,000
	£	£	£
Direct material	8,000	11,000	12,000
Direct labour	16,000	22,000	24,000
Variable overheads	4,000	5,500	6,000
Fixed overheads	7,500	7,500	7,500
Depreciation	2,500	2,500	2,500
	38,000	48,500	52,000

A unifying force?

The second problem of budgeting is that of making sure that it brings people together and does not split them asunder. This is the need to give managers a sense of control and responsibility for their own sphere of influence whilst at the same time recognising that they still fit into the business as a whole.

It must be understood by managers that transferring an expense from one budget to another does not eliminate or reduce the expense, it just puts it somewhere else ('duck-shove' budgeting as it might be called). There must also be a sense of oneness when it comes to capital expenditure budgets. Managers must appreciate that the firm as a whole makes the profit or obtains the cash flow, and to obtain these requires the right investments wherever appropriate. This means that if resources are scarce, they should be directed to those areas of investment which will bring the greatest benefit to the business as a whole. Capital expenditure must therefore always be subject to setting priorities, which may well cross functional barriers. A buyer's proposal to extend the warehouse may have to take second place to the retail shop manager's requirement for new fixtures and fittings, and so on.

Profit centres

In recent years there has been a tendency for managers to become more and more profit responsible. Indeed this has led in many cases to businesses organising their managers within what are sometimes termed profit centres: divisions of the business to which profits can be ascribed. Although this might be thought a most attractive concept, the reality can at times confound the benefits claimed for it. This is when the profit centre, for which a manager is made responsible, is apportioned expenditure and allocated income over which those responsible have little if any influence or control. Such manipulation can destroy the most noble of objectives. Indeed this inclination to provide 'names' and 'titles', within financial controls that sound 'progressive' and 'appropriate', has to be approached with caution and not a little suspicion, whether it occurs within budgetary control or elsewhere.

Profit centres can indeed serve a most useful purpose: a means by which management action can be related to profit measurement. However, it has to be truly measurable because if it is manipulated by means of predetermined expenditure apportionments or income allocations, much of the benefit of management involvement and commitment is lost.

It might also be said that the present development within organisations such as the NHS, the social services and local government of what are termed 'internal markets' bears some comparison with profit centres – and attracts similar criticism in that their success will lie in the extent to which a 'real' as opposed to a 'manipulated' market can be produced.

SUMMARY OF BUDGETARY CONTROL

Policy-makers' needs

Budgetary control is a system of comparison which is designed to serve two purposes: first, to assess the financial credibility of the policies of the business, and as such budgeting confined to the boardroom – to the policy-makers. Budgets around policy will be developed in the context of the business as a whole and it is natural that such budgets will not be confined to the immediate period ahead. They will be made in outline over three or even up to five years ahead. This is especially necessary in the case of capital expenditure, where budgets over the following five to ten years are often set out in outline and in some cases in considerable detail. This is necessary, for example, to provide the required manufacturing capacity or retail outlets to meet the sales and marketing plans for the years ahead.

It must be very carefully noted, however, that if we are to look forward, we must recognise that beyond a period of, say, twelve months, any attempt to be exact will be costly as well as, in all likelihood, inaccurate or inappropriate to situations as they transpire. It is therefore necessary to combine the desire to look ahead with a recognition of its clerical and managerial costs. Here, as so often with financial information, there is a need to strike a happy medium.

Management comparison

The second objective of budgeting, and a growing one, is to use it as a method of management comparison: to enable managers, within their own area of activity, to see the financial implications of what they are doing and to set these out in financial terms in a 'personal responsibility budget'. It is this area of personal comparison that creates the great behavioural problem of people not wishing to be personally compared. It is therefore necessary, when putting people into this position, to make every effort to ensure that they appreciate the need for and objectives of such comparison. This also implies that the relevance and the possibility of the targets or budgets set are very carefully explained and understood by those who need to work with them. Indeed, it might be claimed that without commercial awareness budgetary control becomes a highly dangerous technique in the hands of the modern manager.

Progressing budgets – form and frequency

Having understood this, it is equally necessary to make sure that the progressing of budgets is tailored to the needs and understanding of the different managers. This means that the form of budget presentation and its frequency should be carefully reviewed. The form and/or frequency that might be suitable for a board of directors will not necessarily be ideal for a chargehand, foreman, departmental supervisor or even a divisional manager. Their concern is with the variations: the differences between the budgeted and actual figures as and when they are presented. It is for this reason that they require a frequency of presentation which provides them with dates from which speedy corrective action can be taken. This is a subject which we address in some detail when we discuss standard costing in chapter 11.

Budgeting myths

Finally, we must be aware of the myths of budgeting. First, it will save money only if management understand and appreciate its purpose, and if budgets are being continually reviewed and revised – flexed – in the light of the current situation and activity.

Second, it will bring people together, to understand the business as a whole, only if positive steps are taken, steps that will ensure people see how budgets must interlink and intermix for the benefit of the enterprise as a whole.

Present trends

The recognition of the behavioural effects of trying to avoid comparison is well illustrated by the development in recent years of approaches to budgetary control which take them into account.

One example of this is the re-forecasting of budgets at monthly intervals. Comparisons can then be made not only against annual budgets (which may, through the year, become increasingly remote from reality) but also against revised forecasts, ones that will reflect any current changes in income and expense levels or investment needs.

Another development is that of zero-based budgeting. This technique assumes each budget starts from zero and requires that funds for each budgeted item of expense and investment be justified, and in some cases 'competed for' against other budget-holders.

All these developments are still very much in their initial stages but managers need to be aware of them to see whether or not they are proving effective. Whatever may be the verdict on any particular method of budgetary control, however, what is clear is that it is a developing and changing field of management study and requires constant attention and concern. Certainly at the present time the suggestion that 'many firms would save thousands if they abolished budgeting' could not in all cases be challenged.

Structure of budgetary control

Study carefully Illustration 10.16, which sets out the structure and interrelationships of budgetary control within a business. This text is not an appropriate place to discuss the formulation of policy or the consideration of alternative business plans and strategies. The policies or strategies of a business depend upon management as a whole, although clearly there will, in the short term, be limiting factors to the progress of the enterprise, for example the skills of the workforce or the production capacity of its fixed assets. However, within the context of such limiting factors there will be what might be termed a principal budget factor, which in most cases will be sales – what the business can sell. (Those who wish to study how business policy is formed together with the strategies and limiting factors should refer to more specialised management texts.)

However, a review of Illustration 10.16 will provide an overview of the steps required in building up budgetary control within a business. Study this illustration with particular reference to the way each individual budget prepared by each manager links into the final presentation of the master budget in the form of a budgeted profit and loss account, balance sheet and cash flow forecast.

Once you have completed this review we proceed in the next chapter to examine the second financial comparative technique: standard costing.

Illustration 10.16 Budgetary control: structure and interrelationships

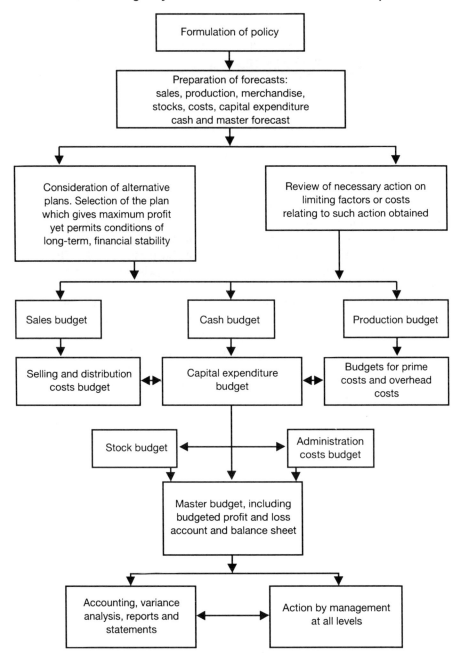

11

STANDARD COSTING

INTRODUCTION

This chapter deals with the second financial technique concerned with comparison: standard costing. Standard costing is not, as might be thought from its name, a different form of costing, but a means of comparison designed to meet the frustration managers can feel when faced with a comparison between actual and budgeted cost or income. The difference revealed will, in most cases, need to be further analysed before corrective action can be taken.

THE ANALYSIS OF DIFFERENCE

To illustrate this point turn to Illustration 11.1, which sets out the actual cost and sale price of a product compared with its budgeted cost and sale price. We also see that there is a third column which sets out differences under each of the four main heads of material, labour and expenses – both direct and indirect – and sales. It is this difference column that can cause the frustration standard costing is designed to tackle.

Illustration 11.1 Standard costing

Product costs (pence)	Actual	Budget	Difference
Direct material	5	4	+1
Direct labour	4	6	−2
Direct expenses	3	4	−1
	12	14	−2
Indirect expenses	6	7	−1
Total cost	18	21	−3
Profit	4	4	0
Sale price	22	25	−3

Material

For example, in the case of material, what exactly makes up this difference? How much is because the price of the material has changed and how much because the usage of material has increased?

Labour

This is equally true in the case of labour. How much of the difference is due to the rate of pay changing from the budgeted rate, and how much to the efficiency of the labour? Have they done the job more quickly or more slowly than the budgeted time?

Direct expenditure

In the case of direct expenditure the difference will have only one cause: that the expense actually involved is more or less than that budgeted. Direct expenditure, as we defined it in Chapter 6, on full costing, is expenditure which is directly related to the unit of cost in which it is included. Examples include a royalty payable to an author on the sale of a book or the fees payable to a solicitor in respect of litigation carried out for a client.

Indirect expenditure

However, the need for further analysis of differences will certainly apply in the case of indirect expenditure. How much of the difference between the actual and the budgeted indirect expenditure on such things as rent, insurance, light and heat, and salaries is a result of the expenditure itself going up or down, and how much has been caused by the activity of the business?

ACTIVITY VARIANCE

To understand the problem of activity turn to Illustration 11.2 and see how the indirect expenses – or overheads – are arrived at in a cost. You will notice that the budgeted overhead rate of recovery set is based upon a particular expenditure – in this case £5,000,000 – and a particular level of activity forecast – in this case 10,000,000 production hours. This therefore means that failing to achieve this budgeted expenditure could be due to either the expenditure incurred or the activity achieved differing from that set. If rents have gone up, for instance, or administrative salaries have changed, this will obviously be one of the reasons that the actual expenditure will differ from that budgeted.

Illustration 11.2 Indirect expense recovery calculation

Budgeted indirect costs for period	£5,000,000
Budget activity measured in production hours	10,000,000 hours
Budgeted indirect recovery rate	£5,000,000
	10,000,000
= 50p per hour	

However, we also have the problem of activity. If we do not achieve – as in this illustration – 10 million hours of production we will not recover these expenses at the budgeted rate of recovery. The 50p per hour recovery rate will prove inadequate for this purpose. Let us assume, for example, that the actual activity achieved measured only 8 million production hours: we would recover only £4 million – 8,000,000 hours x 50p per hour. Further, it is unlikely that the overheads would come down in sympathy with this fall in activity. After all, as we explained in chapters 6 and 7 on full and marginal costing, most overheads or indirect expenses are fixed. They continue whether or not the forecast activity is achieved. Thus, if only 8,000,000 production hours were actually achieved, there would be an under-recovery of £1 million against both and budgeted expenditure. The cause would not be any additional expenditure but the failure to achieve the budgeted activity.

SALES VARIANCES

The same type of problem, with different reasons for variances, arises with sales. In fact the difference between actual and budgeted sales can have as many as three causes: sales may not have been made at the unit price set in the budget; we may not have reached the volume of sales planned in the budget; or, third, the cause could be a failure to sell in the mix we had budgeted.

PRICE, VOLUME AND USAGE VARIANCES

The problems of price and usage and how the differences are calculated can be seen, in the case of materials, in Illustration 11.3, for labour as regards rate of pay and efficiency in Illustration 11.4, and for sales as regards price and volume in Illustration 11.5. These should be studied so that you can follow both the arithmetic and the use which can be made of this data. For instance, in Illustration 11.3 we see that a net variance of only 75p is made up of an unfavourable price variance – possibly outside the control of the purchaser – and a favourable usage variance. The latter variance may well have been caused by the action of the users and, if so, this should be encouraged and if possible continued.

Illustration 11.3 Material cost variances: usage and price

Material budget for unit made up as follows:
    Budget usage   = 10 kg
    Price per kg   = £8
Budgeted material cost per unit:
    = 10 kg x £8   = £80
Actual material cost per unit as follows:
    Actual usage   = 9.5 kg
    Price per kg   = £8.50
Actual material cost per unit:
    = 9.5 kg x £8.50   = £80.75
Net variance per unit (unfavourable) 75p

Made up of:
    Usage variance = (10 kg – 9.5 kg) x 8   = £4.00 Favourable
    Price variance = 9.5 kg x (£8 – £8.50)   = £4.75 Unfavourable
    Net variance per unit (unfavourable)   £0.75

Conversely, in the case of labour the unfavourable efficiency variance revealed in Illustration 11.4 calls for further investigation as to its cause and, if possible, correction.

Illustration 11.4 Labour and cost variances: efficiency and rate

Standard labour cost per unit made up as follows:
Standard labour hours per unit	= 9
Standard rate of pay	= £10 per hour
Therefore standard labour cost per unit	= £90 (9 hrs x £10 per hr)

Actual labour cost per unit made up as follows:
Actual labour hours per unit	= 9.5
Actual rate of pay	= £9.50 per hour
Therefore actual labour cost per unit	= £90.25

Net variance = 25p (unfavourable)
Made up of:
    Efficiency variance = (9 hrs – 9.5 hrs) x £10 per hour = £5.00 Unfavourable
    Rate of pay variance = 9.5 hrs x
        (£10 per hr – £9.50 per hr)   = £4.75 Favourable
    Net variance per unit (unfavourable)   £0.25

SALES MIX VARIANCE

In illustration 7.14 we discussed the sales mix in the context of marginal costing This is shown here as Illustration 11.6 and you will see that, whereas the budgeted sales mix would have given a contribution of 44p per £1 sold, the actual sales mix produces a contribution of only 18p per £1 sold. The difference of 26p between the actual and the budgeted sales mix is not caused by the volume of sales or the sale prices, but by the sales mix. To refresh your knowledge of this topic, refer back to chapter 7 (on marginal costing) and go through it again, very carefully.

Illustration 11.5 Sales variances: volume and price

A Ltd sets its sales budget for the year based on the following facts:
    Standard volume of sales = 10,000 units
    Standard price per unit = £100
Therefore sales budget = 10,000 x £100 per unit = £1,000,000
Actual sales achieved for year:
    Actual volume of sales = 10,500 units
    Actual price per unit   = £90
Therefore actual sales for year = 10,500 units x £90 per unit = £945,000
Total variance = (£1,000,000 – £945,000) = £55,000 (unfavourable)
Made up of:
    Volume variance = (10,000 units – 10,500 units) x £100 =   £50,000 Favourable
    Price variance = 10,500 units x (£100 – £90) £10   = £105,000 Unfavourable
Net variance unfavourable   £55,000

Illustration 11.6 Sales mix example

Products	Sales price	Variable cost	Contribution	Contribution to sales price	Budgeted sales %	mix C/SP	Actual sales %	mix C/SP
	(pence)	(pence)	(pence)	(pence)		(pence)		(pence)
A	10	5	5	0.50	80	0.40	10	0.05
B	15	10	5	0.33	10	0.03	10	0.03
C	8	7	1	0.125	10	0.01	80	0.10
						0.44		0.18

Fixed costs: Budget – £880,000 ÷ 0.44; Actual £880,000 ÷ 0.18
Sales value to breakeven: Budget £2 million; Actual 4.9 million (approx)
Mix variance: 44p less 18p per £1 sales = 26p

STANDARD COSTING

We have now seen that the difference between the actual and the budgeted cost of a unit could be caused by a number of different things. It should also be understood that managers wishing to manage and control their businesses effectively need to know of these differences as soon as they occur, so they can take effective corrective action. To meet this requirement the system known as standard costing has been designed.

Standard costing is a system of comparison which not only brings out the difference between actual and forecast figures but, as we have seen, analyses such differences into their causes. Differences analysed in this way are often referred to as variances. It is therefore the prime purpose of standard costing to produce those variances for management, to help them to manage more effectively.

To illustrate this point, turn to Illustration 11.7, which sets out an actual compared with a standard cost. From this information you will see that the variances are brought out for the use and understanding of management.

Illustration 11.7 Highlighting the variance between actual and standard costs

	Actual cost (pence)	Standard cost (pence)	Variance (pence)
Direct material	10	8	–2 price
			+4 usage
Direct labour	8	9	–2 rate of pay
			+1 efficiency
Variable expenses	4	3	+1 expense
Indirect expenses	6	4	+3 expense
			–1 activity

MANAGERIAL REQUIREMENTS FROM STANDARD COSTING

Having seen the purpose of standard costing let us look at it from a management point of view – in other words, ask ourselves: what is the essential requirement a manager seeks from this technique? And the answer to this question lies, once again, in the credibility that can be attached to the information disclosed. In other words, if we are to go to all the effort required to produce this detailed variance information, it is essential that the information is usable, and to make standard costing usable it must possess three essentials features.

Accuracy of data

The first feature which standard costing must possess is that the actual cost data must be as accurate as possible. After all, if managers looking at variances distrust the actual information upon which they have been calculated they will take very little action, and it is the extent of the action taken which makes the system of any real value to the manager. It is therefore an essential prerequisite of any standard costing system that the actual costs presented are believed, so that the resulting information will be used.

For this reason great care must be taken to ensure that the systems of labour, material and overhead cost control and recording are satisfactory before any system of standard costing is introduced.

Credibility of standards

However, having ensured that this first requirement is met there is still the second: to make sure that the standards available for comparison are recognised, understood and believed by the managers who act upon them. After all, just as the system becomes valueless if the actual data is not believed, so in exactly the same way, if the standards themselves are not believed managers will be reluctant, to say the least, to act on the information produced.

To be told that there is a variance between the actual and the standard usage of materials set and to disbelieve the standard used will again lead to the particular variance being ignored. To provide an effective system of standard costing, therefore, standards will have to be set in the best possible way. For this reason it is often found that before a standard costing system can be effectively introduced work study will have to be applied to ensure that standard times are agreed for the different labour operations.

For the same reason it may also be necessary to introduce production control to produce standard usages for materials which can be believed by those concerned with its control. This would apply equally to pilferage or waste details in respect of a retail business. And it will also be necessary for all those concerned with sales and marketing to agree sales standards – for example sale prices, volumes and mixes.

These then are the first two requirements for a successful system of standard costing – that the actual costs achieved and the standards set for them are believed so that differences or variances between them will be acted upon.

Liability of variances

However, we still have the third and possibly the most important prerequisite that the variances are geographically located into recognisable areas so that corrective action *can* be taken. This requirement affects standard costing in three areas: the usage of materials, the efficiency of labour, and the volume and mix of sales.

Materials usage

To illustrate this point let us review each of these areas in turn, beginning with the usage of materials. Let us take as an example a production manager responsible for the manufacture of a product that passes through several different processes. If the manager is told that the usage of material is, say, 10 per cent greater than the standard laid down, this is only of academic interest. Unless it can be located to a precise process or operation, no positive action can be taken.

In other words, to be told that you are wasting 10 per cent of your material but to know that this is occurring over, say, two, three or even more processes provides no help if you wish to correct the situation. You have no idea from this where you should be directing your attention.

Labour

Again, we need to know, so far as the efficiency of labour is concerned, which particular group of labour is spending more or less time than is set out in the standard. Suppose, again, you as a manager are told that the efficiency of your labour is better than the standard by, say, two hours. This may well be interesting, even gratifying, but unless you know which area of your labour is saving this time, you can take no effective action to ensure that it continues in the future.

Sales

And third, in the area of sales, once again it is essential to know where the differences are happening. To know that you have in fact improved the volume of sales or that the mix achieved gives you a lower contribution than you would have had if you had stayed within the standard mix does not help you to control your salesforce. No corrective action can be taken until the differences are more precisely located. Is it happening in this or that product area? Is it taking place in this sales division or that? Can we trace the difference to a particular salesperson? These are the essential questions which must be answered by standard costing in the sales area.

Purpose of standard costing

Standard costing is very much a technique designed to serve the needs of the line manager.The criterion by which it must be judged is, simply: does it enable managers to locate the cause of the differences or variances more quickly, and if so what effective corrective action can they take? The acid test of standard costing is therefore the positive action it generates. You will see in Illustration 11.8 a series of examples of variances which can be extracted to assist managers manage more effectively under each of the main cost and income heads.

Illustration 11.8 Examples of variances

Cost:	Variance:
Material	Price
	Usage
Labour	Rate of pay
	Efficiency
Expenditure:	
Variable	Expenditure
Fixed	Activity
	Expenditure
Sales	Price
	Volume
	Mix

VARIANCE CALCULATION

Turn now to to Illustrations 11.9 and 11.10 and work through the calculations of the variances under each category of expense and sales, remembering to question the meaning of each variance from a management viewpoint. Once you have mastered these, test your understanding by tackling a similar question set out in Illustration 11.11. Your answers should then be compared with Illustration 11.12.

Illustration 11.9 Standard costing variance data

Calculate the variances which arise from the following data:

Standard product cost for 1 unit

	£
Materials: 30 kg @ 15p/kg	4.50
Labour: 4 hrs @ £1/hr	4.00
Expenses:	
Variable 0.50	
Fixed (recovered at 25p/labour hour)	1.00
Standard product cost	10.00
Standard profit	2.00
Standard sale price	12.00

Budgeted sales for the month are 10,000 units, giving rise to a budgeted profit of £20,000.

The actual results for the month were:

			£
Sales:	9,500 units		118,750
Less:			
Materials:	300,000 kg @ 14p/kg	42,000	
Labour:	40,000 hrs @ £1.10	44,000	
Expenses			
Variable		4,800	
Fixed		11,200	102,000
Actual profit			16,750

Note: There are no stocks.

Illustration 11.10 Standard costing variance analysis

				£
Budgeted profit				
				20,000
Variances		Favourable	Adverse	
		£	£	
(a) Sales	– Price	4,750		
	– Volume		1,000	
(b) Materials	– Price	3,000		
	– Usage		2,250	
(c) Labour	– Rate		4,000	
	– Efficiency		2,000	
Expenses:				
(d) Variable	– Expenditure		50	
(e) Fixed	– Volume		500	
	– Expenditure		1,200	
		7,750	11,000	3,250
Actual profit				16,750

Workings:
(a) Sales – Price: 9,500 units x £12 – £118,750
– Volume: (10,000 – 9,500) x £2 Profit
(b) Materials – Price: (15p – 14p) x 300,000 kg
– Usage: (9,500 x 30 kg) – 300,000 kg x 15p
(c) Labour – Rate: (£1.00 – £1.10) x 40,000 hrs
– Efficiency: (9,500 x 4 hrs) – 40,000 hrs x £1
(d) Fixed – Volume: (40,000 hrs x 25p) – (9,500 x 4 hrs x 25p)
– Expenditure: (10,000 units x £1) – £11,200

Illustration 11.11 Standard costing variance analysis exercise

Calculate the variances which arise from the following data:

Standard product cost per unit

		£
Materials:	40 kg @ 20p/kg	8.00
Labour:	3 hrs @ £5/hr	15.00
Expenses:		
Variable		0.75
Fixed (recovered at £2 per hr)		6.00
Standard product cost		29.75
Standard profit		16.00
Standard sale price		45.75
Budgeted sales for the month are 30,000 units		

Actual results for the month are:		£	
Sales:	32,000 units		1,408,000
Materials:	1,400,000 kg @ 18p/kg	252,000	
Labour:	88,000 hrs @ £5.10/hr	448,800	
Expenses:			
Variable		25,600	
Fixed		192,000	918,400
Actual profit			489,600

Illustration 11.12 Answers to Illustration 11.11

			Favourable £	Adverse £	£
Budgeted profit (30,000 units x £16 per unit)					480,000
Variances					
(a)	Sales	– Price		56,000	
		– Volume	32,000		
(b)	Material	– Price	28,000		
		– Usage		24,000	
(c)	Labour	– Rate		8,800	
		– Efficiency	40,000		
Expenses:					
(d)	Variable	– Expenditure		1,600	
(e)	Fixed	– Volume	12,000		
		– Expenditure		12,000	
			112,000	102,400	9,600
	Actual profit				489,600

Workings:

(a) Sales:

Price	£1,408,000 – (32,000 units x £45.75 per unit)	= £56,000 (unfavourable)
Volume	2,000 units x £16.00 per unit	= £32,000 (favourable)

(b) Material:

Price	(20p – 18p) x 1,400,000 kg	= £28,000 (favourable)
Usage:	32,000 x 40 kg = 1,280,000 – 1,400,000 x 20p	= £24,000 (unfavourable)

(c) Labour:

Rate:	(£5.10p – £5) x 88,000 hrs	= £8,800 (unfavourable)
Efficiency	(32,000 x 3) – 88,000 x £5	= £40,000 (favourable)

(d) Variable expenses:

Expenditure variance	(32,000 x 0.75p) – £25,600	= £1,600 (unfavourable)

(e) Fixed expenditure variance:

Volume	(90,000 hrs (= 30,000 units x 3 hrs) x £2) – (32,000 units x £6 per unit)	= £12,000 (favourable)
Expenditure	(30,000 units x £6) – £192,000	= £12,000 (unfavourable)

STANDARD STOCK VALUATION

It should also be noted that standard costing can be used not only to establish standard costs for the products and services as a whole within a business but also in calculating the standard cost values of stocks in different stages of production. This application of standard costing is set out in Illustrations 11.13 and 11.14 and should be studied carefully. Then test your knowledge by tackling the question set out in Illustration 11.15, comparing your answer with Illustration 11.16.

Illustration 11.13 Standard cost values for stocks exercise

Given the following standard costs, calculate the value of stock held at the end of each stage of production and for finished goods, assuming Stage II completes the production cycle.

Production Stage I
Standard cost of production

Type of material	Standard quantity	Standard price per kg
X	20 kg	20p
Y	10 kg	10p
Z	5 kg	30p

Labour: 4 standard minutes at 25p per standard minute
Overheads: charged at 25p standard labour minute

Production Stage II
Standard cost of production

Type of material	Standard quantity	Standard price per kg
A	5 kg	10p
B	10 kg	10p

Labour: 8 standard minutes at 25p per standard minute
Overheads: charged at 10p per standard labour minute

Final production stage
Standard costing of packing

Materials: standard packing cost 20p
Labour: 2 standard minutes at 50p per standard minute
Overheads: charged at 50p per standard labour minute

Illustration 11.14 Answers to Illustration 11.13

Production Stage I	£	£	
Materials: X 20 kg @ 20p	4.00		
Y 10 kg @ 10p	1.00		
Z 5 kg @ 30p	1.50	6.50	
Labour: 4 minutes @ 25p		1.00	
Overheads: 25p per labour minute		1.00	
		8.50	Standard value Stage I

Production Stage II	£	£	
Materials: A 5 kg @ 10p	0.50		
B 10 kg @ 10p	1.00	1.50	
Labour: 8 minutes @ 25p		2.00	
Overheads: 10p per labour minute		0.80	
		12.80	Standard value Stage II

Final production stage	£	
Materials: 1 standard packing cost @ 20p	0.20	
Labour: 2 minutes @ 50p	1.00	
Overheads: 50p per labour hour	1.00	
	15.00	Standard value Final Stage

Illustration 11.15 Standard cost values for work in progress and finished goods

Assume the following standard cost data and from this calculate the value of work in progress at the end of Production Stage 1 and finished goods stock at the end of the finished process.

Production Stage 1
Standard cost of production:

Type of material	Standard quantity (tonnes)	Standard price per tonne £
C	10	10
D	8	12
E	4	15

Labour mix	Standard times of labour (hours)	Standard rate per hour £
F	2	5
G	1	6
H	3	4

Overheads: charged at 40p per standard labour hour

Finishing stage:

	Standard quantity	Standard price
Packing material:	1 packing case	£4.00
	1 plastic bag	£1.50

Labour: 0.5 standard hours at £4 per hour
Overheads: charged at £2 per standard labour hour

Illustration 11.16 Answers to Illustration 11.15

Production Stage 1:

	Type	Tonne	£	£
Materials:	C	10 @ £10	100.00	
	D	8 @ £12	96.00	
	E	4 @ £15	60.00	256.00
Labour:	F	2hrs @ £5	10.00	
	G	1 hr @ £6	6.00	
	H	3 hrs @ £4	12.00	28.00
Overheads: 40p x 6 hrs				2.40
Standard value of work in progress per unit at end of Stage 1				286.40

Finishing Stage	£	
Packing materials: Packing case	4.00	
Plastic bag	1.50	5.50
Labour: 0.5 hrs @ £4 per hour		2.00
Overheads: charged £2 x 0.5 hours		1.00
Standard value of finished goods per unit		294.90

STANDARD COST PROFIT AND LOSS ACCOUNT

Finally, turn to Illustration 11.17, which sets out how, once standards and budgets have been established for a business, they can be used to prepare a standard cost profit and loss account. The illustration shows that this account can then be compared with the actual profit and loss account results once they are known, so that the variances can be reviewed in detail and in total.

Illustration 11.17 Standard costing profit and loss account

			£000
Budgeted sales			400
Less: Volume variance			10
Standard sales value of actual sales in standard mix			390
Less: Standard cost of such standard sales			240
Standard net profit of such standard sales			150

		Adverse (–) £000	Favourable (+) £000
Variances			
Sales:	Price	5	
	Mix	2	
Materials:	Price	3	
	Usage		2
Labour:	Rate	1	
	Efficiency		1
Variable expenses:			
Expenditure			1

Fixed expenses:			
Expenditure		1	
Activity	2	–	8
Actual net profit			142

SUMMARY

Standard costing is the second of the two comparative techniques used in business finance. The first is concerned with the overall comparison of the budget set for the business as a whole, divided as required into its individual functions and departments, with the actual results as and when they are known, and is referred to as budgetary control.

The second is concerned with the analysis of the variances: the differences between the budgeted and actual cost/income. The technique of tracing them to their causes so that effective corrective action can be taken speedily and effectively is known as standard costing.

CONCLUSION

We have now completed our study of the evolution of financial information, starting from the three primary financial measurements: profit, in the profit and loss account; investment, in the balance sheet; and cash, in the cash flow forecast. We have seen that from these have been developed the techniques of *costing,* which helps us to analyse where the profit or loss is being made, *project appraisal,* which helps us to examine, before committing ourselves to investments in fixed assets and other areas, where money will be tied up – whether or not the investment is worthwhile and will lead to business profit – and *working capital control,* which helps us to analyse time and therefore minimise the amount invested in this area.

We also saw, when we examined the cash flow forecast, how out of this statement information can be summarised so as to express the central problem regarding cash as a whole within any business: are the sources equal to or less than the applications of such cash? In other words, is the business living within or beyond its means? – expressed in a summary termed the cash flow statement.

Finally, we have just completed our study of the comparative techniques of budgetary control and standard costing.

We are now ready to complete our understanding of business finance by studying the approach to and the techniques available for interpreting the information presented.

12

THE INTERPRETATION OF FINANCIAL INFORMATION

INTRODUCTION

We now come to the final step we must take in understanding business finance, possibly the step everyone would like to take at the very beginning – the interpretation of financial information. As was said in the very first chapter, however, financial information does not provide answers, only better questions, and these in turn presuppose knowledge. It is for this reason that interpretation must wait until the end. We have to know and understand what is available, and from where, and from this draw logical conclusions – and, in many instances, pose further questions. This process is known as the interpretation of financial information.

In other words, there is no simple procedure that enables anyone to interpret. It is the result of all the knowledge that has been gained along the way in understanding the information presented and the techniques available to help us do this. There are in fact three steps, set out in Illustration 12.1, which must be taken by anyone wishing to interpret financial information, each of which we will discuss in turn.

Illustration 12.1 Steps in interpreting financial data

Step 1: The data must be **understood**

Step 2: The data must be **organised** using: – a study of cash movement as revealed in the cash flow statement
– full and marginal cost, breakeven and contribution analysis, etc.
– an analysis of profit and investment by means of the added value statement
– current cost accounting adjustments.

Step 3: The data must be **measured** using: – applied common sense
– ratio analysis

Only then can data be **interpreted**.

STEP 1: DATA MUST BE UNDERSTOOD

The first step is to understand what we are looking at – what is available. What can never be over-stressed is that there is no possibility of interpreting information unless we fully understand it. It is indeed this failure to understand financial data which so often creates an inability to interpret its content – and this means a *complete* understanding. It is impossible to interpret financial data if it is only partly understood. For instance, if we understand only part of the balance sheet we will never be able to interpret it. Or if we understand only a portion of the costing data presented we will never be able to interpret and therefore use its contents – or if we do the consequences could be very dangerous indeed.

At the same time, unless you approach financial information with total honesty as to the extent of your knowledge, you will be unable to use it effectively. And what is meant by honesty in this context is whether or not there is an understanding of everything that is presented. If you have the slightest feeling that there are terms or facts presented in the data which are beyond your understanding, questions must be raised and answers sought.

It must always be remembered that there is a basic problem with financial understanding: people do not wish to admit to ignorance. Indeed they are often inclined to hide this from others and in many cases this deception can be highly dangerous – and certainly counterproductive so far as interpretation is concerned. In finance it is essential that you understand everything presented to you, and appreciate that even the simplest terms may require fresh definitions to overcome any confusion.

Throughout our earlier discussions on finance we have mentioned the fact that many areas of confusion are caused by inconsistencies and duplications in the meaning and use of terms. You might call it duplicate and in some cases even triplicate jargon! Consider, the confusion over the terms 'fixed assets' and 'capital expenditure', which as you now know mean the same thing. And sales are often described as turnover, or in some industries revenues, meaning the sales made during a period of time whether paid for or not.

We must also appreciate that within any particular business there may well be 'domestic' jargon, terms which are not used in their usually accepted way. We must also realise that there are very few legal definitions of financial terms and for this reason a clear definition must be sought whenever there is doubt. Indeed, the main purpose of many of the earlier chapters was to create the necessary confidence to ask questions when in doubt.

STEP 2 : ORGANISE DATA

Having understood what you are looking at, the next step in interpretation is to make sure the data is properly organised. In other words, before anyone can interpret information it is vital that the information itself is sorted out.

For instance, if you turn to Illustration 12.2 you will see a profit and loss account for a manufacturing business for this year compared with last. If you look at the illustration you will see that before the reorganisation of the data very strange conclusions could be drawn. For instance, it would look very much as though the expenses as a percentage of sales had fallen from 17.5 to 15.0 per cent. However, if we rearrange the information (as in Illustration 12.3) and divide the expenses between those which are variable and those which are fixed, we find that variable expenses have in fact gone up to 5 per cent of sales, whereas if they had been truly variable they should have remained constant at 3.5 per cent.

Illustration 12.2 'A' Manufacturing Co.: profit and loss accounts for years 1 and 2

	Year 2 £000	£000	%	£000	Year 1 £000	%
Sales		5,000	100		3,200	100.0
Less:						
Materials	2,500		50	1,600		50.0
Labour	1,250		25	800		25.0
Expenses	750	4,500	15	560	2,960	17.5
Profit		500	10		240	7.5

Illustration 12.3 'A' Manufacturing Co.: rearranged profit and loss accounts for years 1 and 2

	Year 2 £000	£000	%	£000	Year 1 £000	%
Sales		5,000	100		3,200	100.0
Less:						
Materials	2,500		50	1,600		50.0
Labour	1,250		25	800		25.0
Variable expenses	250	4,000	5	112	2,512	3.5
Contribution		1,000	20		688	21.5
Fixed expenses		500	10		448	14.0
Profit		500	10		240	7.5

We can also see that the fixed expenses have certainly not remained fixed as they have gone up from £448,000 to £500,000. This may be explainable, but the fact that the percentage comparison (from 14 to 10) suggests that fixed expenses are being well controlled is a false conclusion. If this point escapes you refer back to your studies of the profit and loss account in chapter 2 and those on marginal costing in chapter 7.

Indeed much of what we learned in chapter 7 is relevant to the interpretation of financial data as it applies to the examination of profitability. Contribution per limiting factor and breakeven are both means of analysis which provide valuable further questions and a recognition of how these can be used in the interpretation of data is vital to any examination of a profit and loss account.

All this illustrates the fact that before we organise such information so that, for example, variable and fixed expenses can be identified we might well draw wrong conclusions.

THE CASH FLOW STATEMENT

We have many techniques for organising information. For instance, the presentation of changes in investments and their funding set out in the cash flow statement is very much for the purpose of organising the data so that we can obtain greater meaning.

To illustrate this point look at Illustration 12.4, which shows the balance sheet of a company B Ltd. This sets out this year's and last year's. If you then turn to Illustration 12.5 you will see that the differences between these figures are set out as a cash flow statement.

Illustration 12.4 B Ltd: balance sheet as at 31 December

Last year £	Last year £		This year £	This year £
		Fixed assets		
	120,000	Land and buildings	170,000	
210,000	90,000	Plant and machinery	110,000	280,000
170,000		Investments		160,000
		Working capital		
		Current assets:		
	90,000	Stock	150,000	
	120,000	Debtors	160,000	
	40,000	Cash/bank	20,000	
	250,000		330,000	
		Less:		
		Current liabilities:		
150,000	100,000	Creditors	130,000	200,000
530,000				640,000
		Financed by:		
300,000		Share capital		350,000
160,000		Profit and loss account		200,000
70,000		Loans		90,000
530,000				640,000

Note: Depreciation on plant and machinery for the year is £50,000.

Illustration 12.5 B Ltd: cash flow statement

Source of funds			£
Retained profit			40,000
Add back: Depreciation			50,000
			90,000
Share capital			50,000
Loan capital			20,000
Sale of investments			10,000
		Subtotal A	170,000

Application of funds			£
Purchase of fixed assets			
Land and buildings			50,000
Plant and machinery			70,000
			120,000

Movement in working capital:

	Source £	Application £	
Stock		60,000	
Debtors		40,000	
Creditors	30,000		
	30,000	100,000	70,000
	Subtotal B		190,000
	Negative cash flow		£20,000 (A – B)

This reorganisation of the balance sheet allows us to see that during the present year the business has raised cash for investment amounting to £170,000 from the following sources: from internal sources (its operations, including retained profits, plus depreciation) £90,000; and, from external sources, a new issue of share capital plus new borrowings together amounting to £70,000 and £10,000 from the sale of investments – a total of £80,000. We can also see how this money was invested in fixed assets (£120,000) and working capital (£70,000), a total of £190,000. This means that part of this increase in investment has been paid for by reducing the company's bank and cash balances by £20,000, referred to as a negative cash flow. This therefore explains the reduction in the cash balances in the balance sheet from £40,000 to £20,000.

We can also see from this that the amount of money invested in such areas as plant and machinery, office equipment, motor vehicles, etc., does not bear any relationship to the amount held back as depreciation. This in itself may not be a very important point but if we could see this analysis over the years, it might well raise questions as to whether or not the business is keeping up with the investment required in such items. After all, as depreciation is based on the historical values of the fixed assets, you would expect the amount invested in such things to be more: that the amount invested would in fact exceed depreciation over the long term to take into account new technology, expansion and inflationary price adjustments.

We can also see from the cash flow statement in Illustration 12.5 the increase in the amount being invested in working capital. Here again, because of the reorganisation of this information, it becomes clear to us that increasing amounts are being put into stocks and debtors and also that the business is being financed to some extent by increasing its creditors, the time it takes to pay its bills.

Again, this in itself is not conclusive evidence of things going right or wrong but it does lead us to further questions. For instance, were these increases in the working capital investment planned? Did we intend to invest all this money in these areas, or is it accidental? Again, is it to do with inflation, or with increased sales volumes? After all, if sales increase a business may well have to hold more stocks and finance more debtors or receivables. Inflation may also create a need for more investment as we shall see later in this chapter. All these are questions that can be raised once we reorganise the information in this way.

However, as well as examining where the money has come from and how these funds have been invested, the cash flow statement tells us more: whether the business has lived within or beyond its means. In Illustration 12.5 the business has created funds of £90,000 from its own operations (profit plus depreciation), and £80,000 from share issues, loans and the sale of investments, a total of £170,000. However, it has invested £190,000: £120,000 in fixed assets and £70,000 in working capital. So it has 'lived beyond its means' to the tune of £20,000 and this is reflected in its cash and bank balances being reduced by that amount.

There may of course be nothing wrong in this but it certainly calls for questions about the effect of this reduction in liquid funds within the business. Again, if the reverse situation arose and the business invested less than the funds created the question would be: what is it doing with the surplus funds?

Organising information does not of course give us answers but it does raise more searching questions. We must therefore realise that it is vital to organise information before interpretation can successfully take place.

THE ADDED VALUE LINK

At this stage we could also look at the reorganisation of information in the form of the link between the creation of wealth and its distribution set out in the profit and loss account, and its investment set out in the balance sheet.

This can be done by re-summarising the profit and loss account in the form of an added value statement. If you turn to Illustration 12.6 you will see an example of one in which the added value is calculated at £60,000 – the difference between the sales for the year of £100,000, and the input or 'outsiders' costs of materials and bought-in services such as rent, heat and light, insurance, etc., amounting to £40,000, which have gone into the cost of the goods we have sold.

Illustration 12.6 G Ltd: added value statement for year ended 31 December

	£000	
Sales	100	
Less:		
Materials and bought-in services	40	
Added value	60	
Distribution of added value:		
Employee costs	20	
Dividends	10	} Needs of today
Interest	5	
Taxation	10	
Depreciation	5	} Needs of tomorrow
Retained profits	10	
	60	
Amount available for reinvestment:		
Retained profits	10	
Depreciation	5	{ For reinvestment
	15	{ in fixed assets
		{ and working capital

Analysis of added value

We then see that of this £60,000 added value, £20,000 has gone into the wages and salaries due to the people employed within the business, that £15m has been set aside as interest and dividends on the money invested by shareholders and lenders, and £10,000 is being deducted for taxation on the profits.

We can therefore see from this summary that the amount of money generated within the business during the year for reinvestment in fixed assets, working capital and outside investments, or left to increase the cash and bank balances, is £15,000. This is created by £5,000 deducted as depreciation plus £10,000 retained profits.

This add-back of depreciation, you will remember, is caused by the fact that although depreciation reduces the profit or increases the loss shown in the profit and loss account it does not affect the cash held or owed by the business. Indeed the purpose of depreciation, as you will remember from chapter 2, is to reduce the amount that otherwise could be distributed as dividends (taken out of the business to reward the owners), which amount is limited to the profit shown less taxation. It is because depreciation does not reduce the cash held that the funds created for investment, when profits are made, are the total of profits retained plus the depreciation deducted before calculating such profits.

From the added value statement we can examine the amount of funds the business has generated for reinvestment and see how it compares with previous years. We can also examine the proportion which has been paid out as 'rewards' (dividends to shareholders), as wages and salaries to employees, or as taxes to the government.

All this can be seen in relation to the total added value created and can be compared from year to year. For instance, in Illustration 12.6 wages and salaries are one third of the added value and this could be compared with previous years. The added value can indeed be said to be what the business creates for itself as it represents the difference between what it sells its products, merchandise or services for and what the input costs of these were.

Added value is sometimes used as a measurement of efficiency by comparing the added value per £1 of wages and salaries or per number of employees. In Illustration 12.6 this reads £3 of added value per £1 of employees' costs (£60,000 divided by £20,000), which if set against a budget of, say, £2.75 would show an improvement. However, if the added value were divided by the numbers employed, and assuming the budget was based on £1,500 per employee, then if the actual number of employees for the year was 55, the added value per employee would be approximately £1,100 – a deterioration from budget. This latter comparison has advantages over the former when technology allows the numbers employed to be reduced while wages per employee increase. Both these measurements can be usefully compared from one period to another so that the trend can be examined.

At the same time we can see from the added value statement the relationship between the amount invested in fixed assets and the amount being held back, both as depreciation and retained profits. This will show the proportion of such investment financed from these sources and again, comparison with previous periods will show the trend.

Once again, in the case of the added value statement we are looking at information which does not give us answers but helps us to organise the information in such a way as to pose further and better questions.

Added value also focuses attention on the fact that much of a business's investment has to be financed not from outside but from inside sources. Indeed, once a business is in existence by far the majority of its future investment will have just one source: its own self-generated funds – funds created by the retention of profit and what is held back as depreciation. This means that the health of a business depends not only upon the creation of profit but on its division between what is taken out to reward its employees, investors and the whole community (through taxation) and what is left in for reinvestment.

CURRENT COST ACCOUNTING

Having to make judgements of what is needed for reinvestment led accountants some years ago to consider the problem of inflation and how it should be accounted for in the division of profits. What became clear was that when inflation begins to rise above, say, 10 per cent, the amount required to replace a business's fixed assets and to maintain the same level of investment in its working capital begins to increase. This is not because the business is buying more fixed assets or increasing its real investment in working capital but simply because prices are rising. In other words, during periods of inflation a business needs more money invested in it not to grow but simply to stand still.

However, a problem arises when you look to see from where the extra money 'needed to stand still' is to come. For instance, very few people, whether potential new shareholders or bankers lending money, will want to put money into a business for this purpose. It is because of this that accountants suggested a way of accounting, termed current cost accounting, which would highlight the problem and suggest a solution. This was that whatever profits are generated during such times which would otherwise have been classed as distributable – available to take out as dividends – should be reduced by three adjustments. These are set out in Illustration 12.7 and the calculations for them are detailed in Illustration 12.8. The three adjustments are concerned with:

Illustration 12.7 A Ltd: extract from profit and loss account for year ended 31 December

	£000	£000
Profit calculated in normal way		40,000
Current cost accounting adjustments:		
Additional depreciation	5,000	
Cost of sales	2,167	
Monetary working capital	2,883	10,050
Current cost profit		29,950

(1) *additional depreciation* – to account for the increased cost of replacing fixed assets;
(2) *the cost of sales* – to account for the increased investment required to maintain the same quantity of stocks at increased prices;
(3) *the monetary working capital* – to account for an increase in the investment in credit given less credit taken to maintain the same level of sales and purchases.

Illustration 12.9 sets out these three adjustment needs within the context of the business model. The amounts calculated in Illustration 12.7 total £10.05 million and represent the additional investment needed to keep this business at the same level of activity. As can be seen from this illustration, when such adjustments have been made the amount calculated is referred to as the current cost profit or loss. Its purpose is to highlight how much of the profit of £40 million represents true growth: in this case £29.95 million. In other words, £10.05 million needs to be retained to maintain the present level of investment.

Current cost accounting was tried experimentally in the United Kingdom for some three years, but since 1982 it has not had any widespread use apart from by the newly privatised utilities, i.e. water, electricity, gas, etc. Within these, profits are still announced (and prices calculated) after current cost accounting adjustments have been applied. Whether or not applied, however, the need to maintain and preserve investment remains, as does the question whether or not the right balance is being held between retention and distribution of profits. It is for this reason that the reorganisation of the profit and loss account by means of added value statements, and an appreciation of the principles which underlie current cost accounting, are necessary requirements for those engaged in the interpretation of financial data.

Illustration 12.8 Calculations for Illustration 12.7

				Historical cost £000	Replacement cost £000
Fixed assets subject to depreciation				50,000	75,000
Annual depreciation based on writing off over 5 years				10,000	15,000
Additional depreciation				£5,000	

Cost of sales adjustment

	Historical value £000	Price index	Mid-year value		£000
Opening stock	10,000		100 =	$10,000 \times \dfrac{110}{100} =$	11,000
Mid-year index		110	–		
Closing stock	14,000		120 =	$14,000 \times \dfrac{110}{120} =$	12,833
Difference	4,000				1,833
Cost of sales adjustment			£4,000 – £1,833		= £2,167

Monetary working capital adjustment

	Historical value £000	Price index	Mid-year value		£000
Opening debtors *less* creditors	13,000	100 =	$13,000 \times \dfrac{110}{100} =$		14,300
Mid-year index		110	–		
Closing debtors *less* creditors	19,000	120 =	$19,000 \times \dfrac{110}{120} =$		17,417
Difference	6,000				3,117
Monetary working capital adjustment			£6,000 – £3,117 =		£2,883

Illustration 12.9 Business model showing the areas for current cost accounting adjustment

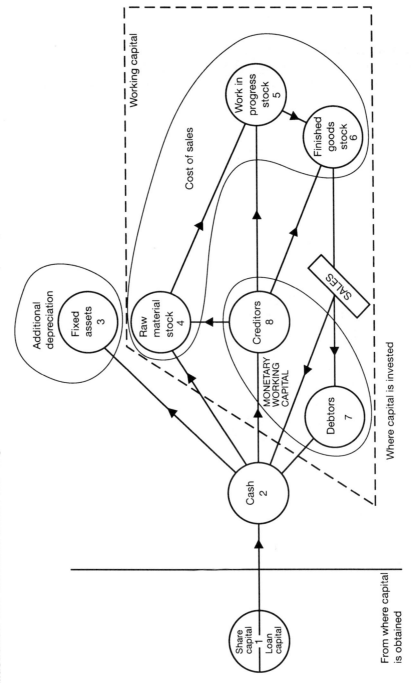

REVISION

We have now seen that in our approach to interpretation, first, we must understand the information we are looking at and, second, in many situations we may
need the information itself to be reorganised. Illustrations 12.10, 12.11 and
12.12 set out a series of statements which require reorganisation to provide the
fullest possible value to someone concerned with interpretation. Try to reorganise these in your own way and compare your answers with those suggested in
Illustrations 12.13, 12.14 and 12.15.

Illustration 12.10 Reorganisation exercise 1

Reorganise the following profit and loss statement in a way which you feel may aid
interpretation.

	£000	£000	£000
Sales			8,000
Cost of sales:			
Factory:			
Material	3,000		
Labour	1,000		
Variable expenses	640		
Fixed expenses	560	5,200	
Sales:			
Commission	800		
Variable expenses	400		
Fixed expenses	100	1,300	
Administration:			
Variable expenses	160		
Fixed expenses	140	300	6,800
			Profit 1,200

Illustration 12.11 Reorganisation exercise 2

Reorganise the following balance sheets in a way which will show the movements
of funds.

		Year 2		Year 1
		£m		£m
Fixed assets		200		170
Outside investments		100		60
Working capital				
Stock	60		30	
Debtors	40		25	
Cash	10		10	
	110		65	

Less: Current liabilities				
Creditors	60	50	30	35
		350		265
Share capital		150		125
Reserves		100		60
Loan capital		100		80
		350		265

Note: Purchases of fixed assets close of year 2 amounted to £40,000

Illustration 12.12 Reorganisation exercise 3

Reorganise the following profit and loss statement to show how wealth was created and distributed in the year.

	£000	£000
Sales		7,500
Less: Materials	2,500	
Labour	1,500	
Expenses for outside services	1,000	
Salaries	500	
Depreciation	200	
Interest paid	300	6,000
Profit before tax		1,500
Taxation		750
Profit after tax		750
Dividends		250
Retained profit		500

Illustration 12.13 Suggested answer to Illustration 12.10

Reorganised profit and loss statement:

	£000	£000	£000	%
Sales			8,000	100
Less: Direct costs				
Factory:				
Material	3,000			
Labour	1,000			
Variable expenses	640		4,640	
Prime contribution			3,360	42
Sales:				
Commission	800			
Variable expenses	400	1,200		
Administration:				
Variable expenses		160	1,360	
Net contribution			2,000	25

Less: Fixed expenses:			
Factory	560		
Sales	100		
Administration	140	800	
Profit		1,200	15

Illustration 12.14 Suggested answer to Illustration 12.11

Reorganised balance sheets:
Cash flow statement

	£m
Source of funds	
Retained profit	40
Add back: Depreciation	10
	50
Share capital	25
Loan capital	20
	95
Application of funds	
Purchase of fixed assets	40
Increase in outside investments	40

Movements in working capital

	Source	Application	
Stock	–	30	
Debtors	–	15	
Creditors	30	–	
	30	45	15
			95
Movement of cash			Nil

Illustration 12.15 Suggested answer to Illustration 12.12

Reorganised profit and loss statement:
Added value summary

		£000	%
Sales		7,500	100
Less: Input materials	2,500		
And services	1,000	3,500	47
Added value		4,000	53
Analysis of added value:		£000	%
Wages and salaries		2,000	50
Depreciation		200	5
Interest paid		300	8
Taxation		750	19
Dividends		250	6
Retained profit		500	12
		4,000	100
Amount available for reinvestment:		£000	
Depreciation		200	
Retained profit		500	
		700	

Illustration 12.16 Hierarchy of ratios

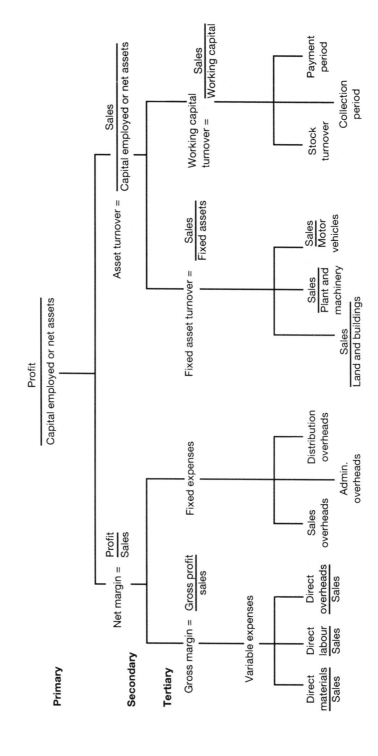

STEP 3: THE MEASUREMENT

Having discussed the first two steps that must be taken in the approach to interpretation, we now come to the third – the measurement of the information itself.

Once we have understood and reorganised the financial data we need then to measure it and to do that we have two major devices: applied common sense and analysis by means of financial ratios – and of the two the more important is applied common sense. However, before we find out how we can use this, we will first consider the use of financial ratios.

FINANCIAL RATIOS

Financial ratios, as they are known, are the indices used in expressing financial data in such a way that it can be compared and trends identified and thus questions can be raised. Ratios may be expressed as percentages or indices or even as ratios. Illustration 12.16 sets out the main ratios in what might be termed their hierarchical order while Illustration 12.17 provides a summary explanation of each ratio.

The primary ratio

From Illustrations 12.16 and 12.17 it can be seen that the primary or number one ratio is profit (or return as it is often called), normally for the year, related to the capital employed or invested (or net assets as it might be described), during the same period. (If you now understand the balance sheet you will realise that these last two measurements are identical – simply the names given to the two sides of the same coin: where the money has gone to – the net assets – and where the same money has come from: the capital employed.) This is the primary measurement for all investment anywhere and in business we start from this self-same point. To admit my generation, it might be termed the Frank Sinatra of all financial measurements.

The secondary ratios

We then see that to investigate the primary ratio more fully we have two secondary ratios: one concerned with profitability (profit in relation to sales) and the other with activity – sales in relation to capital employed or net assets.

The tertiary ratios

Having struck these secondary ratios, we may wish to take our studies further. You can see how from the secondary ratios we can expand into the tertiary ratios.

Illustration 12.17 Ratio analysis

Primary ratio	*Return on net assets*: Profit or earnings before interest and taxation/Net assets (i.e. fixed assets *plus* current assets *less* current liabilities)
Secondary ratios	*Profit margin*: Profit or earnings before interest and tax/sales
	Asset turnover : Sales/Net assets
Tertiary ratios	*Profit/Expenses control*:
	– Gross profit/Sales
	– Variable expense/Sales
	– Fixed expenses
	Use of assets:
	– Fixed assets/Sales
	– Working capital/Sales
Financial status ratios:	*Liquidity/Current ratio*: Current assets/Current liabilities
Liquidity:	*Acid test*: Cash plus debtors/Current liabilities
Stock turnover and credit policies	*Stock turnover*: Sales/Stock
	Collection period: Debtors/Sales x 365 = days
	Payment period: Creditors/Purchases or cost of sales x 365 = days
Solvency	*Gearing ratio*: Long-term debts/Capital employed
	Interest cover: Profits before interest and tax/Interest

Profitability

Here you can see how profitability might be studied from the point of view of gross profit or contribution to sales as a percentage. This can then be expanded by relating direct materials or merchandise, labour and expenses to sales while reviewing the fixed overhead categories as amounts. You should recall this approach to examining profit and expenses by revising chapter 2 and earlier sections of this chapter. Then, if we feel it useful, we could look at the contribution to sales of each of the individual products and merchandise sold or services rendered, again, if this point is unclear revise your study of marginal costing in chapter 7.

Activity (use of assets)

At the same time we could extend our examination of activity by comparing sales separately with fixed assets and working capital. This will reveal how many times we are turning over our investment in these two areas in relation to the sales for the period – in most cases the year. In other words, are we getting value – increased turnover or sales – for money invested? We can also, in this situation, break the activity ratio down into its constituent parts, as suggested in Illustration 12.16.

Financial status ratios

It can also be seen that in addition to ratios concerned with profitability and activity set out in Illustration 12.16 there are those that help us study a business's financial status: the business's ability to pay its liabilities – its bills – and whether this ability is changing because of design or necessity.

Liquidity ratios

In this area we start with the overall ratio discussed when we looked at the relationship of current assets to current liabilities in chapter 3. We also see how this can then be looked at more pragmatically or immediately by means of what is termed the acid test or quick ratio. In this we bring into account only the more liquid current assets such as the debtors or receivables and cash and bank balances before dividing them by the current liabilities. We therefore leave out stocks, which may take some time before becoming cash, from this more immediate measurement.

Stock turnover, collection and payment ratios

We can also see in Illustration 12.17 that because liquidity is closely connected with working capital and its control we have three ratios concerned with stock turnover and the collection and payment periods relating to debtors and creditors. These three ratios need to be read in conjunction with the liquidity ratios to see whether stocks are being controlled and credit policies enforced.

Solvency ratios

Again, the financial status of a business including its ability to meet its liabilities may well be affected by its gearing, the 'pressure' under which it is operating, as you will remember from chapter 1. Illustration 12.17 sets out the calculation of the gearing ratio, and associated with it is the interest cover. This looks at the ability of the business to meet the interest due from the profits available for this purpose.

A worked example

Having studied the hierarchy of ratios in Illustration 12.16 with their explanations in Illustration 12.17, turn to Illustrations 12.18 and 12.19, which set out four years' profit and loss accounts and balance sheets for a particular business. From these statements the appropriate ratios are calculated and shown in Illustration 12.20. These should be studied carefully so that you become familiar with their calculation and their meaning – the questions each poses.

Illustration 12.18 Summarised profit and loss accounts for the year ending 31 December

	Year 1 £000		Year 2 £000		Year 3 £000		Year 4 £000	
Sales		1,440		1,600		2,000		2,400
Less:								
Cost of goods sold		800		1,000		1,200		1,520
Gross profit		640		600		800		880
Selling expenses	160		190		200		240	
Admin. expenses								
(inc. 10% loan)								
interest)	220		240		260		300	
Depreciation	120		130		120		140	
Miscellaneous								
expenses	20	520	20	580	20	600	20	700
Net profit before tax		120		20		200		180
Corporation tax (50%)		60		10		100		90
Net profit after tax		60		10		100		90
Retained profit b/fwd		240		280		260		300
		300		290		360		390
Dividends paid	1.4p per share 20		1.9p per share 30		3.8p per share 60		3.5p per share 70	
Retained profit c/fwd		280		260		300		320
Market value of each share								
at balance sheet date		60p		50p		65p		49p

Illustration 12.19 Summarised balance sheets as at 31 December

	Year 1 £000		Year 2 £000		Year 3 £000		Year 4 £000
Fixed assets							
Land and buildings	1,000		1,260		1,120		1,320
Plant and machinery	240		240		220		340
Motor vehicles	40		20		80		100
	1,380		1,520		1,420		1,760
Current assets							
Stock	600		640		840		840
Debtors	480		500		640		800
Cash at bank	180		140		100		180
	1,260		1,280		1,580		1,820
Less: Current liabilities							
Creditors	240		260		300		440
Accruals	60		70		100		130
Taxation	60		10		100		90
	360		340		500		660
Net current assets		900		940		1,080	1,160
Total assets less current liabilities		2,280		2,460		2,500	2,920
Less: Amounts due in more than 12 months							
Loans		600		600		600	600
		1,680		1,860		1,900	2,320
Capital and reserves							
Share capital							
Authorised and issued £1 ordinary							

shares fully paid	1,400	1,600	1,600	2,000
Retained profits	280	260	300	320
Shareholders' funds	1,680	1,860	1,900	2,320

Illustration 12.20 Ratio analysis from data in Illustrations 12.18 and 12.19

	Year 1	Year 2	Year 3	Year 4
Performance:				
Primary	180:2,280	80:2,460	260:2,500	240:2,940
	7.9%	3.3%	10.4%	8.2%
Secondary:				
PM	180:1,440	80:1,600	260:2,000	240:2,400
	12.5%	5%	13%	10%
AT	1,440:2,280	1,600:2,460	2,000:2,500	2,400:2,940
	0.63	0.65	0.8	0.82
Liquidity:				
Current	1,260:360	1,280:340	1,580:500	1,820:660
	3.5 times	3.76	3.16	2.76
Acid	660:360	640:340	740:500	980:660
	1.8 times	1.9	1.5	1.5
Tax		All 50%		
Solvency:				
Gearing	600:2,280	600:2,460	600:2,500	600:2,920
	26%	24%	24%	21%
Interest cover	180:60	80:60	260:60	240:60
	3 times	1.3	4.3	4
Control of working capital:				
Stock turnover	1,440:600	1,600:640	2,000:840	2,400:840
	2.4 times	2.5	2.4	2.9
Collection period	480/1,440 x 365	500/1,600 x 365	640/2,000 x 365	800/2,400 x 365
	122 days	114	117	122
Payment period	240/800 x 365	260/1,000 x 365	300/1,200 x 365	440/1,520 x 365
	110 days	95	91	106
Investment:				
Return on equity	60:1,680	10:1,860	100:1,900	90:2,320
	4%	1%	5%	4%
Earnings per share	60:1,400	10:1,600	100:1,600	90:2,000
	4.3p	0.6p	6.3p	4.5p
Price/earnings ratio	60p:4.3p	50p:0.6p	65p:6.3p	49p:4.5p
	13.9	83	10.3	10.9
Dividend yield	1.4p:60p	1.9p:50p	3.8p:65p	3.5p:49p
	2.3%	3.8%	5.8%	7.1%
Dividend cover	4.3p:1.4p	0.6p:1.9p	6.3p:3.8p	4.5p:3.5p
	3.1	0.3	1.7	1.3
Use of assets:				
Fixed assets/Sales	1,380:1,440	1,520:1,600	1,420:2,000	1,760:2,400
	96%	95%	71%	74%
WC/Sales	900:1,440	940:1,800	1,080:2,000	1,160;2,400
	62%	52%	54%	48%
Expense control:				
GP/Sales	640:1,440	600:1,600	800:2,000	880:2,400
	44%	38%	40%	37%
Fixed expenses/ Sales	520:1,440	580:1,600	600:2,000	700:2,400
	36%	36%	30%	29%

Investment ratios

Return on equity

Finally, we need to be aware that, as well as management requirements, we have those of investors. The two are, of course, identical but there are certain key areas which are of particular importance to investors. These are set out in Illustration 12.21 and begin with return on equity, which confines its view to the profits belonging to the shareholders – the profit after tax and interest – and relates it to the shareholders' funds: the share capital plus all retained profits and reserves. Applying the ratio formula set out in Illustration 12.21 to the figures in Illustrations 12.18 and 12.19 you can see this ratio calculated in Illustration 12.20.

Illustration 12.21 Investment ratios

Return on equity:	Profit after tax and interest/Shareholders' funds (share capital plus retained profits and reserves)
Earnings per share:	Profit after tax and interest/Number of issued shares
Price/earnings ratio:	Market price per share/Earnings per share
Dividend yield:	Dividend per share/Market price per share
Dividend cover:	Earnings per share/Dividends per share

Earnings per share

Next in Illustration 12.21 we come to what is often considered the central measurement of profitability from an investor's point of view, the earnings per share. It is this ratio which companies try to better year by year and calls for the effort of the whole enterprise to improve what is termed 'the bottom line'. The bottom line is the profit after tax and interest; in other words, that profit which belongs to the shareholders. The calculation for this ratio is set out in Illustration 12.20 and is again based on data in Illustrations 12.18 and 12.19.

Price/earnings

In Illustration 12.21 the earnings per share calculation is followed by the ratio which expresses 'the multiple': the number of times the price of the share exceeds the earnings per share. This ratio is set out for companies with Stock Exchange quotations in what is termed the P/E column in the financial press. The calculation is made by dividing the company share price, which is based on the daily transactions of its shares, by its earnings per share, which stay constant for its financial year.

The net earnings value

If therefore the ratio or multiple rises or falls for a particular company it indicates the popularity or otherwise of its shares in relationship to its last declared profit figures. It also indicates that if a company was purchased, based on its earnings, a value could be calculated from this price/earnings (P/E) ratio. This is arrived at by multiplying its profits after tax and interest by the P/E multiple. This calculation can be seen in Illustration 12.22.

Illustration 12.22 Net earnings valuation

Profits for year	= £70,000
P/E ratio	= £10
Net earnings value of business	= £70,000 x 10
	= £700,000

Dividend yield

However, as well as profitability, investors are concerned with comparing their rewards – the dividends paid to them – with the market price of their shares. This comparison is what is termed the dividend yield and in a sense brings the dividend paid into perspective – what it represents as a return on the real value of the investment made. An example of this is also included in Illustration 12.20.

Dividend cover

Finally, investors are concerned about generosity. In other words, they want to find out what proportion of the profits available for distribution have in fact been distributed. This is calculated by means of the dividend cover ratio. The higher the cover the greater the retention; the lower, the greater the distribution – an example of this ratio is included with the other investors' ratios in Illustration 12.20.

You need to be fully familiar with the logic of ratios, stemming as they do from the primary through to the tertiary measurements, and with how liquidity must also be studied as central to the health of an enterprise. We must remember that a business can be heading for a profit and achieving the right investment activity but it may still have a cash or liquidity problem. At the same time, because managers are wholly responsible to investors, for the investment of money to investors, it is equally important for *them* to become conversant with those ratios that particularly concern investors. Having therefore explained what ratios are and how they are calculated let us consider their use.

USE OF FINANCIAL RATIOS

Ratios are particularly important when building up those questions which are vital if financial information is to be correctly interpreted. Such interpretation must never be based upon snap judgements. Ratios should be used to build up and summarise the evidence available and to create a picture from which, not conclusions, but better questions can be drawn.

Ratios have a very particular part to play in summarising financial data so as to produce the right questions, but it must always be remembered that they do not in themselves in any way provide answers. We use ratios rather as detectives use questions in sorting out alibis – we must therefore use the same care when reviewing ratios as good detectives use with the evidence on which they assess alibis in a particular case.

For example, if a detective asks the husband of a murdered wife where he was at the time of the murder, the husband might reply that he was taking their dog for a walk. In a way this is like the first ratio that we might strike when looking at financial data. However, this would not be enough on its own. Detectives would seek corroboration. They might well seek the evidence of people who may have been along the route of the walk, for example the newsagent on the corner. They might ask: 'Did you see the husband taking his dog for a walk?' The newsagent may say 'yes' and the detective must therefore look at that piece of information with care again because, on the face of it, it corroborates the husband's statement. However, it may also have been given in order to help the husband's case because the newsagent and the husband are in league. Perhaps the wife has not paid her paper bill and this has made the newsagent rather annoyed with her! On the other hand, the newsagent may say 'no', but again this does not disprove the husband's evidence. It may be that the newsagent was engaged in the evil act!

In just the same way the evidence of ratios must be used very carefully. It is important to decide when using ratios what should be taken as the minimum number of periods for the information in question. For instance, if one is looking at the annual results of a company, one would look for a minimum of three years, and preferably five, before drawing any real conclusions based on ratios.

This is equally true if one is looking at short-period statements such as cost summaries. Again, you would want to take a minimum number before you could use ratios devised from them as evidence in creating a satisfactory judgement based on trends revealed.

It cannot be overemphasised that ratios simply 'spark off' intelligent questions. A great number of errors are made by people who leap to conclusions with insufficient evidence. Indeed, ill-informed people using ratios sometimes suggest that they in themselves provide answers whereas in fact, as has been stressed, they simply pose better questions.

It must always be remembered that if making money was simply a question of following a formula or creating the right ratios we would not be wasting our time learning about business finance. We would simply be studying the formula! The creation of wealth is not accomplished by means of a formula – it is accomplished by mixing people with money so as to create wealth, and in that mixture there is much complication, judgement, hard work and – dare we admit? – luck.

However, it must also be pointed out that it is possible in certain situations to create minimum ratios for safety. This can be very valuable when financial judgement is required in such fields as lending money. In such cases minimum ratios have often been applied by, for instance, bankers, who have allowed staff, who in many cases possess a very flimsy knowledge of finance, to make lending decisions. (Mind you perhaps the consequences of this approach in recent years need to be questioned.)

In such situations it is quite possible to lay down certain minimum ratios that we might look for to indicate maximum safety: for instance, that the current assets should cover the current liabilities more than twice. This could be considered to be a very safe situation, as it means the business has twice the amount of money coming in as it will have to pay out to meet its current needs. However, although it is safe it may not be good from the business's point of view. (If that is unclear to you revise your study of working capital in chapter 9 and consider how this 'safety first' view clashes with the objective of minimising such investment.) You could also lay down certain minimum ratios regarding the gross profit to sales, the days' credit allowed to debtors and the turnover of stocks, etc., with equally disastrous effects upon the business's long-term prospects.

These then are just examples of the ratios that can be devised to help in situations where you do not wish for too much freedom of expression in the interpretation of financial data. However, it must never be thought that such 'safe' ratios are in themselves sacrosanct – they are simply convenient to use in certain situations.

It must also be remembered that the creation of wealth involves a mixture of people with money. This means that whatever the money situation, the people who will be handling the money and what it buys are all-important. In the interpretation of the results of a business we must never forget the people investing, spending and earning the money. Their study should always be central to any judgement of a business's financial progress. For instance, good bankers have always understood that behind the figures on which they are lending money people will be spending it. For this reason the people concerned with this must be of equal if not more importance than the soundness or otherwise of the balance sheets, the profit and loss accounts and the cash flow forecasts that are used to support a loan.

REVISION

To consolidate your studies of ratios, go through Illustrations 12.18 and 12.19 again, considering not so much the arithmetic of the ratios set out in Illustration 12.20 but their meaning. Jot down your ideas, indeed in some cases your questions, based on the trends the ratios show and compare your findings with the notes made in Illustration 12.23.

Illustration 12.23 Suggested comments on Illustrations 12.18, 12.19 and 12.20

Performance
1. Profitability is inconsistent, with no apparent trend during the four years.
2. Apart from year 2 the overall profit margin has remained in double figures although the expense control ratios indicate that the company has had problems maintaining its gross profit margin. This could be due to inability to increase sale prices in line with cost increases in material and/or labour.
3. The fixed expenses seem to be in reasonable control as they have decreased as a percentage of sales throughout the years. It would be helpful to see how they compare with budgeted levels of expenditure.
4. Asset turnover, although low, is on the increase. This is a healthy sign as the company has been investing in additional assets, especially in year 4.

Liquidity
1. Working capital has increased each year in line with increases in sales although the requirement per £ of sales has decreased each year. This is shown by the working capital/sales ratio.
2. Both the current and acid test ratios have decreased over the four years, indicating a slight weakening in the liquidity position of the company. This should not give rise to any alarm as both ratios are still in excess of the normal requirement (2:1 for current and 1:1 for acid test).
3. Stock turnover has improved in the last year although with a present stock turn of over four months there is still room for improvement.
4. The credit terms offered by the business need to be known to interpret the collection period ratio as there seems to have been a slackening in collection during the last three years. If the terms are 30 days, customers seem to be taking on average at least three times as long. This could lead to bad debts if the credit control policies are not regularly reviewed.
5. The company seems to have fairly patient creditors although again it would be useful to know the purchasing terms of trade. The increase in creditors in year 4 is not too worrying.
6. The overall financing of fixed assets expenditure is good in that extra cash has come in the main from shareholders plus the depreciation charge.

Asset investment	Year 2	Year 3	Year 4
Opening book value	1,380	1,520	1,420
Less: Depreciation	130	120	140
	1,250	1,400	1,280
Closing book value	1,520	1,420	1,760
Net purchase during year	£270	£20	£480
Financed by:			
Extra share capital	200	–	420
Profit after tax and dividends	(20)	40	20
	180	40	420
Depreciation for the year	130	120	140
	£310	£160	£560

Investment
1. There is not a lot to encourage existing shareholders, particularly as the return on equity does not exceed 5 per cent and the dividend has yet to reach 8 per cent.
2. The company has, however, paid a dividend each year, although it was not covered in year 2.
3. The dividend cover is not very high and year 2's dividend was not covered. This may make shareholders happy in the short term but could result in lower profits and dividends in the future.

THE MEASUREMENT OF COMMON SENSE

We have now seen the first of the two measurements used in interpreting financial information: ratio analysis. However, we still have to consider the second and more important measurement – common sense. It must always be remembered that whatever financial figures are presented about a business, they express a practical situation and it is the investigation and understanding of this practical situation which require the unique gift of common sense.

For example, behind a cost statement there is the manufacture of the goods being sold or the services being rendered. Thus, the first question to ask when looking at any cost statement is: 'Does the information make sense in the context of the practical situation?' For instance, could that amount of material be used in the manufacture of these goods? Could that value of labour be spent in rendering that service? If the merchandise stocks of a retailer amount to so much could the remainder of what has been purchased during this period have been sold? We must always recognise that financial information which has been produced either fraudulently or in error will be illogical.

It could be said that all 'con men' rely on people not applying the yardstick of common sense or logic to the information they present. For this reason everyone concerned with financial analysis must always recognise the paramount need to apply his or her own common sense in assessing financial data. In this respect it is not always the accountant, or the so-called financial expert who possesses this invaluable attribute. There is always a great need to enrol the assistance of practical managers if the commonsense aspect of interpretation is to be fully applied.

This can be illustrated by the situation that happened some years ago in what is still referred to as 'the salad oil fraud'. This was a case in which a company had consistently over-valued its stocks, by fraudulently manipulating its records. In following their customary stock testing routines, however, the auditors had not seen this. They had looked at all the appropriate records and evidence and found them correct. They had examined the bin cards and the store ledgers, and even looked into the vats which contained the salad oil and seen what they presumed to be salad oil floating there. They had indeed found nothing wrong. However, they had never considered the situation from a practical point of view.

In fact it was not an accountant who discovered the situation at all, it was someone who applied his own practical knowledge in the simplest and most direct way possible. He was a chemist and he looked at the balance sheet and saw the stock, or inventories as Americans call it, expressed in dollars and he did what now seems so obvious. He converted the dollar figure into cubic feet of stock, and this proved that no receptacles on earth would hold the quantity of salad oil revealed by the calculation. He needed to look no further. He had no knowledge of course as to whether the stock figure was fraudulent but what he did know was that that amount of stock did not exist. He did not know it from any accountancy records or any study of ratios – he knew it based on his own practical knowledge and common sense.

It can never be over-stressed that everyone within a business looking at financial information must apply his or her own practical experience in assessing whether or not the information is in accordance with this yardstick. Common sense will always remain the most important measurement technique used in the interpretation of financial data. Whenever information is incorrectly expressed, whether fraudulently or otherwise, the clue to its error will always be found to rest here, in the fact that the information does not express a logical picture – in other words, it defies common sense.

It might even be said that the real danger to business of managers not possessing financial or commercial awareness is that they will not use their own common sense or practical skills. They will treat financial information as though it is the province of financial experts only, whereas in fact it is the essence of the business. It expresses the business's activities and its progress and its use and interpretation require the marketing knowledge of the salesperson, the purchasing skills of the buyer, the production knowledge of the engineer, the people knowledge of the personnel executive – and, most of all, knowledge, experience and common sense of the whole enterprise.

CONCLUSION

Having come this far, turn to the final exercise, set out in Illustration 12.24: a case study concerned with the interpretation of financial information. It is important to follow the rules that have been laid down in our approach work to interpretation. First, understand clearly what we are interpreting and therefore read carefully through the notes. Next it will be necessary to reorganise the data – to put it in perspective – so that we can ask better questions. Suggestions about this are also included.

Finally, having reorganised the information, it is necessary to apply the measurements of common and practical sense, and in some cases the ratios we have described in this chapter, which will bring out a greater understanding of the way in which the business has been progressing. These steps of reorganising the data and calculating the necessary ratios are set out as Illustrations 12.25 and 12.26.

Work through the case study at your own speed, and once this is complete compare your 'findings' with those in Illustration 12.27.

Illustration 12.24 Interpretation Ltd: a case study

The board of directors of Interpretation Ltd, having examined the financial statements for the last three years, are worried that the present level of sales cannot continue without an increase in borrowing. They have asked you to analyse the company's financial performance during this time with particular reference to the industry averages they have supplied, and the movement of funds.

Industry averages at present (constant for the last three years)

Net profit to net assets	20%
Net profit to sales	6%
Sales to net assets	3.3 times
Gross profit to sales	20%
Current ratio	2.5 times
Acid test	1.1 times
*Stock turnover	6 times
*Debtor collection period	32 days
*Creditor payment period	25 days
Gearing	10%
Debt to total assets	50%

*Based on year end balance sheet figures

Operating statements for the year ending 31 December

		Year 1 £000		Year 2 £000		Year 3 £000
Sales		6,630		6,886		7,140
Less: Cost of sales		5,304		5,508		5,712
Gross profit		1,326		1,378		1,428
Less: Expenses						
Selling	240		260		280	
Administration	270		302		332	
Distribution	102		214		306	
Depreciation	204	816	256	1,032	306	1,224
Net profit before tax		510		346		204
Taxation		256		174		102
Net profit after tax		254		172		102

Balance sheets as at 31 December

Assets employed:		Year 1 £000	Year 2 £000	Year 3 £000
Fixed assets				
Land and buildings		122	326	306
Plant and machinery		378	296	256
Other fixed assets		72	20	16
	A	572	642	578

Current assets:				
Stock and work in progress		766	1,276	2,066
Debtors		612	694	970
Bank balances and cash		154	72	52
		1,532	2,042	3,088
Less: Current liabilities				
Creditors and accruals		366	530	960
Bank overdraft		–	256	714
		366	786	1,674
Net current assets	B	1,166	1,256	1,414
	A + B	1,738	1,898	1,992
Less: Loan capital		114	102	94
		1,624	1,796	1,898
Capital and reserves:				
Share capital		918	918	918
Reserves		706	878	980
Shareholders' funds		1,624	1,796	1,898

Illustration 12.25 Interpretation Ltd: cash flow statements

		Years	
		1/2	2/3
Sources	Note	£000	£000
Net profit after tax		172	102
Add back: depreciation		256	306
Generated from operations		428	408
Applications			
Net expenditure on fixed assets	A	326	242
Increase in working capital (net)	B	428	636
Loans repaid		12	8
		766	886
Decrease in net liquid funds	C	(338)	(478)
Notes:			
A Net book value previous year		572	642
Less: Depreciation this year		(256)	(306)
		316	336
Net book value this year		642	578
Net expenditure on fixed assets		326	242
B Increase/(decrease) in working capital			
Stock and work in progress		510	790
Debtors		82	276
Creditors and accruals		(164)	(430)
		428	636
C Increase (decrease) in net liquid funds			
Bank balances and cash		(82)	(20)
Bank overdraft		(256)	(458)
		(338)	(478)

Source and application of funds:

1. A significant decrease has taken place in liquidity during the last three years, requiring a large overdraft from the bank.
2. The principal reason for the decrease has been the increased requirement for working capital, over £1 million in two years.
3. The generation of internal cash has come mainly from depreciation rather than profit, which has decreased each year.
4. The total amount invested in fixed assets over the two years of £568,000 (£326,000 plus £242,000) is almost equal to the amount held back as depreciation over the same period of £562,000 (£256,000 plus £306,000). This indicates no real increase in money invested in this area and brings into quesiton the adequacy of the business's investment policies to stay competitive.
5. The company has not sought either additional share capital or long-term loans despite a net investment of £568,000 in fixed assets during the last two years. This has put pressure on the cash resources required for working capital and hence the present overdraft of £714,000.

Illustration 12.26 Interpretation Ltd: ratio analysis

	Note	Year 1	Year 2	Year 3	Industry average
Profitability ratios:					
Net profit to net assets	A	29.3	18.2	10.2	20%
Net profit to sales	B	7.7	5.0	2.9	6%
Sales to net assets	C	3.8	3.6	3.6	3.3 times
Gross profit to sales	D	20%	20%	20%	20%
Liquidity ratios:					
Current	E	4.2	2.6	1.8	2.5 times
Acid test	F	2.1	1.0	0.6	1.1 times
Activity ratios:					
Stock turnover	G	8.7	5.4	3.5	6 times
Debtor collection period	H	34	37	50	32 days
Creditor payment period	I	25	35	61	25 days
Capital ratios:					
Gearing	J	6.6	5.4	4.7	10%
Debts to total assets	K	22.8	33.1	48.2	50%

Ratio workings	Note	Year 1	Year 2	Year 3
Net profit to net assets	A	510:1,738	346:1,898	204:1,992
Net profit to sales	B	510:6,630	346:6,886	204:7,140
Sales to net assets	C	6,630:1,738	6,886:1,898	7,140:1,992
Gross profit to sales	D	1,326:6,630	1,378:6,886	1,428:7,140
Current	E	1,532:366	2,042:786	3,088:1,674
Acid test	F	766:366	766:786	1,022:1,674
Stock turnover	G	6,630:766	6,886:1,276	7,140:2,066
Debtor collection period	H	612/6,630 x 365	694/6,886 x 365	970/7,140 x 365
Creditor payment period	I	366/5,304 x 365	530/5,508 x 365	960/5,712 x 365
Gearing	J	114:1,738	102:1,898	94:1,992
Debt to total assets	K	480:2,104	888:2,684	1,768:3,666

Illustration 12.27 Interpretation Ltd: findings

Ratio analysis
1. The only area where the company seems to be better than the industry is with its debt position, although this is now very close to the average.
2. The remaining ratios highlight a number of problem areas. These are:
    (a) *Liquidity.* Both the current ratio and acid test show a declining position and are now well below the industry average. Unless action is taken to arrest this downward trend it is possible that the creditors and bank may put pressure on the company for payment, which will affect solvency.
    (b) *Stock turnover.* This has decreased at an alarming rate and is only just above half that for the industry. It suggests:
        (i) too much stock on hand, perhaps due to bad sales forecasting, production planning or buying;
        (ii) the possibility of obsolete or deteriorated stock;
        (iii) the true liquidity position could be worse than the current ratio indicates;
        (iv) the valuation may be incorrect. More information perhaps is needed on work in progress.
    (c) *Debtor collection period.* The company seems to have slipped badly in debtor collection. It suggests:
        (i) a poor credit control department in chasing debtors;
        (ii) a slack credit control in accepting orders;
        (iii) an increasing possibility of bad debts.
    (d) *Creditor payment period.* The company now takes more than twice the industry average period to pay its bills, due of course to stock and debtor problems. Pressure from the creditors for payment will affect the solvency of the company.
    (e) *Profitability.* All the profitability ratios indicate that the company is less profitable than the average firm in its industry. The maintenance of the gross profit margin indicates that the company has been recovering cost increases in materials and labour in increased sale prices. The low net profit margin indicates that the sale price increase has not been enough to recover cost increases in overheads. The overhead costs look high, especially distribution.
        Sales to net assets is higher than the industry average due to Interpretation's primary problem in managing its current assets. The decrease in net profit to net assets reflects the low profit margin on sales.

Summary
1. The company shows severe signs of overtrading and needs an injection of capital to support any increase on the present sales level.
2. The company can of course generate funds from its own resources namely:
        (i) net profit plus depreciation;
        (ii) reduction of debtors;
        (iii) reduction of stock.
3. The sale prices will have to rise or overheads be cut back for funds to be generated from profits.
4. There is room for significant reductions in stock and debtors although these

cannot be accomplished immediately. Assuming the stock to be saleable and the debtors collectable, however, it should be possible for the firm to generate a substantial amount of funds from these sources. If it could reduce stock, debtors and creditors to the industry averages this would release £750,000. This would be more than enough to pay off the overdraft and increase sales without requiring additional working capital.

   This will, of course, require some effort on behalf of the management of Interpretation.

5. It would be useful to produce a cash flow forecast for, say, the next six months to show the effect of the action proposed above, and particularly to show the bank manager that by continuing to trade the company can reduce the overdraft, which is now probably reaching its limit.

We have now completed our understanding of business finance. There is of course much more you can learn that has not been included. It must be remembered, however, that real understanding will be gained only by experience and practice, and that the best case study of all is back at work – because that is where it all happens!

Business finance is no academic exercise. It is an expression of life itself and as such requires the respect and understanding and, above all, the experience that only first-hand involvement can provide.

INDEX